DATE DUE

THE PRESS AND THE PUBLIC

The Story of the
British Press Council

By

George Murray, C.B.E.

Foreword by
Howard Rusk Long

Southern Illinois University Press
Carbondale and Edwardsville

Feffer & Simons, Inc.
London and Amsterdam

Contents

Foreword

THE rector of the Church of St. Bride, in Fleet Street, the Reverend Dewi Morgan, on Wednesday, December 9, 1970, conducted the memorial service for George Murray, C.B.E., for thirty years chief leader writer on the *Daily Mail*. The hour was 12:30 P.M., one usual in London for such occasions, yet significant because, on the clock, this half hour is in the no man's land that divides the working day for those who serve the great national dailies and those who labor on the newspapers published in the afternoon. The press was truly represented as were the learned professions, and the branches of government. This Christopher Wren church built after the Great Fire of 1666, on the site of five earlier Christian churches, and restored after the bombings of World War II through the efforts of English-speaking journalists in all parts of the world, is the spiritual home of those who have served the London press since the day of Wynkyn de Worde. Here and here alone, within sound of the presses which seem never to stop, could the men and women of his calling pay their tribute to a man whose accumulated works continue to shape the nature of British public opinion and the performance of the press.

Arthur Brittenden, editor of the *Daily Mail*, said in the address:

George Murray was a man gentle in his ways, passionate in his beliefs, dedicated in his profession.

George was shy, delightful in his sense of fun, and he was very much loved.

And for nearly thirty years he was the voice of the *Daily Mail*.

And yet even when you have said that, there is something more you must say if you are to discern the real George Murray.

And what you must say is what millions and millions of people said through the years.

There was one phrase they used—day in, day out, as they read the Comment column which George wrote with such devotion and skill.

People read George and said: "That's what I think. . . . Now how that needed saying, thank goodness someone has said it."

That was the genius of George Murray. That he knew what was in people's hearts and minds. And when he wrote his words were their unspoken thoughts.

It was all so easy to read.

And behind it there was so much diligence, so much care, so much giving of himself.

Mentioned were the early struggles; the beginning on Fleet Street in 1931. Then the honors: chief leader writer of the *Daily Mail;* a director of Associated Newspapers; Commander of the Order of the British Empire; council member of the Commonwealth Press Union; chairman of the Press Club; chairman of the Press Council.

In the vita prepared by himself, George Murray offered only a few more details of his life. He had always wanted to write, had always wanted to be a journalist. As a young man he wrote news reports and comments for his local newspaper in South London, in his spare time and without pay. He worked for seven years in the provinces, first on the *Farnham Herald* in Surrey. The struggle for a place in Fleet Street took him to the publicity department of the big advertising firm, J. Walter Thompson. On weekends he worked as a reporter for the *Sunday Dispatch.* After eighteen months he was taken on to the staff of this paper as a feature writer and he also did the leaders. Then he was asked to do the editorials in the *Daily Mail* for a week, during the absence of the regular leader writer. He did so and stayed for forty years.

Although he always signed himself simply George Murray, the name registered for him shortly after he was born in London on December 16, 1900, was George McIntosh Murray. He told little more of himself than that he was educated in Archbishop Tenison's Grammar School, that he went to sea for two years, that he took a correspondence course in journalism at this time and later became an insurance agent while seeking a place for himself in newspaper work.

Sir William Haley, editor of the *Times,* writing in his own newspaper under a pseudonym, classed George Murray with Cassandra (William Connor) as writers of the two most successful features in British journalism.

Sir Linton Andrews who considered the contributions of George Murray to contemporary journalism important enough to demand a special chapter in the book published in collaboration with H. A. Taylor under the title *Lords and Laborers of the Press* declared that, "Had his editorials been signed with his name he would have been famous long ago—famous like the American Arthur Brisbane in his heyday, famous like the British Cassandra in the *Daily Mirror*. It is his style, the carefully researched facts, the persuasive progress of argument, the brightly minted phrases, that pierced the screen of anonymity and revealed the kind of thinker and craftsman George Murray is."

It was Murray in the *Daily Mail*, according to Andrews, and not the *Daily Telegraph*, who first criticized the government of Anthony Eden in 1956. It was in the same year that a signed article by Murray made the first responsible reference to Britain as being no longer a first-class power. The statement was contradicted by the *Times*, Harold Macmillan, and many other indignant spokesmen. Now it is commonplace, says Andrews, for the British to refer to the Suez crisis of 1956, cited by Murray, as proof of decline. Other innovations suggested by Murray in his writings and later implemented by the government were a civilian award for heroism during World War II (the George Medal), a pay-as-you-earn tax system, and in 1966 a wages and price freeze for a year or two to cope with Britain's economic troubles.

When the Press Council was formed in 1953, George Murray was one of three representatives elected to this body by the Institute of Journalists. Sir Linton Andrews was the first vice-chairman. The two men, already personal friends through long association in various professional activities, found themselves sharing a concern for the success of a body they both felt essential to the public interest and the future of the British press. It was in the setting of the Press Council meetings that Sir Linton formed the impressions of the Murray talents and the Murray character that come through so clearly in the sketch written for *Lords and Laborers of the Press*. In fact it must have been a conviction of long standing that caused Sir Linton, when asked to nominate a writer to undertake a history of the Press Council, to reply at once, "George Murray is the only man for it." It was Sir Linton who approached Mr. Murray, at the very time he was cutting down on his activities for the *Daily Mail*, with this new project.

The first draft promised in early 1970 actually arrived in Carbondale a year ahead of schedule, hurried along, perhaps, by the author's projected trip to Australia and New Zealand. The design was sound and the text as beautifully written as one would expect from the man who for thirty years had been the chief leader writer of one of London's great national newspapers. But there were problems involving small details dictated by the publisher's requirements, and numerous frustrations for an editor, suffering from an understanding, all too thin, of British practices and procedures, whose author was "somewhere in the South Pacific."

Finally the manuscript was retyped in duplicate. One copy, with a long list of requested clarifications, plus an invitation to revise and to expand was mailed by air to the Murray home in Esher, Surrey. A few weeks later, in March of 1970, there was a pleasant encounter in London with a conference that promised to clear up all problems related to the manuscript. The Murray revisions were to be returned to Carbondale for another typing and collation of the revised pages with those permitted to stand unchanged. Everything seemed to go according to plan. In October the packet arrived from Britain and the revised pages were sent to the typist. Soon the final draft would be ready. Then came the dreadful news in a letter from Sir Linton Andrews: George Murray, at the age of sixty-nine on November 2, after a heart attack, was dead.

There was too much of George Murray in his manuscript to permit abandonment of the project. The need of the British public, and above all the Americans, to be informed about the work of the Press Council was too great to justify further delay of a work so nearly finished. And so it has become the duty of the general editor to see the book through the press without the assistance normally expected from the author. One learns from one's British friends that one cannot let down the side. In this instance, "the side" includes many people: those who labored to found and to bring the Press Council of age; all the journalists of Britain whose profession has benefited; the British people who, because of the Press Council, enjoy a better journalism; the Americans, both public and professional who stand to gain so much by applying the principles of the Press Council to their problems; and, of course, George Murray the great editorial writer for whom this book may become a living memorial.

A rereading of George Murray's account of the development of the Press Council movement from the early stages of discussion and debate, through the preliminary attempts to formulate a plan, and his description of all that followed, seems to show that it would have been impossible for the concept to emerge without the influence of the man who possessed the genius to know "what was in the people's hearts and minds" and whose words "were their unspoken thoughts."

The parallel seems clear enough. First there was the infant council and the reflective analytical mind of the leader writer groping with the others to bring meaning to an ideal. Then with George Murray in the role of vice-chairman the Press Council began to find itself, to assert an authority credible to the public and acceptable to the professionals. Then, in the administration of George Murray as chairman, there came the period of reappraisal and the wise decisions leading to a broadening of outlook and the recognition of the proper role of the people in any effort to improve the quality of the press and its work in the public interest. At this time George Murray demonstrated his willingness to put conviction into practice by yielding the chairmanship to a layman in the person of Lord Devlin.

This book, then, is more than a history, because to some extent it amounts to a report on the personal stewardship of George Murray, journalist. Since the author is not here to defend himself, all errors are those of the general editor.

Carbondale, Illinois   HOWARD RUSK LONG
July 30, 1971

1 The Fight for Freedom

THE British Press Council is the characteristic product of a free society. It was born of the fundamental dilemma of democracy, which is, where to draw the line between liberty and licence.

De Tocqueville said of the press: "If anyone could point out an intermediate and yet a tenable position between the complete independence and the entire subjection of the expression of public opinion, I should perhaps be inclined to adopt it; but the difficulty is to discover this position."

The Press Council represents the first determined effort to resolve that difficulty in a nation where the newspapers had, through the centuries, progressed from entire subjection to complete independence. It is an unconscious attempt to refute another dictum of De Tocqueville (who was so often right) that "there is no medium between servitude and extreme licence; in order to enjoy the inestimable benefits which the liberty of the Press ensures, it is necessary to submit to the inevitable evils which it engenders."

This is so nearly true that the task of the Press Council, in trying to disprove it, has been far from easy. The council was conceived amid antagonisms and contention, its birth pangs were prolonged, and its first decade was marked by outbursts of abuse which tended to drown the occasional praise.

Disgruntled editors called it a Star Chamber, a title which provides a convenient starting-point for a brief review of the gradual unfolding of press liberty which led eventually to the Press Council.

The Star Chamber, a court appointed to uphold the despotic power of medieval kings had, by the seventeenth century, become an instrument for the control of the press. It appointed a messenger to smell out libels (which then meant any criticism of authority), prohibit books, and

1

exercise a tyrannical control over the embryonic newspapers of those days. It could impose fines amounting to the then enormous sums of ten or twenty-thousand pounds and punish offending editors by perpetual imprisonment or loss of ears—a power which (fortunately, no doubt) is denied to the Press Council.

The Star Chamber was abolished in 1641 and the press became free for a few years. Soon further controls were imposed, and it was in protest against these that John Milton wrote his historic pamphlet *Areopagitica,* a plea for the liberty of unlicensed printing. As a result of this powerful advocacy, licensing of the press was lifted, but only temporarily, for it was later reimposed. It was finally ended in 1695, since when there has been no official censorship of the press, except in time of war or other national emergency.

Nevertheless many strangling restrictions were still laid upon the press, and journalists continued to live dangerous cat-and-mouse lives. A ban on the reporting of Parliament imposed in 1660 continued, for in 1688 a judgment of the courts had declared: "No private man can take upon him to write concerning the government at all; for what has any private man to do with the government, if his interest be not stirred or shaken?"

By the eighteenth century the newsbooks and intelligencers of an earlier day had evolved crudely into the modern newspaper pattern— though not into its tradition of freedom. In 1738 the House of Commons resolved that any published account of its proceedings was a notorious breach of privilege, and, of course, no reporting facilities were given. But some bold and ingenious journalists got round this prohibition. One, known as "Memory Woodfall" could make note of an entire debate and reproduce it pretty accurately. Samuel Johnson published reports of the debates in *The Idler,* but the speeches were as he imagined they had been made—and they were doubtless much superior to the originals.

It was John Wilkes, a scamp and a scallywag, but also a fighter for freedom, who changed the adverse current of the times. He had been arrested for criticising the king's speech in his paper, the *North Briton,* discharged, and then rearrested for publishing a dirty essay on woman. He was expelled from Parliament, but the public rallied to his support. Twice he was rejected from the Commons and three times reelected on the cry: "Wilkes and Liberty." Finally, he stayed.

Authority never recovered its lost ground. In 1765 the Privy Council ordered the seizure of the person and papers of John Entick who had criticised the government in his paper the *Monitor,* but Lord Chief Justice Camden decided that the warrant was illegal and void. He did say, however, that he was no advocate of such writings, "for these compositions debauch the manners of the people; they excite a spirit of disobedience and enervate the authority of government; they provoke and excite the passions of the people against their rulers, and the rulers oftentimes against the people." He concluded that "when licentiousness is tolerated, liberty is in the utmost danger"—an opinion which would be shared neither by de Tocqueville nor the protagonists of the permissive society.

Still, despite Lord Camden's disclaimer, things were on the move. In 1771 a printer was arrested by order of the House of Commons for publishing its debates. He was brought before the lord mayor of London, one Brass Crosby, who discharged him and was himself then arrested for breach of privilege of the House of Commons. Lord Chief Justice Grey refused to sentence him because, he said, "we cannot judge of the laws and privileges of the House because we have no knowledge of these laws and privileges." He added: "I wish we had some code of the law of Parliament"—a remark which has been wistfully echoed up to this day when parliamentary privilege remains a trap for journalists, and even M.P.'s.

That the climate of the times began gradually to favour uninhibited expressions of opinion was shown in several significant ways. Junius, who wrote a famous series of letters to the *Public Advertiser* between 1768 and 1772 (and who has never been positively identified), said: "Let it be impressed upon your minds, let it be instilled into your children, that the liberty of the Press is the palladium of all the civil, political and religious rights of an Englishman."

Sir William Blackstone, in his *Commentaries,* first published in 1765, said: "The liberty of the Press is indeed essential to the nature of a free State, but this consists in laying no previous restraints upon publication and not in freedom of censure for criminal matters when published." In English law the freedom of the press, like the Constitution, is nowhere explicitly stated, any more than are the rights of free speech and public assembly. It is implicit in the freedom of the individual to do as he pleases, provided that he keeps within the law. The first time that freedom of the press was protected by law was in the Virginia Bill of Rights drawn up by George Mason in 1776. This said that: "Freedom of the Press is one of the greatest bulwarks of liberty and can never be restrained but by despotic governments."

When the eighteenth century gave way to the nineteenth, horizons extended and outlooks broadened. In 1820 a writer was charged with seditious libel because he had written of cruelties perpetrated by troops in a civil riot—what today would have been an accusation of "police brutality." In dismissing the case, Mr. Justice Best said: "The liberty of the Press is this, that you may communicate any information that you may think proper to communicate by print; that you may point out to the Government their errors and endeavour to convince them that their policy is wrong and attended with disadvantage to the country."

Here, indeed, was a revolutionary change in attitude. It reflected the growing boldness of a free press. In the eighteenth century most newspapers had been the paid creatures of political parties or of individual politicians, but the introduction of advertising by the *Times* had given the British press an independence which it had never before enjoyed, and has since never lost. The way in which it now began to exert its new-found liberty would have been inconceivable to a previous generation.

In 1852 Louis Napoleon of France, thinking that the *Times* could be "bought," approached the foreign secretary, Lord Granville, through Walewski, the French ambassador in London, to secure a modification in the anti-French policy of the paper. The *Times* refused to oblige, and Walewski wrote to Louis Napoleon: "It is possible that third-class papers like the *Sun, Standard,* &c might be purchased. But the enterprises of *The Times* and the *Morning Chronicle* are backed by too big capital, their political management is in too many hands for it to be possible to buy them at any price whatever."

The government used the debate on the address in that year to attack the press for irresponsibility. The prime minister, Lord Derby, said that if journalists aspired to the influence of statesmen they should accept the responsibility of statesmen. Delane, the famous editor of the *Times,* made the historic reply which, once for all, proclaimed the liberty of the press. He wrote: "The statesman collects his information secretly and by secret means; he keeps even the current intelligence of the day with ludicrous precautions until diplomacy is beaten in the race with publicity. The Press lives by disclosures; whatever passes into its keeping becomes part of the knowledge and the history of our times; it is daily and for ever appealing to the enlightened force of public opinion—anticipating, if possible, the march of events—standing upon the breach between the present and the future, and extending its survey to the horizon of the world." At a later date he added: "The first duty of the Press is to obtain the earliest and most correct intelligence of the events of the time, and instantly, while disclosing them, to make them the common property of the nation."

Another clash between press and Parliament occurred in 1854 when Lord Derby denounced the *Times* for publishing a secret proposal of the tsar to partition Turkey. The newspaper replied: "To accuse this or any other journal of publishing early and correct intelligence, when there is no possibility of proving that such intelligence has been obtained by unfair or improper means, is to pay us one of the highest compliments we hope to deserve. . . . We hold ourselves responsible, not to Lord Derby or the House of Lords, but to the people of England for the accuracy and fitness of what we think proper to publish."

These great statements of principle were rounded off by Tennyson, the poet laureate, who wrote:

> *As long as we remain, we must speak free,*
> *Though all the storm of Europe on us break,*
> *No petty German State are we,*
> *But the one voice in Europe; we must speak*
> *That if tonight our greatness were struck dead,*
> *There might be left some record of the things we said.*

Milton would have approved.

By this time the press had thrown off most of the shackles which had tried to bind it to subservience, but several smaller irritants remained. These were the taxes on newspapers, advertisements, and paper—the "taxes on knowledge." The first of them was imposed in 1712 and the last abolished by 1861. In 1868 a case before the courts concerning a report of parliamentary proceedings ended in this declaration by Lord Chief Justice Cockburn: "It seems to us impossible to doubt that it is of paramount public and national importance that the proceedings of the Houses of Parliament should be communicated to the public, who have the deepest interest in knowing what passes within their walls, seeing that on what is there said and done the welfare of the community depends."

But since Parliament is the sole arbiter of its own privileges, this judgment was not accepted by either House, and although the press gallery has been a recognised institution for generations, the reporting of debates remained technically a breach of privilege. This anomaly was ended by resolution only in 1968 – years after the greatest grumble of M.P.'s against the press was not that it reported their speeches but that it all too often ignored them.

From the 1860s onwards, the British press, though always working much more on sufferance than that of the United States, was free, independent, unrestricted in its publications and comments, except for the laws of libel and obscenity which were not aimed specifically at the press but applied to everyone. De Tocqueville's condition of "servitude" had ended. Was a period of "extreme licence" now to begin – a licence which could only be curbed by some sort of controlling authority?

Such as a Press Council.

2 The Unchanging Press

It is a modern, but unfounded, belief that only in our own time has the press become personal, intrusive, interfering, and iconoclastic. It is widely thought that, before the twentieth century, newspapers, especially those of the Victorian era, were models of decorum, with a proper respect for authority. That this was not so has already been shown in the proudly defiant attitude of mid-Victorian journalism. But this was merely one outstanding episode in a long story of criticism and rebelliousness which led many courageous journalists to fines and imprisonment. The press is a thorn in the flesh of authority; it always has been, and, as it values its immortal soul, it always will be. The function of an editor of any paper in any century has been to get the news and to comment on the news—to tell the truth and shame the devil.

But what about the sex and sensationalism, the vulgarity, triviality, and inaccuracy of the modern press? In these respects, also, newspapers do not change except in accordance with changing conventions. The newspaper is the child of its age—the mirror of its time. When Lord Chief Justice Mansfield said, in 1784, that "the licentiousness of the Press is Pandora's box—the source of every evil," he was repeating similar strictures already made, and anticipating many yet to come.

As far back as the civil wars of the seventeenth century, when the Royalist leader Sir John Hopton was many times reported in the parliamentarian newsletters (or Corantos) to have been killed (and such rumors are by no means unknown nowadays), a Cavalier poet wrote derisively:

> There Hopton was slain, again and again
> Or else my author did lie.

In a similar vein a contemporary prayer ran: "We desire the Coranto-makers to be inspired with the spirit of Truth, that we may know when to praise Thy Blessed and Glorious Name, and when to pray unto Thee; for we often praise and laude Thy Holy Name for the King of Sweden's victories, and afterwards we heare that there is no such thing; and we oftentime pray unto Thee to relieve the same King in his distresses, and we likewise heare that there is no such cause."

Through the decades the sins of the press have been constant, and have been as constantly deplored. A periodical called the *Mirror,* published in 1779, castigated contemporaries for "a cruel sporting with the sensibilities of human nature . . . merely to fill the columns of a newspaper." That is the modern accusation of malicious gossip. Another passage said, sardonically, that "it is of the highest importance that the very earliest notice should be given of the near appearance of a figure-dancer." Alter the wording a little, and substitute "pop-singer" for "figure-dancer," and we have "triviality." The *Mirror* also wagged a sorrowful finger because newspapers wrote of the "misfortunes, real or imaginary, of private families. For example: 'We hear that Mrs. Gadabout was lately detected in an illicit commerce with her husband's postilion and the process of divorce will be brought.'" That was certainly a rebuke for "intrusion."

It was in the nineteenth century, when the press really began to ferret out the news and to comment on events with unwonted freedom, that denunciations reached a pitch unsurpassed even in the years which led to the formation of the Press Council. The *Times* was called by various people, including Queen Victoria, "atrocious," "tyrannical," "infernal," "wicked," and "insolent." Greville said that the attacks by this newspaper on Peel, the prime minister, were "as mischievous as malignity could make them." When, in a later age, Mr. Baldwin turned on the *Daily Mail* and *Daily Express* which had long been attacking him, he was no less, and no more, vitriolic. When the *Times* revealed the disgraceful conditions in which British soldiers fought the Crimean War it was accused in Parliament of rigging the market to its own advantage by raising the price of the funds in one week and depressing them in the next. When the *Daily Mail* attacked Lord Kitchener for the scandalous shortage of shells in World War I it was burned on the Stock Exchange. *Plus ca change, plus c'est la même chose.*

Queen Victoria had good reason for disliking the press, some organs of which were enthusiastically republican. The *Times* itself fell under grave suspicion when it published a violent attack on the Prussian court.

Lord Clarendon said that "every condition of treason is fulfilled" by the article which was "a dagger in the Queen's heart." The Prince Consort observed: "Soon there will not be room enough in the same country for the Monarchy and *The Times.*"

The royal family then were treated much more savagely by the press than they have been since – and there was no Press Council to stand between them and the newspapers. When Victoria was still a child the newspapers reported (wrongly) that her legs and feet were so diseased that walking for her was said to be impossible. Later a hostile press said that hers was a "depraved court." Imagine it!

The Queen was furious when, one day in 1844, "a horrid man from the *Morning Herald* got into Windsor Castle and published an alarming report on the Prince Consort's health." How he entered the castle we are not told, but his exploit was not very different from that of a woman reporter who, in 1956, gate-crashed the Duke of Kent's birthday party by arriving in the boot of a motorcar – and was duly censured for it by the Press Council.

Later in the century there were scurrilous gossiping and skits in the press about the relationship of Queen Victoria with her manservant John Brown, of a kind that would not be tolerated today. We may compare the "revelations" of the Victorian press with the discreet silence maintained by twentieth-century British newspapers over the relationship between King Edward VIII and Mrs. Wallis Simpson, until the story had become too important to be withheld.

When the engagement of Prince George (afterwards George V) to Princess May was announced in 1893, the *Pall Mall Gazette* said the marriage would be bigamous because George was already married and had a wife and two children in Malta. This falsehood was current up to 1910, when it was repeated in a paper called the *Liberator,* published in Paris by a man named Mylius. He was charged with criminal libel and sentenced to twelve months' imprisonment.

Facts apart, many passing references to the press may be found in Victorian literature, and they are rarely complimentary. One typical comment – an Anglo-American one – will perhaps suffice. Henry James, in the *Aspern Papers,* published in 1888 makes one character say: "I felt almost as base as the reporter of a newspaper who forces his way into a house of mourning." Even in those straitlaced years reporters "forced their way," and no doubt if the paper had printed photographs, there would have been "picture-snatchers," too. The journalist seemed no better regarded in France. Balzac, writing in the 1840s, has a man say in one of his books: "I was about to take the editorship of a newspaper when I was seized with terror. 'Would *she* want for a husband a lover who had descended so low?' I asked myself."

Some of the business practices of newspaper proprietors, popularly supposed to be introductions of the twentieth century, were not unknown by their predecessors. The system of financing newspapers by advertisements while making a loss on sales was not a twentieth-century innovation, as is shown by the following extract from a letter written by Lord Palmerston to Queen Victoria in 1861:

> The actual price at which each copy of the newspaper is sold barely pays the expense of paper, printing and establishment; it is indeed said that the price does not pay those expenses. The profit of the newspaper arises from the price paid for advertisements, and the greater the number of advertisements the greater the profit. But advertisements are sent by preference to the newspaper which has the greatest circulation; and that paper gets the widest circulation which is the most amusing, and the most instructive.

Northcliffe could hardly have put it better.

It is not true, either, that the absorption and killing-off of rival newspapers by ruthless methods, was unknown before 1900. In the latter half of the nineteenth century there was a continual swallowing of one paper by another. In 1868, for instance, the *Daily News*, which was to suffer a similar fate nearly a century later, suddenly reduced its price from threepence to a penny, thus delivering a mortal blow to its chief rival, the *Morning Star*, which it then consumed at leisure.

3 Why the Press Council?

IF, as I have tried to show, newspapers of today are fundamentally no different from what they have always been, the question that naturally follows is: "Why, then, the need for a Press Council when it was not felt before?"

One answer is to seek an analogy in the traffic on the roads. There were traffic jams in ancient Rome and in the medieval cities of Europe, but little or nothing was done about them because they had not much influence on the life and well-being of the community. It is only in our own age when most people (in the West) are motorists, that the traffic jam has become so serious a social and economic problem that vast sums have to be spent on arterial roads and vehicles have to be controlled and regulated, not only when they are moving but also when they are stationary.

It is surely a similar story with the press. The need for some kind of curb can be summed up in one word—impact. In 1855 the *Times* sold more copies than all the other London papers put together—and its circulation was seventy thousand. By the 1870s the *Daily Telegraph* boasted the largest circulation in the world, with two hundred thousand. The caravan has rolled a long way since then—forward to the million, the diurnal five million. One Sunday newspaper, the *News of the World,* in its heyday sold more than eight million copies every week. The sky, it seemed, was the limit.

To the word impact must be added another—ubiquity. Where the newspaper was once passed from hand to hand, it was beginning to be pushed through every letter box. Where it once confined its attention to the great and near-great, it now began to concern itself with the lives and activities of ordinary people. Actors, actresses, film stars, and later, radio and television personalities, the favourites of the multitude, displaced the personages of society and politics from the front pages. This was an inevitable development of mass communication, mass education, mass entertainment, and an inescapable accompaniment of the egalitarian age. It was the Century of the Common Man.

And it was on the common man that the pressure of the papers began to fall. Intrusion into the castle was more and more becoming intrusion into the cottage—and many cottagers did not like it. When newspaper reports and articles dealt increasingly with the affairs of everyday life, inaccuracies became more and more apparent. Efforts to titillate the million sometimes led editors into indiscretions which became "bad taste." So it was the common man in his century who, in the end, insisted that the press should exercise some restraint and self-discipline.

It was said that with the expansion in circulation there came a diminution in the political influence of the press and, at first glance, this seemed to be true. Before the popular newspaper appeared, the great dailies were, to a large extent, organs of opinion, intended to be read by men who could, and would, influence events and policies. Newspapers sometimes sacrificed profits to such considerations. A notable example was that of the *Westminster Gazette* which, in the years before the First World War, was said to be the most politically influential newspaper in the kingdom. Its editor, J. A. Spender, was so close to the leaders in the Liberal government of 1906 onwards, that he was almost in the cabinet, and his paper exerted considerable authority in the inner circles. Yet the *Westminster Gazette* never sold more than twenty-five thousand copies as an evening newspaper and lost money throughout its career.

It would be a mistake, however, to accept that the press ceased to have any influence on politics when these conditions passed away. What happened was that it came to be differently exercised. The day of the universal vote was dawning and the million-sale newspaper was an instrument ready-made to sway it. Influence, which had once started at the centre, seeping outwards, now began on the circumference, to make its way inwards. The age of the party mandate was also the age of the political slogan which, trumpeted day in and day out by the megaphones of the new press, began to force policies and decisions at Westminster.

Such changes were prodigious but a greater one yet, the one most characteristic of the twentieth century, was to transform the shape and substance of the newspaper press. This was the advent of mass financial power. Many harsh words have been addressed to the "money manipulators," the "financial dictators," the "hard-faced men," but they (or their coevals, the State monopolists) were an essential element in an age which was to cope with the enormous expansion of mass production which rapid scientific progress was making available.

The press could no more escape these gigantic forces than any other institution. It was perhaps more susceptible, for newspapers, if they are to survive, must quickly respond to changing times. It was because so many failed to realise this basic truth that they died or had to sell out to more percipient rivals.

The typical nineteenth-century newspaper was privately owned; more often than not a family property yielding comfortable profits and, if a prosperous daily, conferring a prestige and political influence which its owners would not otherwise have attained. The Institute of Journalists records that when it was founded, in 1883, and for some years afterwards, there was not a single newspaper company whose shares were quoted on the Stock Exchange.

The typical twentieth-century daily newspaper belongs to a chain or group backed by the large financial resources needed to provide expensive worldwide news and photographic services and all the modern features and layouts demanded by readers today. It is a newspaper over which the influence of the editor has declined and that of the manager has become all-important. Journalism is still a profession but it has become a profession within an industry – an industry which pays its employees well and has immeasurably raised the status of the journalist. Many people dream of a return to the Victorian climate which sustained a large number of small, independent newspapers. This is a dream which becomes more remote from reality as the century advances but, strangely enough, it is nourished to this day by some who, at the same time, are foremost in demanding a rising scale of remuneration which only the new, big combines have made possible.

That is one side of the picture. It is the other which aroused such deep and growing public concern that two Royal Commissions were appointed within a comparatively short time to investigate the problems of the newspapers and to make recommendations. For, although it is true to say that the press is just an industry which must expect to be cartelised like the next one, the newspaper is still in a very special category. It represents one of the Four Freedoms which underpin democracy. It is a bulwark of liberty and an enemy of tyranny, and it performs these functions by reason of its own variety and independence. What if that variety is reduced to a point at which independence is seriously weakened? What if the number of newspapers is so lessened that policies come to be dictated by powerful men controlling the organs of opinion, with few remaining correctives to that opinion, or even none at all? These questions, rarely asked at the turn of the century, were increasingly heard as the years passed and hundreds of newspapers passed out of existence.

The distant drumbeats of the new century were audible in 1896 when Alfred Harmsworth (afterwards Lord Northcliffe) and his brother Harold (afterwards Lord Rothermere) founded the *Daily Mail* and other papers. Northcliffe was the journalistic genius and Rothermere the financial wizard, and they formed an unbeatable combination. Their success was phenomenal with nearly everything they touched, and especially with the Daily *Mail*.

It was "a penny paper for a halfpenny." It was "the busy man's daily journal." It provided the first magazine page in British newspaper history. It was just right for those (and there were more and more of them) who were travelling back and forth to their work in new forms of transport and who wanted concise, crisp information. It appealed to women—that vast, untapped market. Its background articles were avidly read by the new literate classes who had benefited from the Education Act of 1870. It bounded forward because it fitted the new century like a glove—and it was the first newspaper whose finances were open to public investment. Northcliffe sensed the unsatisfied national thirst for enlightenment and Rothermere fertilised the multiplying enterprises with his financial aptitudes. They were the pioneers, but had they not lived others would assuredly have followed the same paths, for the demands of an era cannot be denied.

Now, once again, we must look at the other side of the medal. Northcliffe and Rothermere were among the first "Press lords" to feel the vast popular influence which possessors of mighty engines of publicity enjoy. Northcliffe's name became a household word, and at one period during the First World War he was said to be the most powerful man in the country. He was a great patriot, and when he died, the crowds lined the streets for miles to see the funeral procession pass.

But there were times when his demands on the prime minister came perilously close to "government by newspaper"—something novel in the island story. After Northcliffe's death, Rothermere launched many campaigns which he considered to be for the good of the country, but some of which were judged otherwise. Because he lacked Northcliffe's journalistic touch he made mistakes in running his newspapers, but he was no less a patriot than his brother had been. For example, within a few months of Hitler's seizure of power in 1933 he launched a campaign for the building of an enormous force of warplanes to meet the German military menace. He went on making this demand, in season and out, in the face of jeers, scepticism and incomprehension until almost the outbreak of war. Churchill wrote to him in 1939: "When the present regime in Germany was new you were indeed one of the few voices warning Britain of her need for an overwhelming air force and a modernised navy. I know how ungrudgingly you have spent time, energy and money in your endeavours to make the nation aware of its danger and the need to rearm." It seemed, after all, that the "megaphone Press" was not always self-seeking, and that there were some press lords ready to put country before circulation.

At one stage Lord Rothermere joined with Lord Beaverbrook, proprietor of the *Daily Express,* in violent attacks on the prime minister, pursued over a long period. Later disclosures showed that there was some justification for this vendetta, but it was interpreted as an attempt at newspaper domination, and in 1931 Mr. Baldwin hit back in terms reminiscent of ministerial strictures on the *Times,* in the 1850s. This is what he said:

> The papers conducted by Lord Rothermere and Lord Beaverbrook are not newspapers in the ordinary acceptance of the term. They are engines of propaganda for the constantly-changing policies, desires, personal wishes, personal likes and dislikes of two men. What are their methods? Their methods are direct falsehood, misrepresentation, half-truths, the alteration of the speaker's meaning by putting sentences apart from the context, suppression and editorial criticism of speeches which are not reported in the paper. What the proprietorship of these papers is aiming at is power, but power without responsibility—the prerogative of the harlot through the ages.

Strong stuff! The last sentence was to be quoted over and over again in the years to come. It was thought to have been given to Mr. Baldwin by his kinsman, Rudyard Kipling. At all events, the friendship which had existed between Kipling and Beaverbrook became distinctly chilly from that moment.

It might be here interjected that, whatever their sins of omission or commission, both these newspaper proprietors could claim to have done the State some service in the very sphere which Baldwin was criticised for neglecting, namely, the air defence of Britain. In World War I Rothermere was air minister when the Royal Air Force came into being and was warmly thanked by Lloyd George for his "inestimable service to the nation." In World War II, Beaverbrook became minister of Aircraft Production at the most critical period in 1940. Churchill paid tribute to his "personal force and genius" which did much to win the Battle of Britain.

However that may be, Baldwin's "harlot" speech of 1931 summed up fears which had for years been spreading through the community that wealthy men would somehow contrive to control the British democracy through the newspapers, and these fears were given voice in more than one influential quarter.

Lord Hewart, remembered as attorney general and lord chief justice, said in 1922 that the merest caprice and whim of a rich man who chose to put his money into rotary printing machines, "by the mere force of that mechanical duplication may become a danger to the peace of the world." The House of Commons in 1929 gave vent to the growing anxiety when it debated a motion saying that "the maintenance of independent organs for the dissemination of news is vital to the preservation of the standard of public life in this country, and that the consolidation of the newspaper Press in the hands of powerful syndicates, and some of the devices employed by these syndicates to extend the circulation of the newspapers under their control, are contrary to the public interest."

"These devices," many of which were Northcliffe innovations, were new to British journalism. They included free insurance for readers, canvassing, "stunts," gift schemes, and so on. By the 1930s the gift business had reached such a pitch of lunacy that the four principal London dailies were spending a total of sixty to seventy thousand pounds a week on gifts ranging from silk stockings, through sets of books, to mangles and scores of other articles, for people who would order the paper for, say, six weeks. All they were doing was to win and lose circulation, one to another, as readers cashed in on the bonanza simply by continually changing their morning papers.

The "consolidation of the newspaper Press in the hands of powerful syndicates" took a pronounced step forward when the first Lord Rothermere started Northcliffe Newspapers, with the object of founding new evening papers in provincial cities, and buying up existing journals. He announced this great enterprise on February 13, 1928, a date that would never have been chosen by his brother Northcliffe, who was superstitious about the number 13. It proved to be unlucky for Rothermere also. In the following year the Wall Street crash heralded the great depression which froze the marrow of existing newspapers, to say nothing of new journals fighting for a foothold.

Northcliffe Newspapers' struggle was mainly with Allied Newspapers, who were established in many provincial centres. They were challenged particularly in Newcastle and Bristol where Rothermere started *Evening Worlds*. By 1931 there were eleven papers in the Northcliffe chain, mostly bought as existing properties and largely controlled from London. The battle was on, and it was bitter indeed. By 1932 both antagonists were near exhaustion; so much so that they reached agreement whereby Allied kept Newcastle where the *World* closed down, and Northcliffe kept Bristol, where the Allied paper ended. When the "war" finished, four provincial papers had died. It had been a violent episode in newspaper history, but it might have had a happier outcome had the time been better chosen.

Allied Newspapers were bought by Mr. Roy (afterwards Lord) Thomson, in 1959, and are now Thomson Newspapers. Northcliffe Newspapers have been quietly and steadily developed and expanded, with local editors taking full responsibility, until today they are the largest and one of the most prosperous chains in the country. Years after the Northcliffe-Allied war, the second Lord Rothermere told the Press Commission: "We went into the provinces with the idea of showing them how to run their newspapers and they did not take to us. . . . We had to turn our policy completely upside-down and leave them entirely alone, which is what they wanted. We found that highly successful."

Now to go back again. In 1930, Mr. Winston Churchill said: "We should make a great mistake if we exchanged Parliamentary government for newspaper government. The newspapers play a most important part in our modern life, but when they step outside their proper province . . . when they attempt to dominate the State; when they unfairly bias and weight the news they print; when they suppress as far as possible all opinions but their own; when they traduce or belittle all public men who do not show themselves subservient to their will; when they finance and run candidates and confuse elections and split votes; when they dictate policy to party leaders and even demand the right to choose Ministers of the Crown—then they become an abuse which is dangerous to the Constitution and fatal to good government."

It was a formidable indictment. Some of these charges were justified, but was the position really as bad as that? Neither politicians nor press could state an unbiased case for they glared at one another across the healthy gulf of wary hostility which had always separated them, and always should.

Throughout this period, the sniping at the press in Parliament and elsewhere was often accompanied by hints of some form of regulation. In 1935 the home secretary, Sir John Gilmour, replying to a question in the Commons complaining about some newspaper sin said he would prefer to rely on the good sense of the profession to remedy such things, but, if it were unable to do so, "I think it would be necessary to consider seriously whether any other means can be devised of protecting the public from such conduct."

There was also a good deal of soul-searching among journalists. Colonel Lawson (later Lord Burnham), managing director of the *Daily Telegraph* and vice-chairman of the Newspaper Proprietors' Association, representing the London daily newspapers, said newspaper interests should get together and try to arrive at some scheme of self-imposed restraint, otherwise "the freedom of the Press might be seriously menaced in the future."

The Institute of Journalists had drawn up a Journalists' Registration Bill in 1935 in an endeavour to raise journalism to the status of a recognised profession, and though it came to nothing it showed the way the wind was blowing. In 1936 a past president of the National Union of Journalists also spoke of the need for journalists "to impose upon themselves some agreed minimum standard of conduct." In 1937 the home secretary, Sir John Simon, made representations to the Newspaper Proprietors' Association and the Newspaper Society (representing the provincial press) about complaints of intrusion by reporters into the privacy of bereaved persons. Both bodies condemned such methods, but neither did anything effective to end them.

The press also had its grievances. One was grounded in the Official Secrets Acts of 1889, 1911, and 1920, which were intended to protect the national security. When the 1920 Act was passed, Lord Hewart, then attorney general, gave a specific promise that it would not apply to ordinary press inquiries. But in 1937 a Manchester journalist was prosecuted for failing to disclose his source of information about a man wanted for fraudulent conversion. It fell to Hewart, who by then had become lord chief justice, to deal with a case which, as a politician, he said could not occur. Already, in 1932, a London reporter had been sent to prison for obtaining advance information about wills from official sources.

These acts were, without any question, stretched much beyond their original purpose. But who was there to speak for the press, except the press itself? Who was there to question other laws which forbade the publication of full proceedings in divorce cases and the photographing of participants in court cases "within the precincts of the court"? There seemed to be the need for some sort of body which would not only protect the public against the press but also keep an eye on encroachments upon the freedom of the press.

The first mention of such a possibility appeared in a booklet, *Report on the British Press,* published in 1938 by P.E.P. (Political and Economic Planning). This is a body formed in 1931 by members of several informal discussion groups which has since issued hundreds of broadsheets of investigation into nearly every aspect of British life, society, and industry. Before embarking on an inquiry it assembles experts in the fields to be discussed, and each of these groups invites laymen. Anonymity is strictly preserved so that knowledge can be made available from people who might be reluctant to express views if their names became known. By these methods the P.E.P. publications have obtained an acknowledged authority and impartiality.

P.E.P.'s report noted five disturbing tendencies in the press. These were: 1. The replacement of a relatively large number of independent newspapers by a remarkably small number of mass-circulation national journals; 2. The number of separate proprietors of importance had diminished owing to the growth of chains; 3. The cost of launching a national newspaper had become virtually prohibitive; 4. National advertising encouraged the enlargement of popular national newspapers and placed more emphasis on the entertainment side in relation to news and comment; 5. The encouragement of nonjournalistic types of enterprise, such as free gifts and free insurance.

Although the report mentioned the main complaints against the press such as triviality, intrusion, inaccuracy, overemphasis of sex, and so on, it also thought that so far from the public taste having fallen from a once-high level, it had been even lower in the past. It was the rise of mass-circulation newspapers which had made the shortcomings of the press more conspicuous. In other words—impact and ubiquity.

P.E.P. went on: "We therefore attach urgent importance to the redress of these grievances by the action of the Press itself, and propose that a Press tribunal should be set up for this purpose on the joint initiative of the leading proprietors' and journalists' organisations." There should be a lay chairman with judicial experience and two assessors from panels of proprietors and journalists; there would be no legislative authority and no power to inflict fines or punish journalists otherwise than through investigation and publication of findings—"a very powerful sanction." In this way "there would be built up by a series of case decisions a working code of legitimate and illegitimate practice."

When the Press Council came into being in later years it followed almost the exact lines of this remarkably percipient peering into the future. But a long time was to elapse and a torrent of controversial words to be let loose before that culmination. Another idea was put forward by P.E.P. Pointing out that Great Britain was almost alone among leading countries in providing for no continuous scientific study of the press, it proposed the formation of a Press Institute under the auspices of some detached and impartial body, such as the University of London. That proposal has not so far been adopted.

Such suggestions apart, the general observations of P.E.P. on the British press were of great value. Referring to Baldwin's excoriation of popular newspapers it said it was unfair to look at the situation of 1938 in terms of 1930–31. "On the one hand the principal Press magnates have since become much readier to conform with public opinion instead of trying to impose their personal beliefs on their readers. On the other hand, it has become clear that the danger of large circulations enabling one man to influence a wide public through his newspapers was overrated, and it now appears that there is a law of compensation at work. The exploitation of entertainment value prevents such papers from influencing the political views of their readers to anything like the same extent as the 'class' dailies and weeklies."

Whether that was true in 1938 is arguable, though it may have become so in the 1950s and 1960s when the newspapers, even such a "class" journal as the *Times,* were driven to compete with television in entertainment value. It was certainly true that, in seven years, the megaphone had become muted and the stridency softened. This did not, however, stop the "harlot" speech from being quoted against popular newspapers a decade later, when it had ceased to be relevant.

P.E.P. noted some of the changes which had come over the press and its relationships since the nineteenth century. Then, it was the editor who moulded the policy of the paper. Now, it was the proprietor, and it was significant that newspapers were known by their proprietors rather than by their editors. Modern influences on the press included public relations officers, government and otherwise; the paid propagandists of foreign powers and the publicity departments of political parties. Pressures were also exercised by newspaper associations, newsvenders, readers, and the churches. "It would be a mistake to assume that with all these influences and pressures the words of Thomas Jefferson 'nothing can be believed which is seen in a newspaper' are to be taken literally . . . indeed after reviewing all these potentially disturbing influences, it appears creditable that the Press maintains so high a degree of impartiality as it does."

One thing which worried P.E.P. investigators was the inadequacy of foreign news in the British press, especially American news, a good deal of which was "simply trivial and valueless for keeping in touch with events." It went on:

"The difficulty of understanding, and still more of making the English reader understand, the complications of American politics and the American scene generally is very great, and the background is so strange—there are far fewer Englishmen who have been to America than Americans who have been to England. Partly because of the false assumptions about the effects of close kinship, the two nations tend to be rather hasty in simplifying one another's characteristics. America is depicted to England as a territory of crazy politics, gangsters and lawbreaking, divorce and fierce warfare between capital and labour, while England is treated in the American Press with melodramatic bias and an absence of half-tones, British policy in particular being represented as subtly entrapping other countries to serve selfish British interests. Again, the bulk of tendentious material supplied to the Press in America is much greater than in England, and while business and public leaders are much more accessible to journalists, it is more difficult to get reliable data for the interpretation of news, such as is available in London at clubs and dinner parties and elsewhere where people exchange informal views, freely speaking 'off the record.' . . .

"Perhaps the greatest difficulty of all is to convince the British Press that American news in particular is worth more space and more staff than is allowed for it. In fact, from an immediate circulation standpoint, present policies can be strongly defended. On a long view, however, it must be evident that economic and political trends are forcing the English-speaking peoples closer together, and that this must demand fuller information from each other about the other's thoughts and doings."

Even those expert investigators could not have realised how soon, and how dramatically, that last sentence was to be realised. While something of what they said remains true even today, the U.S. gets far more coverage—sometimes amounting almost to blanket coverage—in the postwar British press. Before the war, Paris was the chief foreign news centre in London eyes, but today Washington and New York are by far the most important. The writer remembers when the election of a new American president rated a few inches on the front pages of London dailies. In 1968 it was the subject of splash headlines and background articles for many months, and the election itself could hardly have been more thoroughly covered in the U.S.

That is by the way. One more point made by the P.E.P. booklet was a general dissatisfaction with the educational standards of British journalists, their recruitment training, and general professional competence. Saying that these were customarily, and perhaps inevitably, left to chance, it thought it would be hard to devise a training and examination system which would not hamper rather than facilitate the progress of a born journalist. "At the same time it is very desirable that journalists should have every facility for equipping themselves for what is, after all, one of the most exacting and responsible functions in a modern community. The standard and personnel of the Press can, and should be, very greatly improved." Here, also, was an invaluable suggestion which later led to practical results. A training scheme for journalists was started in 1952, not sponsored, as originally proposed, by the Press Council, but as a separate enterprise.

The war came, and all these matters faded into the background. But not for the duration of the conflict. In 1942, the National Union of Journalists (the N.U.J.) at its annual delegate meeting, discussed a proposal to establish a body representing proprietors and journalists "for ensuring the maintenance of a proper sense of responsibility in the Press and the control of irresponsible newspapers and journalists." Such a motion seemed out of key with the fight to the death for freedom then being waged, and it was strongly opposed by others who believed that "such a body could easily become a most dangerous agency for the suppression of legitimate criticism, and must inevitably lead to a still further invasion of the freedom of the Press."

Later in the year the home secretary met a union delegation on the subject but agreed that the proposal was "unsound and unworkable." This fleeting episode should be noted. The home secretary was Mr. (afterwards Lord) Morrison, and it was not to be long before he and the N.U.J. were working to secure the very thing that both had turned down.

But the matter was not forgotten, and it was the N.U.J. which took the initiative in the demand for a Royal Commission into the press. In 1944 the report of a committee on the union's postwar policy was referred back to the annual delegate meeting because it failed to deal with the "basic question of the trend towards monopoly in the industry." A report advocating an independent inquiry into the press was adopted by the union in March 1945. Early in 1946 the union as a whole urged on the government the appointment of a Royal Commission, and in October 1946, two of its M.P. members opened a debate in the House of Commons demanding such an inquiry.

The Institute of Journalists was not so sure. In his presidential address that year, Mr. W. L. (afterwards Sir Linton) Andrews, doubted whether it lay within the ingenuity of a Royal Commission to devise a formula making the press more useful than it had been during the war, and had continued to be. "The Press has its faults arising out of human nature, but they are not to be blue-pencilled out of existence by political regulation," he said. "Errors of judgment, errors arising from extreme and even misguided loyalty to party doctrine and party leaders are human frailties. The proper remedy for them is a critical, democratic spirit, not intervention by politicians who think they know best what the public should or should not be told, and who alone should be allowed to tell them." The speaker, who was later to become chairman of the Press Council, thus voiced the salutary, and traditional, warning of "Hands off the Press."

Nevertheless, the ball had been set rolling, and it is worth examining the course of events in some detail because of the political issues involved. Those who protested, as many did, that there was no political feeling in the matter, protested too much, for the discussions ran definitely, and often harshly, on political lines. The Labour party, who were in power at the time, were wholeheartedly in favour of a probe into the press. The Conservative opposition were as strongly opposed to it. There is little doubt that had they formed the government there would have been no Royal Commission and therefore no Press Council until, perhaps, Labour had returned to power—and by then feelings might have changed.

As it was, even the Labour government were at first opposed to the idea of a Royal Commission. This was demanded by the N.U.J. early in 1946, but when Mr. (afterwards Earl) Attlee, the prime minister, was asked in the Commons on April 30 if he had considered it, he replied: "I have given careful consideration to this proposal which, however, I do not see my way to adopt."

It was a surprise, therefore, when on July 16, Mr. Morrison, then deputy prime minister, said in the Commons: "All great channels for the dissemination of information to the public would, the Government believe, benefit from having their state of health examined by an independent inquiry from time to time, and we do not exclude the Press from this consideration." He also spoke of the "suppressions, misrepresentations and inventions" of the antigovernment press. Sir Hartley (afterwards Lord) Shawcross, the attorney general, who, fifteen years later, was to head the second Royal Commission on the Press, made similar remarks.

Such words are recalled in order to show a marked antipress sentiment then existing among ministers, though this was denied. Mr. Morrison said in the debate that the abrupt change in the government's intentions was due to a deputation from the N.U.J. who had so impressed them that they felt a request for a Royal Commission was worthy of consideration. "These were exceedingly earnest, anxious and sincere men," he said. "They were really worried about the standing, status and the future of their profession."

Then Sir David Maxwell Fyfe (afterwards Lord Kilmuir), just back from Nuremberg where he had helped to prosecute the war criminals, asked Mr. Morrison whether, in fact, the N.U.J. deputation had come to him before, or after, his statement of July 16. Mr. Morrison said he could not remember, and there the matter dropped—but not for good.

In a debate after the Royal Commission had reported, in 1949, he was asked on what date he had really received that deputation. He replied: "I am not sure. I have not got the date. What does it matter?" But the opposition did not let it go. Mr. Oliver Stanley said the deputation was on July 22 and not July 16, 1946. Mr. Morrison then said this was "a point of some importance," but after saying he could not carry all those dates in his mind he added: "But I see no importance in this point." Mr. Stanley was not to be put off. "I wonder if he would have said the same thing if a journalist had done it," he observed. After some more harrying, Mr. Morrison said: "I will look it up." Later in the debate he intervened to say that "the deputation, it is perfectly true, was received a few days afterwards"—that is, after the government had changed their minds. It was, therefore, not correct to say that the government had done so because Mr. Morrison had been impressed by those earnest men from the N.U.J. The decision to inquire into the press was clearly dictated by other considerations, almost certainly party political in origin.

To return to the 1946 debate. Mr. Haydn Davies, a journalist M.P., moved: "That having regard to the increasing public concern at the growth of monopolistic tendencies in the control of the Press and with the object of furthering the free expression of opinion through the Press and the greatest possible accuracy in the presentation of news, this House considers that a Royal Commission should be appointed to inquire into the finance, control, management and ownership of the Press."

The debate was on a free vote—that is, members could vote irrespective of party policy—and Mr. Davies avowed that it was entirely nonpolitical. But that was not to be. In a winding-up speech, Mr. Maurice Webb, another journalist, said the motion "was designed to protect the little man in journalism against predatory commercial interests." That sentiment, more than the freedom of the press, was the dominant note.

Nor was Mr. Davies himself any less forthright. "We have seen the honourable profession of journalism degraded by high finance and big business," he declared. "We have watched subservience replace judgment, and we are worried about the position. . . . Can we or can we not have real freedom of the Press in a system of combines and chain newspapers? . . . The only freedom of the Press to-day is the freedom of newspaper proprietors. They have the perfect closed shop with the highest entrance fee in history . . . the freedom of the Press has been overwhelmed, not by bad or unscrupulous journalists, but by the power of high finance." And so on. Inevitably came a quotation from Baldwin's "harlot" speech of 1931, which P.E.P. had declared out-of-date as far back as 1938.

Mr. Michael Foot, another journalist M.P., and a member of the N.U.J., who once edited Lord Beaverbrook's *Evening Standard,* attacked Lord Kemsley, then owner of the *Sunday Times* and a large chain of provincial evening newspapers. The unfortunate Kemsley was to be the most hotly criticised proprietor in evidence before the Royal Commission. Mr. Foot said there was no case in grounds of freedom why chain newspapers should be allowed to exist. The main purpose of the Royal Commission should be to inquire into their operation, to stop their spread, and to break up existing chains. (Which seemed rather like judging the case before it was tried!) He said the quality of British journalism had declined in the previous thirty years due to the decline in the power of editors, many of whom had become "little more than stooges, cyphers, and sycophants."

Mr. Wilson Harris, editor of the weekly *Spectator,* who sat as an independent M.P. for Cambridge University, referring to Mr. Foot's attack on Lord Kemsley said: "He accused him of every kind of journalistic crime . . . but from first to last I failed to hear one sentence, one word, one syllable of evidence to support anything he said . . . the unfortunate thing is that hon. members opposite in an attempt to bolster up their case must try to blacken the Press to the utmost degree possible—and I must admit that their efforts in that direction have been pretty creditable."

From the Conservative side Sir David Hamilton Fyfe pointed out that the only tied newspaper (apart from the Communist *Daily Worker*) was the *Daily Herald,* whose policy and outlook were bound by its articles of association to those of the Labour party. While right wing papers accepted articles from left wing contributors, he had never seen an article from a right wing contributor in a leftish paper. "What is behind this motion is not freedom of expression at all," he said. "Members want to saddle the country with a number of newspapers of their own way of thinking . . . it is an attempt to destroy that tolerance of opposition which is the lifeblood of democracy." He said that circulations among national dailies favouring or opposing the government were, at that time, about the same.

Mr. (afterwards Sir) Max Aitken, the son of Lord Beaverbrook, confirmed much of this so far as his own (Conservative) newspapers were concerned. He said that since the Socialists came to power he had published ninety-eight articles by Socialist writers on Socialist ways, whereas the Socialist press had not published one single article from the opposition. Referring to the complaint that the Socialists did not get a fair show in press reports of debates, he said his *Daily Express* had published 1,165 column inches in reporting the government, whereas the opposition had received only 582 inches.

One journalist member on the Labour side, Mr. Mallalieu, said he and many other working journalists would like to go back to the state of affairs when there were masses of small newspapers. "We should get better newspaper writing," he said.

So the debate continued — an historic occasion, in its way. Politicians had many times complained of the press, inside Parliament and out. The new situation was that journalists themselves were now complaining about the press, and — most unusually — some politicians were defending the press against the attacks of journalists; proof, surely, that the newspapers had become one more plaything of party politics.

The end of it all was that a Royal Commission on the Press was appointed. A Royal Commission is the most portentous of the several forms of public or interdepartmental inquiry which form part of the British governmental system.

It consists of a body of persons, men and women, appointed by the government to investigate matters of national importance — not the kind of particular incidents which may be probed by a Tribunal of Inquiry, but deep-rooted influences on the life of the people, such as the police, the taxation system, a great basic industry, and so on.

The members of a commission are usually distinguished in their own spheres and are selected to represent as wide a range of the community as possible. They are unpaid, and their work often covers several years. A commission can demand the attendance of witnesses. It can hold its hearings in public or in private or in both, as it may itself determine.

The Royal Commission on the Press was appointed in 1947 by Mr. Attlee's Labour government, with terms of reference little different from those of the motion debated by the House of Commons. They were "to inquire into the control, management and ownership of the newspaper and periodical Press and the news agencies, including the financial structure and the monopolistic tendencies in control, and to make recommendations."

The commission sat from 1947 to 1949 under the chairmanship of Sir David Ross, classical scholar, philosopher, civil servant, who had presided at numerous commissions and committees over many years. There were sixteen other members representing a wide spectrum of life and activity, not all of whom stayed the course. Among those who resigned was Mr. J. B. Priestley, the novelist, who had criticised the press (though not harshly) while a member of the commission and had been criticised in his turn for doing so. His reason for leaving, however, was his long absences abroad attending meetings of UNESCO in the United States.

The other members of the commission were: Lord Simon of Wythenshawe, Sir Charles Vickers, Sir George Waters, Mr. G. M. Young, Mr. (afterwards Sir) Hubert Hull, Mr. (afterwards Sir) John Benstead, Miss E. M. Owen, Mr. M. E. Aubrey, Mr. N. S. Beaton, Lady Violet Bonham-Carter (afterwards Lady Asquith), Mr. R. C. K. Ensor, Mr. Wright Robinson, Mr. G. G. Sharp, Mr. R. G. Wilson, and Mrs. Barbara Wootton (afterwards Lady Wootton of Abinger).

The Commission held sixty-one meetings, obtained some two hundred written memoranda from all sides of the industry and heard evidence from 182 people. Never in its history had the British press been subjected to such a rigorous examination. And how revealing it was! An intrigued public learned, for the first time, that the Fourth Estate was rent and riven, not only by the customary divisions between employers and employed, but by the hostility felt by one section of journalists for another. The investigation uncovered a host of rumours and beliefs which were unfounded. It disclosed gossip which was untrue. It ploughed through suggestions for "improving" the profession and industry, many of which were either impossible or downright cranky. In the end it came out with only one practicable proposal— the formation of a Press Council which had been mooted long before. But neither its time nor its labours were wasted. The press was compelled to take a good, hard look at itself, and could not be complacent about what it saw. Though a few years were to elapse before the lessons then learned were to sink in, that first Royal Commission was unquestionably a turning-point for the British press.

Let us look, now, at some of the arguments.

4 The Probe

IN its written evidence the N.U.J. disclaimed a connection with any political party or movement. Its main contention was that the production of newspapers could not be governed by the strictly commercial considerations brought to the making and marketing of other commodities. "Our function is in the nature of a public trust and should be so regarded." Referring to the Northcliffe-Allied newspaper war it said those events had had a bad effect on public opinion. Much of the faith and respect which people used to have in the local press had been lost.

"From the purely trade union point of view," said the memorandum, "that is to say the consideration of salaries and conditions of work, there is something to be said for the groups." These, however, "have the disadvantage of lessening the intimate association between the newspaper proprietor and the journalist. And this result, of the shift of emphasis from the editorial to the commercial side, we regard as of the highest possible importance. The *raison d'etre* of the newspaper is its editorial department. No consideration should be superior or even equal to it."

The memorandum quoted Lord Kemsley, the great chain proprietor, as saying: "Within our present system, which is still based on freedom, those who can be held responsible for the conduct of a newspaper are surely fully entitled to determine the opinions to be expressed and the comments to be made on public affairs."

To which the N.U.J. replied that the importance of the business side was not to be ignored; but it insisted "that it must be the consequence of a thoroughly good editorial service to the public and not the determining factor in the editorial service." It went on: "There is inherent in these chain newspapers a public danger . . . the possibilities of abuse are obvious. The appearance of a great public agitation could be given to the desires of a small group of men of certain interests by simultaneous publication in papers all over the country, having the effect possibly of creating some reality behind what was at its inception nothing more than a careful simulation."

The memorandum alleged the existence of "directives" to journalists from Kemsley's London headquarters; the syndication of leading articles in another chain, that of the Westminster Press; the compilation of "blacklists" banning the mention of certain proscribed names in newspapers. Particular mention was made of the Thomson group of Dundee (nothing to do with Lord Thomson) which, by order of its chairman, Mr. D. C. Thomson, had blacklisted Winston Churchill, whose name, it said, did not appear in these newspapers for many years; even during the war when the most famous man in the world was never referred to by name, but always as "the Prime Minister." (As will be seen, this allegation was refuted.)

Then the N.U.J. praised those newspaper proprietors "imbued with a strong sense of public responsibility," who had safeguarded their papers against the dangers of monopoly by creating trusts. These included the *Times, Manchester Guardian, Spectator,* and *News-Chronicle.* (The *Manchester Guardian* was renamed the *Guardian* in 1960.)

At this stage the evidence of the N.U.J. may be interrupted to remove the impression that such trusts converted these newspapers into nonprofit-making concerns and lifted them out of the marketplace. They are commercially owned, like any other newspaper, and depend for their survival on profits. In fact, two of these admirable trusts failed to save the independence of their newspapers. The *Times* was taken over by Lord Thomson, who owns the largest chain of newspapers in the world and runs it, as he has repeatedly stated, to make money. The *News-Chronicle* was bought by Associated Newspapers and merged into the *Daily Mail.*

It might also be of interest to quote the terms of the oldest trust, that of the *Daily News,* drawn up in 1911 by its then owner, Mr. George Cadbury. It read:

I desire in forming the Daily News Trust, that it may be of service in bringing the ethical teaching of Jesus Christ to bear upon National Questions and in promoting National Righteousness; for example, that Arbitration should take the place of War, and that the Spirit of the Sermon on the Mount, especially of the Beatitudes, should take the place of Imperialism and of the military spirit, which is contrary to Christ's teaching that love is the badge by which the Christian should be known. The parable of the Good Samaritan teaches human brotherhood and that God has made of one blood all nations of men. Disobedience to this teaching has brought condign punishment on nations; and though wars of aggression have brought honour and wealth to a few, they have in the long run brought great suffering upon the great majority of conquerors and conquered alike.

There spoke the pure spirit of English liberalism, or Christian democracy in all its idealism and, alas! its unreality. After 1911 the *Daily News* went on to absorb the *Morning Leader,* the *Westminster Gazette,* the *Daily Chronicle,* and the *Daily Dispatch.* When, as the *News-Chronicle* it was itself absorbed, it was agreed that the purchase money should be almost wholly turned over to compensate displaced staff for whom (trust or no trust) such provision had not previously been made.

To continue with the Royal Commission: The N.U.J. dealt with the influence of advertisers on editorial policy, about which much was to be alleged during the inquiry. "We are not able to quote impressive examples of advertisers' direct influence with editorial discretion . . . the influence is negative rather than positive, a recognition that it is 'against policy' to do anything or report extensively any comment which may be considered detrimental to the interests of the big advertisers."

Finally the N.U.J. put forward its proposal: "A British Press Board or Press Council is envisaged, something like the Arts Council, or the Board of Governors of the British Broadcasting Corporation, or the General Medical Council, or the British Board of Film Censors. The Press Board or Council would not be identical with any of these. Its problems are different in shape. It could be an elected body representative as far as possible of every section of the industry, and it should certainly include two or three representatives of the general public."

The Institute of Journalists did not seem to share the fears expressed by the N.U.J. Their memorandum stated that from a populous area served by daily newspapers of high standing Institute members reported that they had no personal experience of the control, management, and ownership of the papers on which they worked affecting the accuracy of the news presented. Editorial directives about space, it was pointed out, were an essential part of day-to-day work in a newspaper office, but these did not dictate any specific line of approach to a subject. The report added: "Working journalists, some of whom have had more than 50 years' experience as reporters, cannot recall any occasion on which their freedom to report what they have seen and heard at public occasions has been interfered with by the managements or owners of newspapers."

The effect of this declaration was somewhat blurred by another paragraph in the memorandum: "Institute members in a county where only independent privately-owned newspapers are published are opposed to the introduction of monopolistic tendencies or chain newspapers, fearing that such changes would limit freedom of expression and lead to news distortion."

The institute turned its main attention to its bitter and long-standing dispute with the N.U.J. over the closed shop for journalists. It remarked that none of the proprietorial bodies had conceded the N.U.J. demand for a closed shop for its own members, though non-union journalists would not be employed by the *Daily Herald* and other Odhams publications, *Reynolds Sunday News* (owned by the Co-operative Society) and the Communist *Daily Worker*. "There are, however, other offices both in London and the provinces, where Institute members who do not hold the N.U.J. card can obtain employment only with great difficulty owing to the antagonism of N.U.J. members, and to the dislike by managements of the internal friction arising from it. Duress and coercion to recruit members have always been repudiated by the Institute as being contrary to the liberal principles which should govern the profession and practices of journalism."

It may here be interjected that this charge was quite true. But abhorrent though it was to these principles, the N.U.J.'s policy of a closed shop for all journalists may have been called into being by the trend towards the so-called trustification of the press. This certainly limited the number of outlets for journalists who also feared that if they were sacked by one big chain or group their chances of employment with another would be prejudiced. Such fears proved to be groundless. As the institute said in its memorandum, the number of journalists employed in areas of multiple ownership of newspapers was almost certainly greater than it had been fifteen to twenty years before.

Nevertheless, it was no rare thing for members of the institute to be frozen out of their jobs by the cold-shouldering of N.U.J. members in the same office, or by consequent requests from managements for their resignation. The N.U.J., in turn, charged the institute with exactly the same practice in some offices in the past. But this would have been on a smaller scale, and not so important except in principle. For many years attempts had been made to end this internecine war and to merge the two bodies, but all had failed over the difficulty of joining a registered trade union with a professional body incorporated by Royal Charter. Sense and reason at last dawned in 1966 when the two bodies, while retaining their separate identities, effected a partnership.

The institute appeared to have no precise feelings, one way or another, on the possibility of a Press Council. It did stress the need for some kind of self-regulation for the profession. "Journalism needs to develop, in institutional form, the professional conscience, and to give precise expression and authority to the code of conduct which is at present traditional, imprecise, and unenforceable."

While the N.U.J. was wholeheartedly for a council and the institute somewhat lukewarm, the British Guild of Newspaper Editors, representing the editors of provincial newspapers, was opposed to the idea. Asked whether it thought the formation of a Press Council would be practicable and in the public interest, the guild replied: "No. We think that all the matters dealt with in this question and its subdivisions should be left to the Press itself."

The two English proprietors' associations were also very much against it. The Newspaper Society, representing provincial newspapers, said that a code of professional conduct was unnecessary because each of the journalists' organisations already had a code in being. Also: "The Society regards the proposal for a Press Council as impracticable, whether an advisory body or one with statutory powers is envisaged. If the former, the Council . . . would do no more than duplicate the work already done by interested organisations. If the latter, it would be discriminatory legislation against the Press and so would be an infringement of the freedom of the Press."

The intriguing part of the inquiry came with the oral evidence, which, even after the lapse of years, makes fascinating reading. On the one side many journalists were out to show that the "tendency towards monopolisation" had wrought great harm to the press and had brought in its train all kinds of abuses, even trickeries, which had not existed before. On the other side, all the proprietors and some journalists were equally anxious to prove the opposite.

Perhaps this part of the story should begin with Lord Camrose, brother to Lord Kemsley, and proprietor of the *Daily Telegraph.* When asked if he could make any suggestion for the betterment of the press he replied: "I do not recognise that the Press is in such a bad way as it is represented to be, and with all due respect to the Commission, I consider it to have been created under false pretences." He said that the speeches made by Mr. Haydn Davies and other M.P.'s who had supported him in the Commons debate were full of inaccuracies. Mr. Davies had talked about papers being "strangled out of existence; they have gone down in the last 20 years by a large proportion of the total."

"I do not find that accords with the facts," said Lord Camrose. He said the N.U.J. had stated that the number of daily papers twenty years ago had been 144 and had come down to 116. Actually, they had come down to 118, which left 26 to be accounted for. Of that number, 13 had gone in one town, Brighton, and these were titles of the same publication. Both he and Lord Kemsley strongly denied statements made about them by Mr. Hannen Swaffer, then employed by the *Daily Herald,* in a characteristically forceful, egotistical, and inaccurate memorandum submitted to the commission.

The quality and tendentiousness of Mr. Swaffer's evidence may be judged by such views as the following: "So-called 'newspaper millionaires' have as much right to print what pleases them and to suppress what does not, as squiredom possessed when it turned political-minded labourers out of cottages. It is no more illegal than was the action of employers who, in the early days of trade unionism, victimised their employees." Mr. Swaffer's remedy for the evils of capitalistic control was the system of group ownership of newspapers which existed in Czechoslovakia, a country, he said, where there were four political parties—Catholics, Liberals, Socialists, and Communists—carrying out a Socialist policy. (In the very next year, it could be said of the parties in Czechoslovakia—"and then there was one"! That one was the Communist party which had bludgeoned the others out of existence.)

In similar vein, Mr. Swaffer alleged that in Britain the most powerful newspaper proprietors included several who had obtained possession of their journalistic machines with money made out of "financial speculation, company promotion and control of industrial undertakings." They would naturally use their newspapers to perpetuate a system which had enabled them to rise from obscurity to wealth and "flatter each other into a semblance of importance which only one or two of them had earned."

Asked to give more specific information, Mr. Swaffer, in oral evidence, said the Berry Brothers (Lords Camrose and Kemsley) had become associated with James White, "a very, very slick operator" who told him that he had lent the Berrys one million pounds and they would soon be millionaires in consequence. Later on, Sir William Berry (afterwards Lord Camrose) "was associated with White over the cotton speculations of 1922 and at least part of the money which was the basis of the Berry fortunes came out of that kind of operation." Mr. Swaffer also said that Lord Beaverbrook's money came out of company promotion in Canada. This must induce "a general attitude of sympathy with speculation" and company promotion.

MR. YOUNG: Would you be prepared to say that Lord Kemsley wields more power by his control of a large number of newspapers in this country than Mr. Hearst does in the U.S.? MR. SWAFFER: Two years ago . . . Canadian editors came to this country. . . . They told me they had met Lord Kemsley that morning in Kemsley House [London] and he said: "From this room I dictate all the leading articles printed in my papers," and one of the editors said to me: "Mr. Swaffer, not even Hearst wields control like that." [The witness added that Lord Kemsley meant that he dictated the policy of the articles, not the articles themselves.]

When Lord Camrose was examined he said it was absolutely untrue that Mr. James White ever lent him one million pounds or any part of one million pounds.

CHAIRMAN: Did you know Mr. White at all? LORD CAMROSE: Yes, quite well; a most interesting character; but I never speculated in cotton as Mr. Swaffer stated, and he never lent me a penny piece.

Lord Kemsley also said there was not a word of truth in Mr. Swaffer's statement about James White. Asked whether it was true that he had said what he was alleged to have said to the Canadian editor, he replied: "Certainly not; like most of Mr. Swaffer's evidence."

Lord Kemsley, defending newspaper chains and groups, said that had the system not developed, the reduction in the number of newspapers would probably have been larger. "The system has been the means of preserving some local papers and has established others more firmly. The financial position of all the papers acquired by Kemsley Newspapers has materially improved while the fact that, in every case, the circulation has increased substantially is evidence of public approval." As to "monopolistic tendencies" in the true sense of the word, no press monopoly existed, and certainly his own group had no monopoly. Out of a total estimated circulation of national morning papers of 15,300,000 Kemsley's commanded 800,000; out of a total circulation of national Sundays of 28,700,000 it claimed 4,900,000. In the provinces Kemsley morning papers sold 1,400,000 out of a total circulation, in that field, of 18,500,000. "The total circulation of all the Kemsley morning papers is not much more than a third of the circulation of the national morning newspaper with the largest sale."

All this having been said about the newspaper scene regarded from the central point of London, outwards, it was interesting to hear something of what it looked like from the periphery, inwards. Questions on this aspect were put to Lord Rothermere, the chairman of Associated Newspapers, which owns Northcliffe Newspapers.

MR. MIDDLETON: In the plan which your father published on 13 February 1928, it was proposed that the provincial papers should share the news services of the *Daily Mail* and the photographic services of the *Daily Mirror* [then owned by the first Lord Rothermere]. Has that intention been carried out? LORD ROTHERMERE: The intention has not been entirely carried out because it was not found to be practical.

Q.: Why was that? A.: The needs of the provinces were found to be very different from the needs of a national newspaper, and although advantages were found in having a central organisation in London to supply the provincial papers with news, advertisements, and so on, when it came to supplying the foreign service of the *Daily Mail* to the provinces most of the editors said they did not want it.

Q.: The photographic service also? A.: I think that was also made available to the provincial papers, but they did not want it.

Q.: It just gradually broke down, one newspaper after another declining the central service? A.: Yes. We had no experience of the provinces at all when we started this, and we found that they were very different from London. Their ideas and wishes were entirely different.

Another view came from Sir Ivo Thompson, managing director of the Yorkshire Herald Newspaper Company, which sold out to Kemsleys. This was done after he had approached Lord Kemsley and not the other way about.

CHAIRMAN: So that any suggestion that a big paper came in and squashed a struggling local paper would be untrue? SIR IVO: Absolutely.

Q.: How does your paper benefit from being part of a large group? A.: We get a much better service than we could possibly afford if it was a small paper. We get direct representation all over the country which we had not got before and could not possibly have afforded.

MR. AUBREY: Has there been any local feeling or resentment about people from London taking over a local paper? A.: There was at first. Everybody thought it was the end of the world.

Q.: That has completely died down? A.: Yes, and the circulation has increased enormously.

When Lord Beaverbrook was asked whether he thought there was a threat to the freedom of the press because of the concentration of interest, he replied: "No. I think new men will break in if it is profitable. It is a pleasant occupation. New men are sure to break in. Competition will be quite severe again, like it used to be in the past."

Asked by the chairman what was his main purpose in conducting his newspapers, Lord Beaverbrook made the now famous reply: "I ran the paper purely for the purpose of making propaganda and for no other object."

CHAIRMAN: Propaganda, I take it, on particular issues rather than general? LORD BEAVERBROOK: Particular issues; my own issue, the issue I have advocated all these years. [He was referring to Empire Free Trade.]

He added that to make the propaganda effective the paper had to be successful. "No paper is any good at all for propaganda unless it has a thoroughly good financial position. So that we worked very hard to build up a commercial position on that account, but never sacrificing propaganda; always making propaganda, but never in the news."

SIR GEORGE VICKERS: Do you recall an occasion when there was a tendency among the editors of the different papers to take different views on an Empire matter? LORD BEAVERBROOK: Occasionally.

Q.: What happened then? A.: I talked them out of it.

That was one attitude in the proprietor-editor relationship. Another was reflected by Lord Rothermere, when he was questioned about bread rationing which was introduced in 1946. His newspaper, the *Daily Mail,* had vigorously opposed bread rationing but he said he personally thought it was necessary. The editor of the paper, however, thought otherwise. "That shows your control is not tyrannical," remarked the chairman.

The question of directives from proprietors to editors and the existence of blacklists forbidding the mention of names of certain specified persons in newspapers, occupied a good deal of attention. The blacklist was one of those mysterious institutions which most journalists had heard about, but few had seen. The N.U.J. in its evidence had said: "They are the lists of persons—and sometimes firms and organisations—mention of whom is completely banned in all circumstances in the columns of the papers concerned. These lists are constantly being extended and amended according to instructions from proprietors, editors, advertising managers and other leading executives. Every journalist knows of their existence. . . . We consider them to be a gross abuse of the personal power of those who compile them."

However, when Mr. Bundock, the general secretary of the N.U.J. was asked for a list of papers which had blacklists—"a firm list which you could stand by," said the chairman—he replied: "I am afraid I cannot do that. That is more within the knowledge of my colleagues."

The truth is that blacklists did exist in some offices before the war, that they were blown up by journalists (who do not lack imagination) into something much bigger than they really were but by this time they had, for all practical purposes, disappeared. What is certainly true is that directives, not merely on policy but on the shaping of news, were known in some offices. This regrettable phase in British journalism was also killed off by the war.

Mr. Bundock said he had had a number of directives from proprietors in his hands but unfortunately had not kept them. One, however, which he did have, and issued to the Kemsley group papers, read: "Arkinstall to editors all evenings, Sundays and mornings. Please do not give Tom Driberg [a Labour M.P.] Parliamentary Question about Hess. Please do give Vansittart motion on atrocities, but it is important only his Motion and not any Press Association write-up which may follow." Mr. Bundock said he did not know the purpose of this directive "which might have been good." It was just an example of what he had in mind.

Another directive to editors of the Westminster Press group of provincial papers was to give maximum publicity on the front pages to the current Liberal party conference. "The directors desire the conference treated as first-class front-page news. Will you please give this your personal attention," it read. Lady Bonham-Carter (a daughter of Mr. Asquith, a former Liberal prime minister) suggested that it was legitimate for a newspaper director to give such instructions, which could not be called "unwarrantable interference" with editors. Mr. Jay, the then president of the N.U.J., agreed. It was merely another example of directives which were going out.

Persistent efforts were made to show that proprietors of groups and chains dictated what news and comment should, or should not, go into their papers, and what names should, or should not, be mentioned, but the evidence was for the most part either unconvincing or nonexistent. Mr. Harry Carr, who had been employed by Kemsleys for thirteen years, said the system pursued by the group as it related to the treatment of news was detrimental to good journalism and the freedom of the press. Speaking of blacklists he said he had never seen one but their existence had been alleged at meetings of the editorial chapel. He agreed that a blacklist guarding against libel was a reasonable precaution, "but I am sure the Kemsley blacklist extended far beyond that."

CHAIRMAN: Can you give us definite examples? MR. CARR: No.

Q.: Can you remember reading of any specially flagrant example? A.: No.

Mr. Carr had been a reporter on Kemsley's *Sheffield Telegraph*. On one occasion, he said, he was sent to a local constituency during the general election of 1929 with instructions to give the Conservative candidate a good write-up each day but not to bother to call on the Liberal and Labour candidates. Mr. G. F. Gardiner, the editor of the paper, who had not been there in 1929, said both the chief subeditor and the chief reporter of that time denied any knowledge of such instructions. "There were photographs and biographies of all three candidates," said Mr. Gardiner. "The allegation is entirely without foundation."

The supposed dictation of leading articles from London to provincial newspapers (and, once again, Kemsley's were said to be the chief offenders) led to many questions. Mr. H. N. Heywood, vice-president of the Newspaper Society and a Kemsley executive, said the editorials in the provincial papers were written by men on the spot. "There is nothing written in London." During the war, when the leader nearly every day was on a war subject based on conferences at the Ministry of Information, it became necessary to write them in London. Mr. Gardiner and Mr. R. Clough, the editor of the *Newcastle Journal*, confirmed this testimony. After the war, the central influence gradually loosened and there was no "line" dictated from London. Both denied that the loosening took place when it was known the commission was about to sit. It had already occurred.

Lord Kemsley, who was examined, confirmed that some of the changes made about directives to his newspapers were due to a confusion between wartime and peacetime conditions.

CHAIRMAN: Before the war was any guidance from the centre about the treatment of news given to the local papers? LORD KEMSLEY: No.

Q.: Your own practice now is what it was before the war? A.: Exactly.

Q.: And really only differed during the war? A.: Yes.

Lord Kemsley repudiated the evidence of some subordinate members of his staffs that some news was suppressed and other news given improper prominence.

CHAIRMAN: How do you think that impression has arisen? LORD KEMSLEY: From the accusations of people who have no right to make them, starting with Mr. Morrison and continued during the debate in the House.

Continuing with the Kemsley Press, Mr. Michael Foot, M.P., said his main objection to it was that it was the biggest of the newspaper chains. "I think it is probably the most inefficient of the chains and is most disgracefully conducted."

CHAIRMAN: Can you give examples of misrepresentation in the Kemsley Press? MR. FOOT: There are examples given in the memorandum of the N.U.J. on the subject of bread rationing, and I think there were other examples in their evidence.

Q.: Have you any detailed evidence to offer on that matter in addition to what appeared in the N.U.J.'s statement? A.: Not on the Kemsley Press.

Asked if he had information about misrepresentation in other chain papers, Mr. Foot cited the Harmsworth chain which had bought up local papers in Devon and Cornwall. Since then, he added, there had been a great deal of difference in the fairness of their reporting.

CHAIRMAN: That is an expression of opinion. I asked for details? MR. FOOT: I have no evidence of detailed cases of misrepresentation with me. It would be easy to make an analysis.

Mr. Foot thought the growth of chains was illegitimate, whereas the growth in circulation of a single newspaper, though it might be undesirable beyond certain limits, was a more healthy or legitimate growth.

SIR GEOFFREY VICKERS: Why illegitimate—because he has got more money? MR. FOOT: Because he has got more money and can stand the strain longer.

Later he said that, on the whole, the invasion of the provinces by chain newspapers was against the will of the local people.

CHAIRMAN: Can you give us details of such a case? MR. FOOT: I do not know the figures.

He then spoke of cases where a local paper had been put out of business by an invader, even though the local paper's circulation was bigger than that of the invader.

The chairman asked if he had some case actually in mind. Mr. Foot said: "No."

MR. BOWMAN: Did you, while editor of the *Evening Standard,* find that the encroachment of the newspaper proprietor [Lord Beaverbrook] interfered with what you would regard as your proper duties as editor? MR. FOOT: I think I did. I had a tacit agreement that I did not publish anything I knew the proprietor would be opposed to publishing, and he never required me to publish anything I was opposed to publishing, and on the whole it worked. However, the arguments became so frequent that it was impossible.

CHAIRMAN: What evidence can you give us about the existence of blacklists on papers? MR. FOOT: When I was on the *Evening Standard* from 1939 to 1944 there was a blacklist.

Q.: Have you seen it? A.: Yes, I think in origin the blacklist is probably quite legitimate. It started as a means of protecting the newspaper against libel actions.

In reply to a latter question he said a lot of names were put on the list for quite different reasons. "The kind of names, for instance, that I remember on our blacklist at one time or another . . . were Paul Robeson and Noel Coward and Haile Selassie—partly because there had been a libel action—Claire Luce, Sir Thomas Beecham. I think they were on the list because there had been a quarrel with the proprietor . . . names were put there in order that the person concerned should not get publicity."

When it came to his turn to be examined, Lord Beaverbrook re-

ferred to this evidence. He said: "Some people call it a blacklist. In
the *Evening Standard* it is called the 'cautionary list,' and in the *Daily
Express* office the 'warned list,' and it has been in existence many years.
There has never been a political name on it in the whole history of my
connection with the newspapers. . . . Robeson's name was never on
the list. In the time when these names were said to be on the list
Robeson was mentioned on 26 occasions in the paper from 1939 to
1947, and Claire Luce's name was mentioned 82 times in the papers,
and Clare Luce, the actress, was mentioned 12 times. I have seen
Robeson twice in my life . . . and we have never had the slightest
quarrel."

Lord Beaverbrook quoted letters from his lawyers on the *Express*
and *Standard* saying that the names on the lists were those of persons
because of litigation or threatened litigation by them. The *Evening
Standard* barrister said the names of Paul Robeson, Claire Luce, and
Noel Coward had never been on the list.

Referring to Mr. Foot's statement on directives, Lord Beaverbrook said: "I do not look upon what I have said to [my] newspapers
in the past as a directive. I look upon what I have said as advice.
. . . It was really advice, particularly to Michael Foot. He came to
me without any experience at all in daily journalism and not much
experience in journalism anyway. He is a very clever fellow, a most
excellent boy. And then suddenly he was projected into the editorship
of the paper before he was ready for it. The circumstances of the war
necessitated our putting him up swiftly, almost at once. At that time,
and indeed for some time after he became editor, Michael Foot himself
believed I had made him a journalist. He took the view that I allowed
him immense freedom of expression and he certainly thought he had
more freedom with me than he could have had with anyone else."

Never before had the relationship of proprietors and editors of
newspapers been so thoroughly probed. In this connection one piquant
revelation came from Mr. Ensor, a member of the commission, during
the questioning of Mr. Maurice Webb, M.P., one of the N.U.J. representatives. Mr. Webb had agreed that the press had always worked on
the profit motive and had been owned by private individuals, but until
recent times, he said, the editor had been a much more important
person with pretty nearly absolute power.

MR. ENSOR: Are you quite so certain about that? MR. WEBB: Quite
certain about it in my own mind, from my own study of the problem.

Q.: Will you take this case? I wrote leaders for C. P. Scott, who I think you will agree represented a very high level in journalism? A.: Yes.

Mr. Ensor added: "He was then editor of the *Manchester Guardian,* not proprietor. The proprietor was his uncle. Constantly Scott would say to me: 'You must not do that because uncle does not want it done.' Not only did that apply to questions of policy, but it not infrequently applied to the sort of personal points which are represented in the case of the *Express* and the blacklist. Now that happened in the old days in the most conscientious of offices under one of the most powerful of editors."

(The same editor, Mr. Ensor, might have said, who afterwards gave famous expression to the ark of the journalist's covenant when he wrote: "A newspaper is of necessity something of a monopoly and its first duty is to shun the temptations of a monopoly. Its primary office is the gathering of news. At the peril of its soul it must see that the supply is not tainted. Neither in what it gives nor in what it does not give nor in the mode of presentation must the unclouded voice of Truth suffer wrong. Comment is free, but facts are sacred.")

When Mr. Ensor was trying to elucidate the difference between an editor receiving a direction from an office controlling a lot of papers and a directive from one proprietor, Mr. Jay, for the N.U.J. said it was the degree of influence of the directive which mattered. In the one case an editor was getting it directly and it would be limited to his paper. In the other, the field was far wider and therefore the damage, if any, much greater. Mr. Webb said that, of course, instructions were received from editors but "we are in contact with our editor . . . we have the means of discussing things together. But this remote person in London is quite outside our sphere of activity."

MR. ENSOR: I could not make submissions to Mr. Taylor, the uncle of C. P. Scott and proprietor of the *Manchester Guardian.* He was in Bournemouth at that time and we were working in Manchester. MR. WEBB: Yes, but I am saying that is equally wrong.

Pursuing the theme of proprietorial interference with the judgment of editors, Mr. Hannen Swaffer mentioned the treatment given to the Peace Ballot of 1935 which was signed by eleven million people in support of collective security through the League of Nations. Mr. Swaffer charged that the results of this ballot were inconspicuously printed on inside pages of the *Times,* the *Daily Telegraph,* and the

Morning Post, while the *Daily Mail* ignored the results and the *Daily Express* gave twenty lines on an inside page.

To this Lord Camrose replied that the *Times* and *Telegraph* only had inside pages at that time because the front pages were given over to advertisements. In any case, the first leader in the *Telegraph* was devoted to the Peace Ballot when the result was announced, and the matter was mentioned twenty-five times in the paper between May 1934 and July 1935.

Mr. Swaffer had also said that when the Jews in Germany were "approaching their Gethsemane" in 1933, no notice was taken of them in the British press for weeks. But Lord Camrose replied that he had had this checked, and found that the *Manchester Guardian* referred to the subject 56 times, the *Times* 69 times, the *Morning Post* 4 times, and the *Daily Telegraph* 258 times.

Whether editors were the paid creatures of proprietors, or possessed wills of their own, drew such contradictory evidence that the commission must have had some difficulty in making up its mind where the truth lay.

Mr. Francis Williams (afterwards Lord Francis-Williams), a former editor of the *Daily Herald,* said: "In the great range of the popular newspapers the editor is entirely at the present time the executive agent of the proprietor, without independent life and without independent policy-making rights or functions."

As against this, Mr. A. Marshall Diston, who had been employed by Kemsley's, said he knew of only two general principles laid down by Lord Kemsley. The first was that a due sense of responsibility should be observed in comment, as in news; the second was a "guidance" that the new Labour government should be given a fair chance.

Mr. W. L. Andrews, then editor of the *Yorkshire Post,* did not agree that what witnesses had termed directives from proprietors or editors in chief pointed to any diminution of traditional editorial independence. "If Lord Northcliffe gave instructions to his various editors he was exercising editorial independence himself and in no way whittling down the freedom of the Press."

When Mr. Haydn Davies was asked if he could give definite examples of twisting news or direction of opinion from above, he said he had worked for the *News-Chronicle* and *Star* where that sort of pressure did not exist. "But I know plenty of Fleet-street gossip about it," he added.

CHAIRMAN: We want something more than gossip. MR. DAVIES: I have had no personal experience of it. I have never been told to write a story against my own conscience.

So the cut and thrust continued. Whatever the extent to which proprietorial influences were at work in the "capitalist" press, it emerged that the *Daily Herald* was the most tightly bound of all, through its connection with the Labour party and the trade unions.

Mr. Francis Williams said that Odhams (who printed and published the paper) held a majority interest and were supposed to have the final voice on commercial policy. The trade unions, the minority shareholders, were supposed to deal with political and industrial policy.

"It is laid down that the general political policy of the *Daily Herald* is the political policy laid down at the annual party conferences of the Labour Party," he said, "and the general industrial policy is the industrial policy as laid down at the annual conferences of the Trades Union Congress, and that in between whiles decisions in political and industrial policy shall be a matter for the trade union directors."

Mr. Williams said there were "a number of cases in which leading articles were altered by the commercial side. I know of no case in which a leading article was altered by the political side."

Mr. Foot, however, gave it as his opinion that "the editor of the *Daily Herald* has got more authority in policy matters than the editors of most other popular papers."

CHAIRMAN: We heard Mr. Francis Williams about that, so I will not ask any further questions there.

As a footnote, Mr. George Edinger told the commission that in 1933 the *Daily Herald* editor wanted him to act as their special correspondent in Berlin. "The Trades Union Congress representatives on the board objected as I was not a member of the Labour Party and could 'not be trusted to give the Labour angle.' "

On this point, a previous witness, Mr. Diston, had said that as a former active Socialist he knew from experience how much more rigid control is in the case of left wing publications than in that of the so-called capitalist press.

Before leaving the editor-proprietor complex, the story of the D. C. Thomson newspapers of Dundee deserves a section to itself.

Mr. H. B. Boyne, a journalist formerly employed by the Thomson-Leng papers (the two had merged), said they had had a monopoly in Dundee for twenty years. They owned, among other papers and magazines, two morning papers in Dundee, the *Courier* and the *Advertiser,* one Liberal, the other Tory. That these two apparent rivals should be owned by the same man was the subject of a sardonic comment by Mr. Winston Churchill in 1922. After the General Strike of 1926, Mr. D. C. Thomson amalgamated the two papers and his firm became a 100 percent nonunion house.

Mr. Churchill, who ceased to be M.P. for Dundee in 1922, said: "You get the same man behind these two absolutely differently served-up dishes, hot or cold, roast or boiled, seasoned or unseasoned according to taste, and both brought out by the same cook from the same kitchen. Behind these two, I say, you get one single individual, a narrow, bitter, unreasonable being, eaten up with his own conceit, consumed with his own petty arrogance, pursued from day to day and from year to year by an unrelenting bee in his bonnet."

The speech was reported in the Dundee *Advertiser.*

Mr. Boyne said that from that date until 1945 he had seen from the cuttings index only two occasions on which Mr. Churchill's name had been mentioned in D. C. Thomson newspapers. This was in 1932 when Mr. Churchill was rebuked by the Lord Provost of Dundee for referring in one of his books to Dundee's "bestial drunkenness."

CHAIRMAN: It is almost inconceivable that his name was not mentioned in 1940? MR. BOYNE: When he became Premier I think it is absolutely certain that his name must have appeared, but afterwards he was referred to when it was necessary to refer to him, as "The Premier" or "The Prime Minister."

Mr. D. C. Thomson, the chairman of the Thomson-Leng group, then aged eighty-seven, did not attend the commission's hearings, but submitted a written memorandum, in which he said: "I do not agree with the proprietors of other papers who leave all the policy to the editors, for I hold that the proprietor is ultimately responsible for every word published. I see no sense in raking up the past by Mr. Boyne, who was not in our employ at the time of the Churchill incident. Much of his evidence, therefore, depended on hearsay, and, anyway, seems to me irrelevant for the purpose of the commission. In anything we did or did not do I am satisfied we treated Churchill fairly. . . . In a vile temper at the papers not supporting him Churchill attacked me. We gave a full report of his attack and we also replied in plain language. No instructions were issued by me or with knowledge on my part to keep his name out. I have no regrets over the part we played against Churchill's arrogant attempt to bully us. There was no vendetta on my side."

On the alleged blacklisting of Mr. Churchill, Mr. F. R. Simmers, the editor of the *Courier* and *Advertiser,* said: "Boyne's suggestion that between November 1922 and 1945 Churchill's name appeared only twice is nonsense. He also suggests Churchill's name was not given in the *Courier* when he became Prime Minister. In fact it had a double-column heading. . . . I gave instructions to have our files searched for the period mentioned by Boyne. We found so many references to Churchill in 1922 and 1923 that I told our searchers to take a jump or two and take two or three months in 1930, 1935, 1940, and 1945 and give me a list of the times his names were mentioned. There are hundreds of references."

The blacklisting of the name of a firm of solicitors in the Dundee papers also came before the commission. Messrs. McCash and Hunter, the largest solicitors in the city and county of Perth, obtained damages of twenty-five pounds from the Dundee *Courier* and *Advertiser* for a client who had been incorrectly reported in the paper. From that day the Thomson newspapers refused to accept any advertisement from the firm, and ceased to use their name or the name of anyone representing them who appeared in cases before the court. This meant that no advertisement for properties in which they were concerned as solicitors ever appeared in the local papers, and no legal notices.

On this matter Mr. D. C. Thomson said: "I agreed with my colleagues we should refuse to continue business relations with McCash and Hunter in view of their grossly offensive treatment following the friendliest treatment on the part of our staff. We cannot do business with people who are abusively arrogant and set out to bleed us for money."

Turning to newspaper finance, the N.U.J. had said that "as the financial interest in newspapers becomes more and more than of a speculation and shares are held by insurance companies and city houses we cannot feel that the public interest is secure."

CHAIRMAN: Can you give us any examples of evil consequences arising from that particular thing? MR. BUNDOCK: No; I do not think we are referring here to particular facts so much as we are to tendencies and possible dangers to the public welfare from the fact that newspapers are becoming increasingly commercial propositions.

Mr. Sharp asked whether the N.U.J. agreed with the definition given by Wickham Steed (a former editor of the *Times*) that the disease of the press was "the use of the Press as a source of pecuniary profit to an extent wider than to ensure the moral, political and financial independence of journalism." Mr. Jay replied: "Yes, most definitely, that diagnosis of Steed's holds good to-day."

Mr. Benson said: "The commercialised paper sells news as scented soap, and we do not hold that news is scented soap, and that is part and parcel of the system these papers have created, whether due to the profit motive or not." Mr. Bundock added: "I think we have diverged from the general lines of our case if we are understood to be opposing the profit motive. . . . So long as we are living in a society constructed as this is, the profit motive is bound to operate, and we recognise that all papers, to succeed, must make a profit. The whole point is how important is the profit in relation to the public duty of the newspaper and what you do with the profit when you have it."

Considerations of finance led to questions of the influence, if any, of advertisers on editorial policies. The chairman asked whether, in ordinary times, newspapers tended to maintain optimism about the economic situation in order to stimulate buying, and what was the reason for the tendency. Mr. Hutt said: "It was purely, in my experience, that this would please the advertisers and make it easier for the advertising department to attract more advertising."

CHAIRMAN: Did you get actual instructions to that effect? MR. HUTT: I would not say I actually got instructions but that was the tone of the discussions I had with my superiors.

The chairman asked if there was any evidence of financial interests having made illegitimate offers to city editors to boost a particular company, or the like? Mr. Webb replied that they had no direct evidence, but his colleague in the Commons, Mr. Mallalieu, who was in the City office of a newspaper, had said in the debate on the commission: "When I hear experienced journalists seriously telling the House that advertisers exert no influence, I can only say that they are too innocent to live."

Two representatives of the London Press Exchange (a large advertising agency), Major G. Harrison and Mr. F. C. Mitchell, were called by the commission. Major Harrison said his concern might order more advertising space than any other in the country and in his experience editors were not influenced by advertisers either to insert or to suppress news. They would lean over backwards to keep the name of an advertiser out of an ordinary news item.

CHAIRMAN: There is no doubt that the British Press as a whole did not warn us sufficiently [before the war] about the danger of Germany. Do you think it was due to the fear of losing advertisements if they had notified the danger of coming war? MAJOR HARRISON: I do not think for a minute this is so. I would know if there had been any concerted action on the part of manufacturers because we did act for many leaders in their own field.

Q.: It is alleged that the Press refrained from criticising the brewing trade and the patent medicine trade because they are of such value as advertisers? A.: For four years we did handle the brewing industry cooperative campaign. I can assure you that never, during the whole of those four years, did I make a single representation to the newspapers about brewing, and they were spending a very large sum of money.

Major Harrison said his agency did not handle patent medicines, "but there have been cases where the newspapers have definitely attacked them, even though they are running the risk of a libel action."

The representatives of the Newspaper Society, Messrs. R. A. Gibbs (president), H. N. Heywood (vice-president), H. R. Davies (director), spoke on this subject. Mr. Davies said that no attempts at advertisers' pressure on editors had been reported to them.

MR. HULL: Are you saying that you have never heard of any manufacturer ever threatening any newspaper that he would withdraw his advertisements if the newspaper did not change its line on a topic affecting the manufacturer? MR. DAVIES: We are saying, sir, that such an approach has never come to the Society's notice.

Q.: You are not saying that as an individual, are you? MR. HEYWOOD: I have been a journalist for forty years and I have never in that time been approached by an advertising man or firm to do anything in the way of leaving out, putting in, or distorting or anything like that.

Mr. Davies said he was certain the small provincial papers were as capable of resisting, and were prepared to resist, undue influence, as were the larger papers.

Asked if the Newspaper Society papers got a lot of government advertising, Mr. Davies replied: "More than they can cope with in the present size of newspapers."

CHAIRMAN: Does it make them disinclined to criticise Government action? MR. DAVIES: It has no effect whatever.

Q.: Would you say that would be equally true whatever Government was in power? A.: Unquestionably: the two things are poles asunder. You do not let your advertisers, whoever they are, influence your editorial policy.

Mr. R. J. Minney, the editor of the *Sunday Referee,* spoke about the corruption of critics. He said there were three possible methods of bribing film critics: 1. By offering a substantial sum to a critic to write a film script shortly before the release of a new film by that producer; 2. Asking critics to read the script of a film and offering money for their opinion; 3. By direct bribes. This information was at secondhand and he did not know how widespread these practices were.

MR. ENSOR: All the instances you have given were of temptations held out by British film producers? MR. MINNEY: Yes.

Q.: Were similar temptations held out by American film interests? A.: Yes, and still are. The practice is much worse in America itself, where I have also worked in films. There is more direct bribery there.

The commission turned its attention elsewhere. For those witnesses who objected to newspaper chains and groups, the obvious alternative was a return to a larger number of smaller newspapers. Some witnesses advocated this course without considering how the clock could be turned back, or what the consequences might be. Others, remembering that smaller newspapers would mean thinner pay packets, took a more practical view. The result was a confused and contradictory line on this crucial question.

Mr. Foot thought "an enormously greater number of newspapers would be an advantage," and Mr. Webb believed that any circumstances which would encourage the development of more independent newspapers would be good, "whatever the proposal is."

Mr. Jay was asked whether he would be willing to sacrifice the higher wages, fixed hours, and improved conditions brought about by amalgamations, for what might be called the spiritual values. "Yes," he replied. "I think the fact that so many of our members are willing to come forward, even to their personal detriment, or possible detriment, is an indication that our people have a higher view of things than a purely materialistic one." But when Lady Bonham-Carter inquired whether this represented the views of the N.U.J. rank and file, he said there might be difficulty in moving people to accept lower wages and conditions, but the great majority of responsible journalists would be prepared to be less well-off if standards could be maintained.

These idealistic sentiments were not shared by the union's general secretary. Mr. Bundock said that from the trade union point of view there was a good deal to be said for larger papers because they could meet the demands of the trade unions more easily. They were criticising chains and monopolies rather than large newspapers, but "we are not saying you can reverse the development. It has happened, for good or bad."

The N.U.J., in its memorandum, had given examples of what it considered to be serious inaccuracies in newspapers. It contended that inaccuracy, overwriting, and overpresenting arose from the pressure on journalists to produce exciting and entertaining news which, in turn, was blamed upon the commercialisation of the press. The *Daily Express* N.U.J. chapel (union branch) denied the charges relating to their newspaper and said the N.U.J. was out to give "an impression of inaccurate, irresponsible reporting by a British Press which fails sadly in its duty." If the N.U.J., they said, could find no better material than they had produced after an exhaustive search of the daily and weekly newspapers, then the press emerged very well from the scrutiny.

Mr. John Gordon, editor of the *Sunday Express,* read extracts from instructions he gave to his staff, which began: "I want to worry, worry, worry again about this fundamental matter of accuracy," and said, among other things, "the plain fact is, and we all know this to be true, that whenever we see a story in a newspaper concerning something we know about, it is more often wrong than right." Other editors quoted similar homilies, and Mr. Andrews said the true picture of a newspaper staff in his experience, was of men and women continually striving after accuracy.

That members of the commission had the idea of a Press Council in mind was shown when they asked representatives of the various organisations, and other witnesses, what they would think of such a body. The N.U.J. is already on record as suggesting it. Even so, opinion within the union was divided. Mr. Webb said that, although he was surprised at the amount of support for the idea, some of their members would be violently opposed to it on the ground that it would in some way infringe the freedom of the press. Mr. Jay said they would prefer a council to be run by the industry itself without any statutory provision.

Lord Burnham, for the Newspapers Proprietors' Association (the N.P.A.), said he did not think his organisation had considered it, and did not know what their view would be. "I have seen codes of conduct which are the commonplace of every school of journalism in America," he said. "They are terribly woolly and not at all practical." Asked if he would prefer such a council to be on a voluntary or a statutory basis, he answered: "Both are equally impracticable."

Mr. Davies said the Newspaper Society would be averse to any outside organisation whose activities could infringe the freedom of the press. Mr. Heywood added that this was the strong, unanimous opinion of a committee appointed by the society to consider the matter. "We believe that the public is a safe enough judge of newspapers."

Mr. C. F. Carr, president of the Guild of British Newspaper Editors: "We are strongly opposed to the proposal for a Press Council with outside representatives because we regard it as the beginning of a Press control. We think it will create a focal point for the operations of all the cranks and borderline cases in Britain. . . . We are dead against it."

Lord Rothermere: "It would depend on the status of the Council, on its reputation and on its position in regard to public opinion. If it were looked upon as a court of honour then I think it would have great influence. If it were looked at with enmity I do not think it would have any influence. It entirely depends on how it is received and how it works and whether everybody is prepared to accept its objectives, whatever they might be. With those things agreed, I think it might have very great influence. . . . I would not like the public to be on it, but I would not mind an independent chairman. . . . I think you should come gently to these things. If you come too fast you will get great antagonism. You have to appeal to the better elements of everybody and get them to come along with you."

Lord Kemsley: "I would rather rely on the reaction of public opinion than on the endowment of such a body as a Press Council with statutory powers. . . . I cannot believe that such a tribunal, even if it were possible for it to be established, would be able to enforce its findings or have behind it any strength of professional or public opinion."

Lord Beaverbrook: "I think the Press has come out of this inquiry so far wonderfully well. These lads, a splendid lot, who initiated this agitation for a Royal Commission, have said everything they could, but what they have said amounts to very little. . . . I would leave the Press as it is, since they are doing a good job. . . . And since proprietors all seem to be guiltless of most of the charges that these young lads have made against them, I would not hold them up to any restrictions or limitations at all."

Mr. D. C. Thomson: "I am very doubtful indeed whether it would serve a really good and useful purpose or be wise in the long run."

Mr. Percy Cudlipp, editor of the *Daily Herald:* "I would personally not have the slightest objection to a Press Council. . . . No harm would be done by warning those of us who have charge of newspapers that we may have to account to an impartial body for what we do. . . . I would say there is a positive argument in favour of establishing a Press Council."

5 The Verdict

HAVING digested the evidence (of which the preceding pages have offered only a fraction), the commission wrote their epoch-making report.

It began with a warning that the abnormal state of the press must be kept constantly in mind. At that time severe newsprint rationing had reduced the national morning papers to four pages, which meant the elimination of nearly everything except extremely condensed news. They were making a profit on sales, some of them for the first time in their history, and all were in the happy position of having advertisers queueing up for space. Such exceptional conditions naturally had reactions on the editorial side – hence the commission's warning.

In 1921 there had been 169 daily and Sunday newspapers in England, Wales, and Scotland, but by 1948 this number had fallen to 128. In 1947 there were 1,162 weekly newspapers compared with 1,485 in 1921. Against this background the report ruminated about why people published newspapers. "Purposes are seldom single, and motives seldom unmixed; the desire to make money, the desire to make opinion, and the desire to make a good newspaper can, and do, insensibly blend. . . . If there is in almost all newspaper ownership some admixture of commercial motives, we believe that it is also true that most newspaper undertakings conceive themselves to be rendering a service to the public. The strength and clarity of this conception vary according to the character of the undertaking, and so do its consequences in the conduct of the paper; but its existence should always be allowed for in discussing either the present or the future of the Press. There is still widespread among Pressmen a sense of vocation. . . . even Alfred Harmsworth, the high priest of commercialism, did not wholly escape it."

We might break off here to remark that, in thus damning Northcliffe with faint praise, the commission was being less than fair to him.

Journalism was his whole life, and the great fortune it brought him, though naturally welcomed and enjoyed, was far from being his primary consideration. Financiers who bought newspapers and regarded them merely as extensions of the commodity markets he called "Monsters of the Fleet-street deep." Lord Northcliffe gave voice to this concern at a time when it was rumoured that Mr. Carnegie, the American steel tycoon, had threatened to buy up the British press. "I object to being a member of a combination in which capitalists, ignorant of Fleet-street, dictate terms to those who have spent their lives trying to understand the complex question of a newspaper," he declared.

When a printers' wage demand in 1922 seemed likely to lead to industrial trouble, he said: "I am not likely to join combinations of rich men to grind down poor men." And again: "Some of the multi-millionaires who have plunged into Fleet-street in the past five years are trying to drive the men's wages down." He did more to raise the status of journalists than anyone in the history of the British Press. In 1912 he wrote to the newly formed N.U.J.: "It is my proudest boast that the changes and competition I have introduced into English journalism have had the effect of increasing the remuneration of every class of newspaper writer, as well as greatly adding to the number of those engaged in journalism." In 1917 he wrote, again to the N.U.J.: "I am one of the few newspaper owners who have been through the mill of reporting, subediting, and editing, and I have very vivid and painful recollections of underpaid work for overpaid millionaires."

Now, after that digression, to continue with the report. It said the complaint that the authority and status of editors had declined through the formation of groups and chains appeared to have been misconceived. "The truth is, not so much that the status of editors has declined, as that a new kind of paper has been created which calls for a new kind of editor." The members of the commission found little substance in instances given them of proprietorial directives from the centre, and those cited were more often than not the result of temporary wartime conditions.

The power of proprietors to dictate opinions "is not an unlimited power, because its arbitrary exercise would defeat its own ends. . . . Such a power, if it were improperly exercised, might lead to a serious distortion of the news by a particular newspaper; but this is merely to say that all power, wherever it resides, is capable of abuse."

In twenty-seven years, forty-four provincial dailies had ceased publication, but they were not all killed by the chains. "In only six cases out of the 44 does the activity of the chains seem to have been a major factor in the disappearance of a paper." The existing nine national morning papers was not considered so small as to prejudice either the free expression of opinion or the accurate presentation of news. There was no virtue in multiplicity and the public interest did not require that smaller schools of thought should find expression through national newspapers.

Then came one of the key sentences in the report—destined to be quoted to prove two opposite cases in the years to come: "We do not, therefore, see cause for alarm in the decrease in the number of national morning newspapers from 21 in 1921 to 9 in 1949; but while the number is not alarmingly inadequate it is not so large that any further decrease could be contemplated without anxiety."

After studying all the arguments the report concluded that the case against the chains had been overstated. It did not consider that chain ownership was necessarily undesirable, but in certain circumstances it might become so. The critics of the press sought to show that ownership of newspapers by large commercial undertakings resulted in commercial considerations and the political policies of the chief proprietors taking precedence over good journalism and public interest. In remarking that some of the evidence proffered did not stand up to examination, the report rebuked the N.U.J. for failing to produce much positive evidence in support of its contentions.

"The Memorandum submitted to us by the Union was not a survey of the Press as a whole, but rather an attack on the Right Wing portion of it. In the light of what follows in this chapter, the fact that the *Daily Worker* and the *Daily Mirror* [a Labour supporter] were the only daily papers not criticised by name, while the *Daily Herald* was scarcely mentioned, is some indication of the selective nature of the document. The Memorandum gives no coherent and comprehensive picture and no means of reaching general conclusions about the extent and character of the abuses which had been said to exist."

One common complaint was that news was coloured by opinion, either by selection of news or by misstatement of facts. The commission found that extreme forms of this practice were rare, though the political factor in the selection and presentation of news was in all the national newspapers. It could often be accounted for by legitimate differences of opinion on news value.

The existence of blacklists might seriously prejudice the free expression of opinion and the accuracy of news presentation, but there was no evidence of widespread blacklisting on personal or political grounds. On accuracy, the report said that a daily newspaper could seldom be certain of its facts "in the sense in which a nautical almanac can be certain of its facts. Facts which are not beyond dispute are often news and news is too ephemeral to acquire the authenticity conferred by investigation and proof."

On this point the commission had a grievance. It was itself the subject of an inaccurate report and it jumped well and truly on the offender — the Sunday newspaper *Observer,* which printed a "think" story about the commission's recommendations before they were made. The statements in the article, said the report, were "not only untrue but devoid of any resemblance of the truth. Whatever information and deductions were the basis of this article, to present speculations as categorical statements of fact is a flagrant breach of the standards which the Press professes to set for itself and results in an inexcusable misleading of the public."

Turning to triviality, sensationalism, and intrusion, the report said these resulted in a competition to attract more readers by lowering standards, and produced a tendency to abandon rational conceptions of relative importance. "It is no doubt legitimate for a newspaper to entertain its readers by reporting events which are in themselves entertaining; but it too easily loses the distinction between what will entertain and what is intrinsically important. . . . The 'human angle' is not infrequently so remote from the central issue that what catches the one travesties the other." An attractive layout was all to the good, but it was possible for a newspaper to become the slave of its own typography.

Intrusion on privacy might be no more than an annoyance and bereaved people often derived comfort from a paragraph in a newspaper. But it was very different for a bereaved person in some tragedy to be harassed by telephone inquiries and besieged by photographers and reporters. "The pain given to individuals is only part of the evil of this practice. The greater evil lies in the degradation of the public taste which results from the gratification of morbid curiosity and in the debasement of the journalists who, whether willingly or otherwise, minister to it."

The report next dealt with the influence of advertising on editorial policy. The only specific example of its alleged pressure on general policy was the "there will be no war" attitude of some part of the press in 1938–39. A witness for the N.U.J. had said it was commonly believed that the Advertising Association had urged that the possibility of impending war should be soft-pedalled because of the injury that would otherwise be done to trade. Mr. Wickham Steed had written in his book on the press that certain large advertising agents had warned that advertisements would be withheld from certain papers if they played up the international crisis. The commission invited Mr. Steed to give evidence on this point. "At his own request he was interviewed privately, but gave no precise information about newspapers, and none of the organised pressure on them by advertising agents."

On particular policy, the Pharmaceutical Society in a memorandum to the minister of health had said that "the advertising of proprietary medicines is so extensive that the influence of advertisers prevents any ventilation of reforms in the public Press, and so derogates from the freedom of the Press." The commission asked the secretary of the society for evidence in support of his statement but he was not able to provide any from which a clear inference could be drawn.

On film advertising, Mr. Francis Williams had said that when he was on the *Daily Herald* there was "a general recognition on the part of the film critic that the advertising side of the paper was concerned in getting advertisements of film companies and that that should be borne in mind." But Mr. P. L. Mannock, who had been film critic on the paper during that period, told the Commission that this statement "had not the faintest foundation in fact."

The case was different with financial advertising. Mr. Williams, who had been financial editor of the *Daily Herald* before becoming editor, said that although he may have adopted a "very critical line" in some City matters he was never aware of any definite, implicit or concrete effort to influence what he wrote, nor was he subjected to pressure from inside his own office. The commission reported that it had been given no evidence that such pressures had been anywhere applied, and some evidence to the contrary.

So, on the question of advertising in general, "we have some evidence that individual advertisers occasionally seek to influence the policy of a newspaper or to obtain the omission or insertion of particular news items. Any attempt by an advertiser to exploit his position in this way is to be condemned, and we are glad to record that such attempts appear to be infrequent and unsuccessful. We have no evidence of concerted pressure by advertisers to induce newspapers to adopt a particular policy."

There is one other way of bringing pressure to bear on newspapers and muddying the clear waters of truth. That is by the intervention of public relations officers, more especially information officers employed by government departments. The commission remarked on the danger that government P.R.O.'s would "consciously or unconsciously" present information from the point of view on their own department and would tend to be less zealous in giving news which was to its discredit. Evidence did not suggest that any harmful influence was being exerted on the press through government information services—"but if newspapers get out of the habit of finding their own news and into the habit of taking all, or most, of it unquestioningly from a Government Department, they are obviously in some danger of falling into totalitarian paths. Future developments, therefore, need to be closely watched."

Since that was written, the "hand-out" system and the appointment of P.R.O.'s has been greatly intensified. Through their information officers, ministers try to "manage" the press much more than they did at the time the commission sat.

Discussing bias and the colouring of news through political prejudice, the report had this to say: "In the popular papers, consideration of news values acts as a distorting medium even apart from any political considerations: it attaches supreme importance to the new, the exceptional and the 'human,' and it emphasizes these elements in the news to the detriment of, even the exclusion of, the normal and the continuing. Consequently the picture is always out of focus. The combination, day after day, of distortion due to these factors with the distortion arising from political partisanship has a cumulative effect upon the reader. It results, where it is carried farthest, not only in a debasement of standards of taste, but also in a further weakening of the foundations of intelligent judgment in public affairs."

"We consider that the Press does provide adequately for a sufficient variety of political opinion. But we think it desirable that it should cater for a greater variety of intellectual levels. . . . The gap between the best of the quality papers and the general run of the popular Press is too wide and the number of papers of an intermediate type is too small." It was also considered that the standards of education prevailing generally in journalism were not high enough to enable it to cope adequately with the increasing complexity of events which the modern journalist must deal with.

So, having weighed the pros and cons, having heard the prosecution and defence, having listened to a catalogue of press crimes hardly balanced by the list of claimed virtues, the commission concluded that "the public can dismiss from its mind any misgiving that the Press of this country is mysteriously financed and controlled by hidden influences, and that it is open to the exercise of corrupt pressure from self-seeking outside sources. There would still be danger to the public interest if we had found marked monopolistic or quasi-monopolistic tendencies in the organisation of the Press. Certain large concentrations do undoubtedly exist, and are known to exist. But over the field as a whole we have found no such trends."

And, finally: "It is generally agreed that the British Press is inferior to none in the world. It is free from corruption: both those who own the Press and those who are employed in it would universally condemn the acceptance or solicitation of bribes." This was, indeed, a handsome vindication of a much-maligned institution, but the commission still had the task of recommending what steps, if any, should be taken to remedy those defects which it had found.

First it had to examine the proposals it had received for dealing with those "monopolistic tendencies," which were the gravamen of the charge. Though all of these, however cranky or impractical, were carefully examined, little time need be spent on them now. Here they are, with the brief reason for dismissing them.

1. Papers should be owned by government-licensed corporations: This would be an "unwarrantable interference with the liberty of the individual and the freedom of the Press."

2. A limit should be set to newspapers' profits: "Such a limitation would be both unfair and undesirable and would not achieve the purpose intended."

3. There should be a limit to the size of circulations: This "would involve depriving the reader of freedom of choice."

4. Trust ownership: "A trust does not necessarily convert a newspaper from a commercial to a non-commercial concern."

5. A public corporation to provide finance to start new newspapers: "This proposal does not appear to us to touch the root of the problem."

6. A limit to the advertising revenue a newspaper of any given size might carry: "We do not think these proposals would necessarily achieve their ostensible object."

7. Tax reliefs for new newspapers in competition with established journals: "Taxpayers should not be asked to subsidise newspapers."

8. Make newsprint cheaper for smaller newspapers: "One section of the industry should not be compelled to subsidise another."

9. Proposals for breaking up the chains: "Since we do not consider chain ownership undesirable in itself or concentration of ownership at present so great as to be contrary to the best interests of the public, we do not recommend measures to break up existing concentrations."

10. The Board of Trade to conduct a periodic investigation of newspaper companies and report to Parliament: "This does not seem to us to be necessary."

11. A journalists' registration council with power to strike a man off for professional misconduct: This would mean turning journalism into a closed profession and "that, in our view, would be disastrous."

12. Intrusion should be corrected by legislation: "Extremely difficult to devise legislation which would deal with the mischief effectively and be capable of enforcement."

13. A column should be reserved in every newspaper for outside critics to comment on misleading statements in the paper the day before, and to express different views from the paper: "To make the adoption of this proposal compulsory would, in our view, be open to objections of principle as well as to practical difficulties."

Those were about all the suggestions made by people thirsting to improve the press. That last crackpot idea was actually the brainchild of an editor.

Having thus cleared the ground, the commission came to its conclusions and recommendations. It remarked, very truly, that "if the Press is not aware of its responsibilities to the public it cannot perform its functions adequately; but if it is not free it cannot perform them at all." From this it followed that "the amount of pressure which society can afford to put on the Press is very limited." Except in certain, well-recognised fields publication, or nonpublication, could not be controlled because that would dam the free flow of information and undermine the independence of the press. "Whereas it is a question of opinion whether State control should be extended in other directions, nearly everyone would agree that State control ought not to be extended to the Press."

The report thought it remarkable that there was no one organisation representing the interests of the press as a whole. It recommended the creation of a central organ for this purpose, which it proposed to call the General Council of the Press. First, however, it wanted to consider in more detail the functions which the council might perform.

One of these would be to raise the general educational level of journalists by improving the existing haphazard methods of training and the "normally low standards" of education among those who embarked on a newspaper career. For while "the hard-working and the gifted no doubt can, and do, educate themselves, there must be many who are content to learn as much as their employer requires of them, and no more."

The proposed council might promote readership surveys and surveys of the subject matter of newspapers and its treatment. It might study the long-term development of the press and the social and economic factors which affected it, particularly any tending to produce greater concentration or monopoly; it might "study scientific developments in the transmission of news and pictures, and possibly the development of additional sources of newsprint." At this point the report broke off to observe: "This is not, of course, an exhaustive list . . . but it serves to indicate what we have in mind."

What it had further in mind was that the council might provide all sections of the press with guidance on advertising; speak for the press to central and local government; study the proper relationship between the newspapers and government information officers; represent the British press at the United Nations and with institutions representing the press of other countries.

The commission preferred a voluntary to a statutory body. It recommended that it should have a lay chairman, a person of standing unconnected with the press, and a lay membership comprising about 20 percent of the whole. The lay members should be entirely independent of the government and should be nominated by the lord chief justice of England and the lord president of the Court of Session of Scotland. Also, "we consider that the chairman, on whom a heavy burden of work will fall, should be paid."

Summing up, the commission said: "We hope, therefore, that the

Press will take the earliest opportunity of establishing an institution, the principal object of which will be to maintain those standards of professional responsibility and integrity which, we are happy to learn, are acknowledged by proprietors and journalists alike."

Then came the sentence which was to be the guiding light of council procedure in the years to come. "The body we have in mind . . . would depend for its effectiveness on its moral authority rather than on any statutory sanctions. It would derive its authority from the Press itself, and not from statute."

The commission tabulated the proposed articles of association for the Press Council. They were:

1. To keep under review any developments likely to restrict the supply of information of public interest and importance;

2. To improve the methods of treatment, education, and training for the profession;

3. To promote a proper functional relationship among all sections of the profession;

4. By censuring undesirable types of journalistic conduct, and by all other possible means, to build up a code of conduct in accordance with the highest professional standards. In this connection it should have the right to consider any complaints it may receive about the conduct of the press or of any persons towards the press, to deal with these complaints in whatever manner may seem to it practicable and appropriate, and to include in its annual report any action under this heading;

5. To examine the practicability of a comprehensive pension scheme;

6. To promote the establishment of such common services as may from time to time appear desirable;

7. To promote technical and other research;

8. To study developments in the press which may tend towards greater concentration or monopoly;

9. To represent the press on appropriate occasions with the government, with the organs of the United Nations, and with similar press organisations abroad;

10. To publish periodical reports recording its own work and reviewing from time to time the various developments in the press and the factors affecting them.

The council has never even discussed some of these suggested duties, either because there was no need, or because it was inappropriate that they should do so. Training for journalists, for example, has become an entirely separate endeavour. A training scheme was set up in 1952 and has since flourished. Devised by all sections of the profession and industry, it is run entirely by newspapermen for newspapermen. While most countries have schools of journalism or university courses in the subject, the British system is to train young people in journalism after they have become journalists, thus marrying theory and practice in a way which gives everyone the same chance on an equal footing. The budding journalist must first get a job on a local newspaper where he will receive the help and advice of senior members of the staff. In addition he will attend classes on one day a week in such subjects as shorthand, English, civics, newspaper law, and so on, at a local technical college, or college of higher education. At the end of three years there is a proficiency test by which he will stand or fall.

There is no general pension scheme for journalists, though some individual offices make their own arrangements, and the Press Council decided that this did not lie within its sphere of activity. Nor has it ever encroached upon the advertising side of the press, which is adequately dealt with by that profession's own bodies. Article No. 3 in the above proposed constitution also remained a dead letter because nobody has ever understood what it meant.

What was left, however, consisted of a mountain of work which could be tackled only by a large organisation with experts heading the various specialist sections, and with properly equipped offices. Such tasks were far beyond the capacity of the Press Council which did emerge, starved of funds, short of staff, working in two attic rooms and run by busy journalists and managers, all of whom gave voluntary service, and all employed on full-time jobs in the press. It is perhaps not surprising that it should have met, at times, with scathing criticism, often from newspapers which took no part in it. The wonder is that the council, in its first ten years, succeeded as well as it did in impressing itself on the country.

But this is to anticipate. Although the recommendation for a Press Council was made in 1949, it took four years of meetings among the various sections, of argument, often bitter, and of prodding from Parliament before the council came into being. This reluctance may have been due, in part, to the encomiums in the commiission's report. Newspaper proprietors may well have thought: "If the British Press is about the finest in the world, what need to restrain it?" Certainly the newspapers had hailed the report as a vindication, and in such enthusiastic terms that Sir George Walters, a member of the commission and a former editor of the *Scotsman,* thought it necessary to register a rebuke.

"I have been seriously disturbed by the selective treatment the Report received from the editorials of newspapers," he said. "The Commission never intended this to be a whitewashing report; nor is it. It has been hailed as a complete vindication of the Press, or, in any case, as a vindication. It is nothing of the kind." Perhaps this mistaken euphoria demonstrated, after all, that there was real need for a Press Council.

But first, Parliament had to have its say. After Mr. Morrison had moved that the House of Commons would welcome all possible action by the press to give effect to the commission's recommendations, the debate resolved itself largely into the views of those who thought the press had been vindicated, and those who said it had been condemned. The government endorsed the proposal for a Press Council including a lay element. "We think it important that the Council should be a really effective body," said Mr. Morrison. "We believe it can be of assistance to the Press and not a nuisance to newspapermen, and it would in no way interfere with their freedom. . . . If it should turn out that the Press should not be willing to take steps for the appointment of a General Council the Government and Parliament would have to consider the situation which would thereby be created."

Mr. Oliver Stanley, for the Conservatives, said his party believed that the decision to set up the Royal Commission was an "almost naked, certainly ill-conceived party political attack, not upon the Press as a whole but upon that section of the Press which opposed Labour. The whole of this debate and that in 1946 was set up to damage the Right Wing Press." But Mr. Haydn Davies said there were no deep machinations behind it. The movement was prompted by the genuine feeling that all was not well with the newspapers and the time had come to look into the question before the trends became more and more exaggerated.

Mr. Foot made an *amende honorable.* He had said some hard things about Lord Kemsley in the original debate, but now he thought it right to pay tribute to the candour with which he gave his evidence before the Royal Commission. But, added Mr. Foot, "we cannot always be assured that Lord Kemsley will be in charge. . . . If this cool cautious Bismarck of Kemsley House is succeeded by a Kaiser Wilhelm, or if this Solomon is succeeded by a David, what a calamity would occur."

So much for the M.P.'s. In spite of Mr. Morrison's veiled threat of compulsion the newspapers, for the most part, were very unwilling to form the council. Almost the only section which did not drag its feet was the N.U.J. which, at a special delegate meeting in 1948, before the report was even published, had already outlined the shape of a future council. Mr. H. J. Bradley (who was soon to become the union's general secretary) tentatively suggested a body consisting of six representatives of the proprietors, four of journalists, two of the printers' unions, and an independent chairman. He went on to outline methods of procedure remarkably like those adopted five years later when the council came into existence. Mr. Bradley encountered some strong opposition, but in the end the N.U.J. approved the idea of a Press Council, though it rejected the inclusion of the printers and the public, apart from an independent chairman.

The institute, having examined the report, emphatically opposed lay membership. "The Council should be given absolute authority to select its own members in order to prevent any external attempt to capture a controlling interest in it, and through it, the newspapers," it said.

The Royal Commission's report was presented in June, 1949, and the first meeting of the N.P.A. was held in July by a committee appointed to consider the report and "advise what steps, if any, should be taken." Thus, the proprietors lost little time in getting down to the question, though those two words, "if any," were significant of the spirit in which the idea had been received. A committee of the Newspaper Society was also appointed.

At this first meeting, the N.P.A. committee opposed the idea of a Press Council because "it would necessarily involve censorship of the printed word and would be highly dangerous and contrary to newspaper interests." It also thought that most of the proposed objects were already secured by existing organisations. However, a questionnaire sent to member newspapers showed a majority in favour of establishing a Press Council without a lay element. The members of the Newspaper Society also favoured a council, but by a much less decisive majority.

Early in 1950 the N.P.A. were ready with their suggestions for the composition of the new body. They thought it should comprise half editorial and half managerial representatives, to be appointed by the newspapers and not by the various organisations. The chairman and vice-chairman should be the chairman of the N.P.A. and the president of the Newspaper Society, who would occupy the chair in alternate years. The secretaryship would be shared by the secretaries of these two bodies. Obviously, this would be a cosy little council completely dominated by the proprietors, and though the Newspaper Society went part of the way to meet the idea, they thought working journalists should also be represented through their organisations, the N.U.J., the institute, and the Guild of Editors.

Then the Newspaper Society came out with its own proposed constitution. There should be twelve managerial representatives and six editorial members, all elected by newspapers. These eighteen would elect another six editorial men, two each from panels nominated by the three journalists' organisations. But this, too, though an improvement on the N.P.A. scheme, would obviously have given undue weight to the proprietors' chosen nominees. In the next few months the other bodies which now included the Scottish Daily Newspaper Society put forward their own ideas and there was one abortive meeting in which they all got together. But the whole thing lacked fervour, except from the N.U.J., which was pressing enthusiastically for the council. By March 1951, the union's patience was wearing thin, and Mr. Bradley told "recalcitrant proprietors" that if genuine round-table talks were not held, Parliament would be asked to reconsider the situation.

In spite of this warning nothing more was done in 1951 though some unrecorded and inconclusive meetings were held and a year elapsed before anything more positive emerged. Then a new impulse was given in February 1952, when Mr. (afterwards Sir) Eric Clayson, the then president of the Newspaper Society, who had been most active in the discussions, took the chair at what became the first of many genuine round-table meetings of most, or all, of the organisations concerned. Progress began to be made, and in April 1952, Mr. Bradley offered to compromise on the lay chairmanship if some of his other views were met. It was now agreed that about twenty-five members would form a suitable Press Council, of whom ten should be managerial and fifteen editorial. By this time the N.P.A. was ready to agree that the council should appoint its own chairman, if he were a newspaperman and not an outsider. In the following months there was a good deal of tedious jockeying about the representation of the various sections of the press, including, respectively, morning papers, evenings, Sundays and provincial dailies and weeklies.

By this time the public had begun to wonder what was happening, or, rather, why nothing apparently was happening. The Labour party, in 1952, expressed concern at the continued failure of the press to form the council. Lady Bonham-Carter began a correspondence in the *Times*. The Conservatives were now in power, and in November a Labour M.P., Mr. C. J. Simmons, presented a private member's bill in the Commons aimed at establishing a statutory Press Council. As usual, this was supposed to be a nonpartisan measure but, as usual, the debate fell into party lines. Mr. Simmons said the prejudice and stubbornness of the press were standing in the way of a Press Council. If it was not formed voluntarily it would have to be done by statute and one clause in the bill would have given a Press Council power to do anything to facilitate the proper discharge of its duties – even, perhaps, to closing down a newspaper. The bill, which would have had a better chance of becoming law had Labour been in office, came to nothing. But it did have the effect of giving a new spurt to the long-drawn-out discussions. Two months later a committee of the organisations concerned, under the chairmanship of Lord Rothermere, then chairman of the N.P.A., announced agreement on draft proposals for a Press Council, which would have to be approved by all six.

By May 1953, approval was given. The annual delegate meeting of the N.U.J. accepted the draft constitution but thought representation of journalists was inadequate, regretted that lay members were not to be appointed, and deplored the absence of a comprehensive pension scheme for journalists. Mr. Bradley said the N.U.J. was the only organisation that favoured lay membership and that the union and institute were alone in pressing for a pension scheme. He paid tribute to the part played in the negotiations by Mr. Norman Robson and Mr. Stewart Nicholson (general secretary) of the institute, and to the chairman of the joint committee, Mr. Clayson, for the part they had played in bringing the constitution much closer to the proposals of the Royal Commission. Although the union had rejected lay members (apart from a chairman) in 1948, while he had favoured them, it was now disappointed that they had been excluded. However, Mr. Bradley did not think their omission at the present stage outweighed the benefits of a Press Council.

The institute had already expressed the view that if lay members were excluded it thought the council would be an experiment well worth trying, and accepted its establishment with adequate safeguards against political and all other outside interference. It regretted that the commission did not condemn in explicit terms the N.U.J.'s policy of the closed shop.

The N.P.A., which had insisted that only complaints against newspapers from persons affected should be received by the new council, had given way on this point also. It was agreed that it could consider complaints from whatever source they came if the council itself so decided. This it did at its first meeting. It was a decision which ensured the public that, legal procedures apart, they now enjoyed a medium through which to air their grievances. Such an assurance did much to establish the council as an authentic body of arbitration in the minds of the people. And, although this procedure annoyed some editors, it did have the effect of reducing the number of complaints made directly to the newspapers. Instead, many of them came to be channelled through the council's secretariat who were able to explain things, or clear up points of contention without recourse either to the newspapers concerned or even to the council.

The warm thanks of the final, drafting committee were given to Mr. Clayson for his wise and diplomatic conduct of the business, and to Mr. Bernard Alton, secretary of the N.P.A., for his skilful drafting and administrative abilities. Mr. Alton was asked to undertake the setting-up of the council and the calling of meetings until the appointment of a secretary. This he did, and thus gave valuable service to the embryo body.

It had been seven years since the Royal Commission was demanded by Parliament, an interval which, though perhaps justified by the important issues involved, had tried the patience of many eager exponents. At last the long trail had come to an end. The new one, now to begin, would show whether all the bother had been worth while, or whether it had been a waste of time.

The council was to consist of twenty-five members, fifteen of them editorial and ten managerial, all of whom would be employed full-time by the press, including free-lance journalists. Representatives were three editors of national newspapers, four provincial editors, one Scottish editor, four nominees of the N.U.J., three of the institute, four managerial nominees of the N.P.A., four of the Newspaper Society, one of the Scottish Daily Newspaper Society, and one of the Scottish Newspaper Proprietors' Association. The editors were nominated by national and provincial editors of newspapers in membership of the N.P.A and the Newspaper Society and the Guild of Editors. The chairman and vice-chairman were to be elected annually, and members were to retire by lot, subject to reelection. The meetings would be quarterly. An official of each constituent organisation was to be permitted to attend meetings, and could speak but not vote. Council members would be entitled to travelling expenses but not to subsistence or other remuneration.

The Articles of Constitution finally adopted were:

1. To preserve the established freedom of the British press;

2. To maintain the character of the British press in accordance with the highest professional and commercial standards;

3. To keep under review any developments likely to restrict the supply of information of public interest and importance;

4. To promote and encourage methods of recruitment, education and training of journalists;

5. To promote a proper functional relationship among all sections of the profession;

6. To promote technical and other research;

7. To study developments in the press which may tend towards a greater concentration or monopoly;

8. To publish periodical reports recording its own work and reviewing from time to time the various developments in the press and the factors affecting them.

It was a formidable programme, but only three of these articles, numbers 1, 2, and 8 had life or validity, at least during the council's first ten years. The others remained a dead letter, not from unwillingness to tackle them, but from sheer inability to do so.

The initial income was fixed at £2,500 a year, but this proved so insufficient that it was soon raised to £3,000. This total was divided into 120 parts and allotted among the constituent members in accordance with their capacity to pay. At the beginning, the N.P.A. were assessed on 40 parts (£1,000), the Newspaper Society on 32 (£800), the N.U.J. on 16 (£400), the institute on 12 (£300), the guild on 8 (£200), and the two Scottish bodies on 6 each (£150 each). These proportions changed as time went on, with the proprietorial bodies taking a greater share of the expense and the journalistic societies less. But money was a constant worry, and from the first the council's financial basis was much too slender to enable it to fulfill anything like the burden of duties laid upon it. The less wealthy journalistic bodies, notably the institute and the guild, had difficulty even in paying their allotted shares.

From this meagre revenue the council had to find £1,450 for a part-time secretary and a full-time assistant secretary; £550 a year rental for its attic rooms; £500 a year for the fares of members travelling to London. After losing £100 on the annual report in a typical year, this left only £400 for postage, telephone, insurance, furniture, a press cuttings service, office equipment, and incidentals. In 1959 the income rose to £4,100 and in 1962–63 to £5,287, but by 1960 it had become obvious that such income levels were much below what was required if the Council was to continue as an effective body.

The council's one committee, which made a special inquiry into finance, estimated that another £2,000 a year would be required. "It is becoming more and more clear that our present basis is too narrow," it reported. "The idea that the Press Council needs only a part-time secretary with full-time assistance is no longer acceptable." The amount of work had increased in volume and importance even in twelve months and the demands made by the Royal Commission on the Press (the second one) and the police had put heavy strains on the staff. The office was open all day and every day, except at weekends, and an efficient and continuous service was maintained. "In these circumstances the Committee thinks it both unfair and unrealistic to regard the secretary as a part-time employee." It recommended that his salary as full-time secretary should be raised from £1,200 (which it had then reached) to £1,800 a year and that his assistant should also be paid more.

The committee's statement, which reflected the council's "narrow basis," went on: "Both the secretary and his assistant are called upon for such duties as stamping letters, taking messages, running office errands and so on, which normally fall to a junior employee. The time has come when it will be necessary to recruit the services of a junior girl to perform these tasks." A sum of £180 was allotted for the purchase of office equipment and furniture, both badly needed. "The furnishing and equipment of the office are not commensurate with the standing of a Council which represents in the public mind the newspaper profession and industry," said the Committee. "The one typewriter is an antiquated machine and most of the furniture was picked up second-hand at bargain prices from the offices of the *News-Chronicle*. A photostat machine is essential to an organisation which issues a mass of duplicated material."

Recalling that when a previous increase in income was requested, some of the less wealthy organisations were unable to oblige, it was now recommended that the additional £2,000 needed should be contributed by the four proprietors' associations. In the event, the income was raised to £5,787. It was not until the new council, with lay membership, came into being in 1963 with a subsequent income of about £20,000 a year that the funds approached anything like an adequate figure, and even that was considered far from ample.

Such a peer into the future at this point was necessary to indicate the financial handicap under which the council worked—a body whose influence was rooted, not in statutory sanctions, but, as the commission had enjoined, in "moral authority." It had no power beyond that of persuasion and publicity—but if the force of public opinion means anything, these should be among the most powerful of all.

The council depended on the cooperation of editors and on being taken seriously by the press and public. It relied upon newspapers publishing rebukes against themselves, however harsh they might be—and it did not rely in vain. In the whole history of the council there have been only two cases of editors refusing to give space to adverse adjudications. But, naturally, all this took time. It was only gradually, and reluctantly, that the council came to be accepted as something to be reckoned with but as, month by month and year by year, it built up its code of "case law" it became less of an irritant and more of a refuge for aggrieved members of the public, besides being a useful guide to, and corrector of, the press.

6 The Council Finds Itself

THE initial meeting of the press council was held on July 21, 1953, in the Press Association-Reuter Building. The members looked at one another with a "wild surmise," and, if not silent upon a peak in Darien, were perhaps a little tongue-tied on a pinnacle of Fleet-street. It was the first assembly of its kind in the history of the British press. Never before had proprietors and employees, editors and managers, the N.U.J. and the institute sat together round a table to pursue a common purpose; and that purpose mainly to put a snaffle on the untamed and spirited creature they all served.

It would not have been surprising had they felt some diffidence about the responsibilities awaiting them. They had to feel their way, make their own rules, define their own scope. But they shook down into a homogeneous body with remarkable speed and by the second meeting the feeling that they represented different interests in the profession and industry had largely disappeared (except when industrial relations were to be discussed) and had been replaced by a spirit of corporate existence. The members are not elected to "represent" the constituent bodies – nor are they answerable for their actions to their nominators.

The first chairman was Lord Astor of Hever, then the chief proprietor of the *Times,* and a much-loved and respected figure in the national press. He had for many years been president of the Commonwealth Press Union and of the Newspaper Press Fund, and his presence in the chair gave status and dignity to the untried council.

A General Purposes Committee was appointed to sift complaints against newspapers and make recommendations for approval, or otherwise, by the full council which would meet every three months. It was also agreed that a complaint against any publication should be first addressed to the editor. If this did not settle the matter, the nature of the grievance, the correspondence with the editor, and all other relevant

73

details should be submitted to the council who would take over from that point.

Another decision, which subjected the council to a good deal of subsequent criticism, was that its meetings should be closed to the public. It was to be attacked many times as a "secret tribunal" and a "Star Chamber"—taunts particularly wounding to men who themselves demanded free access to information on every possible occasion. But this uncongenial course gave a necessary measure of protection to a body often listening to highly libellous utterances without the privilege accorded to the courts of law and some statutory councils.

The pattern of work was soon established. It took time for the council's presence to be realised and most of the cases in those early days were of small importance. A large number of letters called for no action. Many complaints were flimsy or frivolous and were from people with bees in their bonnets or who wanted easy publicity. But none was neglected. If there was the slightest basis of a case it was thoroughly investigated, taking time which it may not have deserved. Many people failed to distinguish between news and comment and wrote furiously to the council about "biassed reporting" when they disagreed with views expressed in editorials.

As time went on the burden placed on the council, but more especially on committee members sifting complaints, became extremely onerous. Every feasible case was investigated with the utmost care within the limits imposed by the council's slender resources. It was not uncommon for members to be presented with briefings running to 10,000 to 15,000 words on a single inquiry, and dossiers of 40,000 to 50,000 words were not unknown. As just one example, a complaint from Carlisle concerning the reported protests of schoolgirls about the way they should wear their hats, and an alleged demonstration by boys against their school's amalgamation with another, ran to some 19,000 words. Such case histories had to be read line by line by the committee who, often after long discussions and numerous amendments to the text, made their recommendation to the council. This was then subject to further arguments, alterations, and suggestions until the final decision was reached. Some of these cases were, on the face of them, of the utmost triviality, but the council took the view that what appeared of little consequence to the world at large could be of great importance to the persons concerned, and to the reputation of some local newspaper. In any case, the principle at stake would be the same.

That the Press Council had really arrived was demonstrated by a statement issued from its first meeting which, to use a newspaper cliché, burst on Fleet-street like a bombshell. The name of Princess Margaret had been linked, in terms of a possible marriage, with that of Group Captain Townsend, and the affair had been a matter for speculation and gossip for some time. The *Daily Mirror* came out with a poll among its readers on the question of whether they approved, or otherwise, the idea of such a marriage. The council discussed the matter and decided on the following rebuke: "That this meeting of the Press Council, while conscious of the great interest of the public in the lives of members of the Royal Family, strongly deprecates as contrary to the best traditions of British journalism the holding by the *Daily Mirror* of a public poll in the matter of Princess Margaret and Group-Captain Townsend."

That first bulletin put the council on the front pages. It was a warning to the press that henceforward it would have to mind its p's and q's. But while some newspapers approved, others intensely disliked it. Some of the initial criticisms, which more or less cancelled one another out, were: "A good beginning"; "dignified"; "pettifogging"; "utterly ineffective"; "responsible"; "too hasty"; "certainly not hurried"; "succeeded in making a prodigious ass of itself"; "a threat to the freedom of the Press." Lord Beaverbrook's *Evening Standard* said the council ought to be ashamed of its Princess Margaret resolution. The *Daily Mirror* made no immediate comment but later wrote sardonically that the seventy-two thousand readers who had taken part in the poll were feeling thoroughly ashamed of themselves.

Mr. Cecil King, then chairman of the *Daily Mirror,* had said at his annual meeting in 1953 that the proposed Press Council was "an entirely unacceptable compromise," and went on: "I was never very clear what the idea of the Council was, but as time wore on it has evolved as a body on which the Mrs. Grundys of the Press will make disapproving noises at their gayer and more prosperous contemporaries. When this body comes into existence it is therefore likely that it will frown on sensationalism—which usually only means big type—or pin-up girls and crime stories—while passing lightly over their own sins of timidity, political bias and inaccuracy. Personally I would judge that the Council is doomed to futility before it starts, and it was with that conviction that we voted against it in the N.P.A."

Mr. King was not the only powerful newspaper proprietor who regarded the new council with either hostility or contempt, and whose enmity was a handicap at the start of its career. But Mr. King's pre-judgment proved to be wrong. While it is true that the first "disapproving noises" were made at his own lively newspaper, there were many other times when "sensationalism" was upheld and what was considered by laymen to be bad taste was defended in the name of press freedom.

The council was often to be strongly criticised for being "too kind to the Press," and acting as "judge and jury in its own case." Since only newspapermen were sitting in judgment on newspapermen there was, no doubt, some substance in the latter charge. This did not prevent the condemnation, from time to time, of nearly every national newspaper represented on the council. When cases against these papers were heard, their representatives took no part in the discussion. If the complaint concerned something for which a journalist actually on the council was responsible, he absented himself until a verdict had been reached.

At his annual meeting in 1954, Mr. King said the council had reduced itself to a "minor joke" and he renewed his criticisms from time to time thereafter. It is fair to say that, in spite of this disapproval, the *Daily Mirror* was always most helpful in assisting the council when a complaint was made against it. From the beginning Mr. King favoured a lay chairmanship for the council and, when the time came, was instru-mental in obtaining it.

At that time growing concern was expressed by clergymen, religious bodies, women's associations, and others about the emphasis on sexual matters in the press. This was given impetus by the treatment of the Kinsey Report, and the serialisation of *Forever Amber* in the *Sunday Dispatch*—features which, a few years later, when homosexuality, con-traceptives, abortion, premarital intercourse, and nudity on the stage became of common discussion and report, would have seemed innocuous enough.

Mr. Randolph Churchill kept up a sustained attack on the news-papers. He said the London press "dished out a cataract of filth every day. So deep and lush and fast-flowing had become the river of por-nography and crime which streams to-day from Fleet-street, that there has been some talk behind the scenes that the more important por-nographers and criminologists should receive some public recognition of their tireless labours." Mr. Churchill had himself contributed a regular column of comment to the *News of the World,* itself among the foremost purveyors of articles and news items with a sexual flavour.

At this point it may be asked how much responsibility the press has in such matters. For it to go beyond certain limits is indefensible, but although the newspapers are often made to take the blame for the sins of society, it can be argued that their main purpose is not to give a moral lead but to reflect the age in which they live and operate. It is not the press which evolves topless or see-through garments for women, or invents the Pill, or delves scientifically into sexual irregularities. These things must occur before the newspapers can take notice of them and to ignore them would be to neglect their own function, which is to tell of what is going on in the world.

It is for the public themselves to accept or reject what the newspapers are offering them. The *Sunday Dispatch,* mild as was its alleged transgressions, decided to become more restrained and to model itself on the more "respectable" papers. Its circulation at once began to fall, and in two years it was dead.

Here, of course, we arrive once more at the fundamental dilemma. Popular newspapers which believed in "giving the public what it wants" were castigated as being corrupt, immoral, or even – as we have seen – "pornographic." But if they neglected this commercial principle they invited disaster and sometimes succumbed to it. Where to draw the line? That was the question which brought the Press Council into existence and those newspapers which answered it the most skillfully were those who survived and prospered. It was a question which even moral institutions always ready to criticise the press found it hard to answer.

Lord Samuel, the venerable and revered leader of the Liberal party in the House of Lords, said that "sexual laxity is much more than it has been in earlier generations . . . adultery is regarded as a jest and divorce as a mere unimportant incident . . . the vices of Sodom and Gomorrah, the cities of the plain, appear to be rife among us." Yet only a few years later it was the House of Lords which led the way in legalising homosexuality among consenting adults.

Thus the way of manners and morals – and thus, also, the way of the press. Perhaps the last word in this digression should be with Ogden Nash, the American writer, who said in a letter to his daughter: "You should be intelligent enough to know that in various eras of history it has been fashionable to laugh at morals, but the fact of the matter is that Old Man Morals just keeps rolling along and the laughers end up as driftwood on a sand-bar."

To return to the Press Council. After considering the many letters and resolutions received, it issued the following statement from its second meeting in October 1943: "That this Council, while defending the right of the Press in the contemporary world to deal in an adult manner with matters of sex, is deeply concerned by the unwholesome exploitation of sex by certain newspapers and periodicals. It places on record its view that such treatment is calculated to injure public morals, especially because newspapers and periodicals are seen and read by young persons. It is also contrary to those standards of journalism which it is the Council's duty to maintain. The Council intends to keep this matter under review."

One case in 1953 which led to an important statement of editorial principle arose, not from a complaint by a member of the public, but by a journalist against a newspaper. Mr. Tom Hopkinson, a guest critic of the *Daily Sketch,* complained of alterations in his notice of the film, *Front Page Story.* He had written that "this is not a great film" and was asked to drop the phrase. He declined, but said he would not object if the sentence were altered to read: "This is not a great film, but a good one." When his article appeared, further changes had been made. In particular he objected to "a fulsome and undeserved compliment to the film's technical director" who was the editor's wife. Inquiries showed that the alterations had been made by the editor, who thought the article did not do justice to a film with which he had been associated. He said he had given instructions for Mr. Hopkinson's name to be removed, but owing to a misunderstanding this was not done. He had admitted the error and tendered a private apology to Mr. Hopkinson.

The council thought this was not enough. An apology should have been published in the paper with an explanation that the article as published did not represent Mr. Hopkinson's views. Nor could it agree that it was proper for an editor to allow his association with a film to affect his newspaper's judgment upon it. In its adjudication, the council deplored his action which had fallen below the best journalistic standards and was deserving of censure. It gave its complete support to the principle that a critic had the right to insist that where his name was to be published with an article, no alterations, apart from those of normal subediting or those necessary to protect a newspaper against legal action, should be made without the sanction of the critic or his agent. Furthermore it did not support the view that if a critic's name were removed from his work, the editor was free to make use of that work in any way he pleased.

This judgment met with general approval. The *Observer,* later to be a critic, said: "The Press Council has made its mark decisively for the first time with its strongly worded resolution. . . . The result shows that endeavors to enlist the aid of the Council for the ventilation of grievances against newspapers can be worth while." The *New Statesman* said the council was the right kind of tribunal to deal with such a case. "Its sensible and unequivocal findings will no doubt make editors and sub-editors more careful about how they treat contributors' copy." The *Economist* pointed out that threats of legal proceedings had been flying about in the case, and, not being a privileged body, a possible invocation of the law must have made the council's quasi-judicial function doubly difficult. "Its job is to censure but it can apparently be brought before the courts if it is unduly censorious."

Not long afterwards the council took out insurance against libel. That no case has ever been brought is perhaps a tribute to those maligned newspapermen who delivered tricky judgments for ten years without legal advice, and with chairmen unversed in the law as a profession. Yet, as the council rightly claimed, on no occasion had it toned down judgments for publication for fear of the law.

The pattern of the annual reports was laid down in the first number by the vice-chairman, Sir Linton Andrews, in association with Mr. Guy Schofield (then editor of the *Daily Mail*) who suggested the title, "The Press and The People," which it has borne ever since. That first number, looking back over the initial twelve months, found no reason to be displeased with what had been done.

"The Council wishes to emphasise," said the report, "that it considers its prime duty to be that of preserving in full the existing liberty of the Press. . . . The Council therefore holds the view that such disciplinary authority as it wields should be exercised against those practices which, by bringing the Press into disrepute, threaten that priceless liberty and weaken the confidence which should exist between the citizen and the professional journalist." It continued: "With millions of the less cultivated in the land now buying a paper there is a proper and important place for what, without priggishness, can be termed a vulgar Press. It should be remembered that what we here style vulgar papers often disclose public abuses which would not come the way of the others."

The main ethical questions dealt with during the year had been:

1. The alleged invasion of private life by reporters and photographers and the disclosure of secrets which officials and others wished to remain secrets; 2. The reporting of crime; 3. The treatment of sex.

On crime reporting, people complained that some papers gave criminals a kind of glamour which tempted moral weaklings to follow bad examples. "Most of these complaints appear to us to be grossly exaggerated. . . . The Council agrees, however, that criminals should not be painted as reckless heroes who have gambled for great gain, and lost." On sex, the report said the editor who knew his business would draw a clear distinction between reports with a sex element which might excite imitation of wrong conduct and those in which the interest was scientific, or arose from a healthy curiosity about the mysteries of human existence.

The question of intrusion gave the council a great deal of thought and, as the years went on, was destined to give it even more, for this has always been one of the major causes of public complaint. The first report said that "those who criticise the Press most are unlikely to know of the acts of self-denial by the best types of editor who detest callous methods." But it also said that badgering and intrusion sometimes arose from the sheer numbers of reporters and photographers sent on a sensational story and suggested that the conscience of the profession should insist on a search for a remedy. (None has yet been found.)

"Some critics," it went on, "when they refer to alleged Press intrusions, cherish the simple belief that they can suppress a piece of business or a document of which the public ought to be apprised, merely by labelling it 'private and confidential' and that the Press ought meekly to consider themselves in honour bound to respect the injunction. Many a fussy little jack-in-office would like to set up his own Official Secrets Act in this way. Every experienced editor will refuse to be fenced off. If hushing up a matter is against the public interest, the duty of the Press is clear: it must tell the public what is happening."

It was as well that the council attempted to define attitudes in such an important matter thus early in its career, for it was to crop up time after time in later years. The complainants were usually local authorities accusing newspapers of publishing secret information although, they plaintively said, the document from which it was taken was labelled "private and confidential."

But the council's observations led to some misunderstanding for in its second annual report, in 1955, an attempt at elucidation was made. The new statement said: "The Council did not intend the reader to gather some meaning hinted at but not expressed by those words and to suppose that 'private and confidential' should be treated as a disregardable formality. If a citizen sends a letter so marked to a newspaper it is an obligation of honour not to publish the letter. That does not mean that whatever information is contained in it must be regarded for journalistic purposes as permanently vetoed. The same information may come to the editor from other sources. The letter may be merely a specious attempt to secure suppression of something that ought to be known. The writer is not entitled to say: 'I tell you this secret so that I may put you on your honour never to disclose it.'

"Some officials send out documents which, though marked 'private and confidential' contain information which will flow into a newspaper office from various sources and is of such public importance that to continue to suppress it would be against the public interest. . . . The editor's duty is to decide whether a document was marked 'private' for good or bad reasons and to make his decision whether to publish or not according to the sense of responsibility of all concerned.

"It is not for the editor to suppress what the public ought to know merely because an official or a public authority finds it far more convenient if the Press keeps quiet about it. Indeed, it is not for a newspaper to promote any private interest contrary to the general welfare."

Lord Astor, to the great regret of the council, was obliged to resign the chairmanship on account of ill health in April 1955, and Sir Linton Andrews, for many years the distinguished editor of the *Yorkshire Post,* was elected to the chair. It was under his guidance during the next four years that the council took shape and substance and began to build up the body of precedents which proved so valuable then and in the future. In 1954 Mr. Alton had established the executive framework, earning the grateful thanks of the council, and Mr. Alan Pitt Robbins, who had retired after long service with the *Times,* latterly as news editor, had become part-time secretary.

Few noteworthy cases occupied the council in its second year. At the end of it, the new chairman in his foreword to the annual report of 1955 said that it was passing from the experimental stage and becoming an institution widely accepted in the national life—"though it has not yet grown to its full strength and cannot do so until its methods have been perfected." He said its appeal to conscience and fair play had not been in vain. "The Council may be settling into a routine but it has no complacent belief that its methods are already adequate. Disparagement of the Press is too widespread for our happiness and must be dealt with. . . . We think it our duty to encourage a fuller and fairer appreciation of the merits of British journalism."

Apart from the chairman's foreword, articles appearing in the annual reports of the council's earlier years were unsigned. They were written by individual members but were published only after they had been approved by the council, which therefore became responsible for them. From 1961 onwards, the council occasionally asked distinguished journalists, lawyers, and others to write articles for the annual reports. These were signed.

An article in the 1955 report entitled "The Public and the Press Council" said it would be something gained if the council could get rid of the false notion that newspapers were callous enterprises with no thought for any damage they might do in printing the news. "One obstinate problem is that of the alleged 'invasion of private rights' about which the American Society of Newspaper Editors very properly says: 'A newspaper should not invade private rights or feeling without some sure warrant of public right as distinguished from public curiosity.' " The article continued: "But how is private right to be distinguished from public right, and public curiosity from the public interest by mere ingenuity of definition? The Press Council can only hope to establish a code of sound practice slowly by its decisions on specific cases brought before it."

Another matter mentioned was the relationship between the press and the hospitals. It was noted that some hospitals gave information to reporters freely while others showed sheer obstructiveness. Some medical men had an exaggerated notion of professional secrecy; some journalists had an equally exaggerated notion of the lengths to which they could go to get news. The question was complicated by the large number of newspapermen who converged on an unusual occurrence and could impede the work of a hospital. The council welcomed a conference with press representatives called by the British Medical Association to try to work towards smoother relations.

A year later, in its third annual report for 1956, the council was able to report that agreement had been reached on procedures to be followed in sickness and accident cases. In particular, hospitals were asked to appoint a responsible officer to answer press inquiries at all times. A decade later, however, the council had to inform the then minister of health, Mr. Kenneth Robinson, that the arrangements were not working well. They were being interpreted in widely differing ways by hospitals, some of which still failed to provide adequate press facilities. On the other side, the minister said that on occasion the press had published exaggerated or distorted reports based on unofficial information and had used methods which gave grounds for complaint. He nevertheless reminded hospitals of the 1956 agreement, asked them to observe it, and to give further thought to good relations with the press.

An article on "The Popular Press" in the second annual report was, in effect, though not in intention, a reply to those who sneered at the council as a body of old-fashioned stick-in-the-muds only too ready to frown on the bright boys. It referred to a leading article in the *Times* which had said the race for mammoth circulations had led in some cases to a disgraceful lowering of values. "The baser instincts are being pandered to, not only in lasciviousness—the influence of this can be over-rated—but in social attitudes and in conduct as well."

The council's article said: "There is much truth in these strictures. If there were not, the Press Council need never have been called into existence. . . . Having made these points, however, it is easy to go on to condemn the popular Press, root and branch. But that would be a mistake." "To expose injustice, to right wrongs, to give advice, to befriend the friendless and to help the helpless—these are among the services which these newspapers are constantly rendering to people who could not otherwise obtain them. The Council could never condone the vulgarity, triviality and sheer bad manners of some journals. But it is fair to point out that the Council has also defended from charges of sensationalism, distortion and falsehood some of the very newspapers it has rebuked on other grounds."

The phrase "to expose injustice, to right wrongs" collected the usual quota of derision from superior persons. But the "yellow Press could justifiably claim that, in many ways, it showed more public spirit than the "quality" journals. Such papers as the *News of the World* and the *People,* for all their alleged faults, have on many occasions served the nation well by disclosing fraud and corruption and by publicising wrongs and cruelties to humble, distressed, or handicapped people. The quality papers may be more sober, responsible and intellectual but they do not indulge in the kind of "revelations" which affect the mass of the people. Nor do they normally pursue the sort of public-spirited enterprise which is the constant preoccupation of the middle-range newspapers.

The chairman's claim that the Press Council had become an institution was justified when the press secretary to the Queen began to consult it on the proper relations between palace and press. This interesting development is fully dealt with in a later chapter.

An article on the "Lessons of Three Years" in the third annual report said the council had done something significant to improve the tone of the press and had had an increasingly sound and healthy effect on public opinion. "But not everyone would agree with these claims," it said. True—for not everyone did agree. Some M.P.'s and others were extremely critical.

One question people were asking, the article added, was: "Have you stopped the unscrupulous exploitation of crime and sex in some Sunday newspapers?" The answer was: "Opinion differs widely on how sex should be presented to young people. Some believe in shielding them from knowledge of evil as long as possible. Others believe in training them, stage by stage, for the world in which they will have to live. At a Methodist Conference one leading speaker said in a debate on moral evils: 'It is no use peevishly and genteelly calling this problem vice when we really mean pimps, prostitutes and pansies.' Are sections of the Press to be condemned because they are not evasive and genteel in dealing with sexual evils? There will not be a unanimous answer."

So the council went steadily on with its work which, as Sir Linton Andrews noted in 1956–57, was growing mainly because the frequent publicity given to it had prompted many persons to refer grievances to it. The General Purposes Committee was meeting twelve or more times a year and the main council four times a year, while the burden on the staff and the committeemen became more onerous.

What was not known by people who imagined the Press Council to be cocooned in complacency was that twice in those early years it held soul-searching sessions to examine what it had done, what it might do, where it had failed, and where it was going. In 1956, on the suggestion of Mr. Clayson, the chairman invited members and the constituent bodies to submit memoranda for discussion at a special meeting to be held in January 1957.

In preparation for this meeting, Sir Linton asked the members: "Have we done all we should have done? If not, how shall we make good our failing?" and, "If we have done what we ought not to have done how can we guard against repeating our mistakes?" Criticism and self-criticism, he said, should be directed to asking whether the machinery was adequate, whether it was fulfilling its purpose, and how its methods could be improved. He said the crippling effect of a small budget had been obvious when it came to investigating mistakes, when extra council or even committee meetings had been proposed, and when propaganda addresses by the secretary away from London had been suggested. Each meeting of the council cost one hundred pounds and any suggestions for a special session, however justifiable, caused misgivings on account of the expense.

The chairman went on to say that the council had been criticised for not having done enough to carry out some of its stated objects, especially the one requiring it to review developments in the press and the factors affecting them. Among things it had been asked to investigate were the newspaper strike of 1955 and the closed shop in newspaper offices. But the council had kept off such subjects up to then because, as one member had said cynically, they were too difficult. Ought that attitude to be reconsidered? The most persistent criticism was that the council was almost entirely occupied with complaints of injustice, many of them of small importance to the public, and did little to restrain the kind of journalism so often condemned at religious meetings and by individual citizens. Should the council investigate such criticisms, ignore them, or answer them? Should it issue a pamphlet in reply? The most awkward critics were those who resented much that the press did and, because the press went on doing it, assumed that the council must be ineffective. They regarded the council as part of the system and would never be satisfied until lay members were included. Should the question of a lay element be reconsidered?

There had been complaints about the council's private deliberations ("another secret tribunal"), its alleged excessive reliance on documentary evidence, the insufficiency of investigation, and the brevity of the bulletins. On questions of taste, the council had never been sure of its duty. Ought it to formulate some rule to guide it through this difficult territory? Many critics had said it should be armed with greater powers but presumably all the members believed that moral persuasion was more effective. But ought they to set forth their views about it more forcibly than by the curt *non possumus* that had hitherto been their answer?

Thus the chairman, and in reply some good and useful points were made by individual members. The answers from constituent bodies, however, were to a large extent predictable. The N.P.A. was still opposed to the introduction of lay members, while the N.U.J. still favoured it. The institute returned to its grievance about the closed shop and, like the N.U.J., thought the Press Council should do something about a pension scheme for journalists. The union was opposed to the council trenching upon matters which belonged to the field of normal industrial relations.

All these points were discussed by a special meeting in January 1957, but things remained very much as they were, the crucial factor being, as usual, the absurdly small financial basis upon which the whole operation rested.

When it was five years old the Council said in its annual report for 1958 that "if the brightest hopes have not been fulfilled, it is certain that the darkest fears have not been confirmed. Neither those who said it would be submerged under complaints, nor those who thought it would find nothing to do, had been anywhere near the mark." The council had done its best to be fair and the bitterest criticisms had almost always originated with reprimanded offenders or disappointed complainants. "Looking back over five years we think the voluntary Press Council has established itself as a useful and well-known, if controversial, element in our national life."

A special committee was appointed in 1958 to consider the future constitution and powers of the council in the light of its five years' experience. In particular it was to look once more into the possibility of lay membership. A canvass of council members showed that there was little support for a lay chairman because it was thought such an appointment would shake public confidence in the council rather than strengthen it. There was less opposition to the idea of ordinary lay members and the committee recommended that four should be appointed, one to be a woman, one a lawyer, one a representative of local government, and one an educationalist. This proposal was not accepted by the council, which continued with an all-press membership. Certain recommended changes in the constitution were also rejected. It was decided, however, that to expedite business there should be five council meetings a year instead of four. Later this was increased to six.

7 The Press Attacked

DURING these years the popular newspapers were falling in public esteem, and not only the Press Council but the press as a whole was the subject of successive waves of criticism. Before the Royal Commission had reported, Mr. Aneurin Bevan, a left wing demagogue who was then minister of health, had said in a typical diatribe that the British press was "the most prostituted in the world" – though he had himself enjoyed a long and close association with Lord Beaverbrook. Talking of press intrusion on another occasion, Mr. Bevan said: "If Cabinet Ministers cannot have domestic privacy from British newspapers, neither should proprietors of British newspapers." It was a sad irony that one of the first big cases of alleged intrusion investigated by the Press Council concerned Mr. Bevan himself when he lay dying in hospital.

A P.E.P. pamphlet of 1956, called *The Performance of the Press,* said: "By and large, the popular Press is not respected by the public; it is treated as something of a joke. Its sales stand notably higher than its prestige. This loss of public regard is something which has happened during the last 30 years or so" – since, in short, the rise of mass communication. It went on to ask whether the formation of the Press Council would prove to be an outstanding event in the history of the British press or merely an elaborate piece of window-dressing.

P.E.P. remarked that the council had offered no comment on the prolonged newspaper strike of 1955 and, in view of the duties laid upon it, called this a "startling omission." That was only one of many criticisms of what was regarded in some quarters as a serious lapse. Some members of the council, in a discussion on the stoppage, did urge that a statement should be made, but others took the view that the council had no business to interfere in industrial relations for which ample machinery already existed within the industry. On such matters the council tended to fall into its separate, and sometimes opposing, elements.

The P.E.P. pamphlet said it was clear that the basis of the Press Council was too narrow to allow it to carry out the institutional aspects of its work satisfactorily. In some ways the composition of its membership could debar it from detached consideration of many problems.

"The Press Council," it continued, "began its work without any cut-and-dried rules of professional conduct as its guide. Various attempts have been made to formulate a code of ethics, notably that of the American Society of Newspaper Editors, but these have generally fallen down when it has come to a practical interpretation. The majority of the members of the Council appear to have recognised the difficulty of drawing up a complete set of rules able to cover, in umbrella fashion, papers as different as the *Daily Mirror* and *The Times*. . . . The Council has not the authority, facilities, staff or rules of evidence of a court of law, but its rulings on specific complaints against individual newspapers seem in the main to be fair and reasonable. Its decisions cut both ways; editors are sometimes upheld, sometimes opposed; the public is sometimes considered to be right, sometimes not. These decisions are gradually establishing precedents but the process will undoubtedly take time, and the approach must in the main remain empirical. . . .

"Although the Council may have made mistakes, its affairs have, on the whole, been conducted adroitly and with skill. It has acted on the belief that everyone responds to the expressed approval or disapproval of his fellows, and there can be little doubt that the methods adopted have already gained for it some real influence. The Council must be given a reasonable time to demonstrate whether it is possible to establish a complete code of conduct in this way.

"Editors who are criticised do not like it, and often reply in their own columns by criticising the Press Council. Certain proprietors and journalists have always been opposed to the Council and lose no opportunity of trying to discredit it. There is a tendency among some journalists to grumble about the Press Council in such a way that it might be supposed that the Council is responsible for all the faults of the Press; but few of these journalists have reported to the Council the abuses of which they claim to have knowledge. . . .

"The Press as a whole gives the Council its support and respects its decisions. But there is a recalcitrant element which flouts the decisions and this gives rise to suggestions that the Council should be given powers of sanction, such as the imposition of fines on newspapers which consistently disregard its ruling. Powers to impose sanctions would completely change the character of the Press Council as a voluntary body and might prejudice the freedom of the Press. . . . If the Press continues to offend, there will be the danger of government intervention: the Press is not subject to Parliamentary control, but the other two great channels of information and comment, radio and television, are. If the Press Council were not allowed to succeed there might some day be a much more powerful and very different council in its place."

Finally, this valuable and independent analysis said: "In the general field of Press conduct, the Council has been very active. It has provided a possibility of appeal both for the public and for journalists themselves. In its public statements, the Council has, on the whole, said the sort of thing which people who want to uphold good standards would expect of it. It must have made many people think twice before leaving the way open to criticism. But on many of its objects the Council has done next to nothing. It will never develop into the kind of body P.E.P. envisaged in its 1938 pamphlet, or the Royal Commission, unless it extends its activities – particularly since in this country there are no other organisations which could undertake many of its tasks. The next stage should be to strengthen and develop the Press Council to enable it to carry out all its professed objects effectively. If this proves impracticable, there may be need for fundamental reconsideration."

That last thought had already occurred to others. In 1955, a Labour M.P. had asked the government to establish a statutory Press Council. The prime minister, Mr. Eden (afterwards Lord Avon), said "No" and indicated that he was "very, very chary of acting" in anything concerning the freedom of the press. This was one of several similar demands made from time to time by politicians, and always refused.

But that great principle was not held in awe by everyone. Mr. Randolph Churchill had written in the *Spectator* in 1955 that "a lot of bosh is talked about the freedom of the Press. The original sanctity of the phrase has been much corrupted by those who have wished to enlarge its true meaning to serve their own purposes. The freedom of the Press . . . does not mean that a handful of rich men and their servants have rights denied to others to poke their noses into the private lives of their fellow subjects. This is the abuse of the power of the Press which has led many people to add a fifth freedom to Roosevelt's Four Freedoms, namely Freedom *from* the Press."

This attack was mild compared with another launched by Lord Selborne, a peer who had held office in the wartime government. In a letter to the *Daily Telegraph* in 1955 he wrote: "For too long we have writhed under the excesses of the gutter Press. These organs specialise in exploiting every conceivable morbid sensation, whether it can be extracted from the scum of police court reports, from murders and other crimes, from civil actions, from accidents or even from operations and confinements. No matter the source so long as something can be written about it which can be connected with sex, and can be made to look disgusting, sordid or shameful. No domestic privacy is safe from the attacks of these jackals. They pry into hospital wards and subject surgeons engaged in the most critical cases to third-degree interrogation. They exploit the grief of the bereaved in every tragedy. The pallbearers of the coffin are shot at by the cameras of these ghouls, and discharged criminals are greeted at the prison gates with the searchlight of merciless publicity."

Lord Selborne had actually prepared a bill to set up a three-man authority to license and control newspapers which failed to reach a required standard. The standard was to be "that evinced by *The Times* newspaper during the month of May in the year 1956." This foolish proposal, which would, in time, have frozen the *Times* itself into an outmoded mould, was widely condemned. Lord Selborne said he had introduced it because of the "ineffectiveness" of the Press Council. The council replied that his suggestion was "misguided and reactionary." The *Daily Mail* said it was "a Bill to make the gods laugh—if they did not weep at such stupidity."

But cockeyed though the earl's ideas may have been they did bring a response from people who were thinking and saying much the same things about the press. He claimed to have received about one thousand letters, no more than half a dozen of which were opposed to his campaign to clean up the newspapers.

This feeling was certainly reflected in a Commons debate in 1957 when Mr. Kershaw, a Conservative M.P., moved that the House "viewed with concern some recent examples of newspaper reporting, and is of the opinion that a vigorous effort by the industry itself to maintain a high standard of conduct is desirable." The Press Council came in for some rough handling, but it also found some champions.

Mr. Kershaw initiated the debate because he thought the press was unreasonably exploiting pornography and crime, that the pursuit of the exceptional and sensational had been carried too far, and that there had been intrusions into private grief. The elevation of the trivial in some newspapers had reached a point where it was almost impossible for readers to form any coherent idea about public affairs. He charged the Press Council with complacency, but was himself opposed to lay membership.

Mr. Allaun, a Labour member, thought there had been some improvement in the press since the formation of the council, which had done an excellent job. The same view was taken by Mr. Deedes, on the Conservative side, but Mr. Victor Collins (afterwards Lord Stonham) for the Opposition belaboured the council which had "failed lamentably to deal with the major difficulties and shortcomings of the Press." By and large the Socialists favoured either lay membership or statutory powers, or both, while the Tories were opposed to these measures. Mr. Anthony Greenwood, who was to be a minister in the next Labour government, thought that in the circumstances, lacking power, the success achieved by the council had been greater than many people thought possible. This, however, did not justify the self-complacency which was the keynote of its first three annual reports. The debate, as nearly always happened when the press was discussed, ended inconclusively, with the government hastening to assure everyone that it had no intention of interfering either with the newspapers or with the council.

In 1961 another attempt to legislate against the press was launched by Lord Mancroft who introduced into the House of Lords a Right to Privacy Bill providing for members of the public to be able to claim damages for the "unjustifiable publication of matter concerning private and personal affairs." He called his bill "an extension of the age-old protection against eavesdroppers, Peeping Toms and Paul Prys" and added that "the Press Council does its best but sometimes it is like cleaning the Augean stables with a feather duster." The press protested strongly and Lord Arran (who was writing a weekly column for the London *Evening News*) said he would attempt to kill the measure. But it was given a second reading, despite the government's view that it would prove unworkable. But neither Lord Goddard, a former lord chief justice, nor Lord Denning, the master of the rolls, agreed. The lord chancellor, Lord Kilmuir, for the government, said it would be difficult to restrain the invasion of privacy without interfering with the reporting of matters that ought to be publicly aired.

In the end Lord Mancroft withdrew his bill "for the time being." He said: "It is not dead. It is for the moment sunk, but not without trace. It will come to the surface again."

So far it has not done so.

Thus, nothing was altered. The press, like the proverbial dog, had been given a bad name, and it stuck. During these years charges against newspapers tended to be accepted without question and their actions to be condemned before these had even begun to be investigated by the Press Council. Two examples were the case of Mary Kriek and the Munich air crash of 1958, both of which attracted wide publicity, and both of which were minutely probed by the council.

Mary Kriek was a Dutch girl employed on a farm in Essex who was found murdered in 1957 and whose murderer was never brought to justice. On January 17, 1958, the *Times* published a letter from a man who lived in the neighbourhood and was a friend of the girl's family in Holland, condemning "a majority of the national newspapers" in pursuing their inquiries. He said that "within five minutes of the murdered girl's family in Holland being told of her death, reporters from British papers had swarmed into their flat, even penetrating to the girl's bedroom, before being thrown out. No reporters from any other country, even Holland itself, took part in this disgraceful scramble. . . . Can nothing be done to stop this disgusting type of thing?"

Had such serious accusations been levelled at any other persons or institutions there would at least have been a pause to see whether or not they could be confirmed. But because the press was in the dock, these charges were at once accepted as true, even by some newspapers. The *Times* rushed in with the comment that "things are done in the name of the Press which must make any decent-minded, let alone sensitive, journalist, feel ashamed." The *Guardian* was equally incontinent: "Instances like this have been suffered and complained of for a decade now . . . things are getting worse, not better."

The Press Council got to work. The complainant was invited to attend the committee meeting, where he was thoroughly examined, and other evidence, oral and written, was also taken. Eventually it was found that no British reporters had visited the flat in Holland. They were all Dutch. The "swarm" consisted of six reporters. It was not true that they penetrated to the girl's bedroom, nor were they thrown out. They were invited in and were later asked to leave, which they did. The complainant had also described how his car containing Mary Kriek's father and sister had been chased along the road from Harwich; how he had been besieged in his home by reporters and photographers, and how one reporter had made a false statement in his paper. At the end of it all the council reported: "That while the complainant has failed to substantiate his charges made against the 'majority of the national daily newspapers' there was one case of serious inaccuracy in a report; there were also two cases of badgering intrusion, i.e., the Press cars' pursuit of the family on the road from Harwich and the Press photographers' entry into the garden of his home. These matters are strongly condemned."

This affair had a grim sequel. Some years afterwards the complainant was found dead in Australia with his second wife, a young Dutch woman, whom he was presumed to have murdered. It was then reported that he had himself been suspected by the police of the murder of Mary Kriek. Hence, no doubt, the "badgering intrusion" of the reporters who might, after all, have been trying to assert a public right rather than to satisfy public curiosity.

The publicity attending this case was far exceeded by that of the second one a few weeks later, for this was worldwide. On February 6, 1958, an aircraft carrying the Manchester United football team crashed at Munich airport, killing a number of footballers and journalists who were travelling with them. On February 11, a letter appeared in the *Times* from Mr. (afterwards Sir) Anthony Milward, the chief executive of British European Airways, who was there at the time.

In this letter he spoke of the German nurses and doctors working with devotion in their beautiful, modern hospital to care for these critically injured countrymen — "how great a contrast with the horde of British cameramen who were gathered in the corridors waiting for a chance to photograph the victims in the wards. . . . I hope I may be spared from seeing again the flash of camera bulbs from six or more photographers at a time as they walked into the ward in which three men were fighting for their lives, in order to photograph an unconscious man lying in a critical condition in an oxygen tent. . . . I believe, sir, that the time has come for the Press Council to take action to stop this scandal of our times."

This letter was followed by the customary flood of denunciation from the public before the facts had been unearthed. But the newspapers were now a little more cautious. The *Guardian* wrote that "much of the clamour about the shortcomings of our newspapers is wild and wide of the mark. Some of it has been pure McCarthyism, the smear technique at its worst." The N.U.J. expressed concern at the "growing tendency for complaints against the Press to be exploited in some quarters as matters of fact without corroboration or investigation." Mr. (afterwards Sir) Max Aitken, the chairman of Beaverbrook Newspapers, called Mr. Milward's letter a "disgraceful document." He said Mr. Milward should be concentrating his attention on the causes of the shocking disaster at Munich instead of writing criticisms of the press, "thus establishing a standard of operation which would enable both footballers and newspapermen to travel in safety." But even that letter was cited as an example of the shameful attitude of newspaper proprietors.

Sir Linton Andrews wrote to the *Times:* "May I suggest that private critics might keep their judgment under some restraint until the facts are fully known? It is not without precedent to find the following sequence of events: first an emotional complaint about some incident concerning the Press; then a flow of letters from masters of invective who assume with no further inquiry that the complaint is justified in every respect; next, on patient investigation the discovery that some of the original statements, though well-intentioned, were not true." Which is exactly how it turned out in the Munich case. But Sir Linton's reasoned appeal for fair play did not prevent thirty-five M.P.'s, even before matters had been investigated, putting down a motion in the Commons deploring the conduct of "a certain section of the British Press after the Munich disaster."

The Press Council's inquiry was long, patient and exhaustive. The committee spent many days in questioning Mr. Milward (who appeared personally) and getting and examining statements from sixteen reporters and photographers, besides members of the medical staff of the Rechts der Isar Hospital in Munich. What emerged from all this evidence was the impression of cooperation from the hospital authorities who had not only given permission for news and pictures to be obtained but had invited the newspapermen into the hospital for that purpose. One man said: "Accustomed as the British reporters and cameramen are to the usual rudeness, arrogance and sheer bad manners displayed to the Press in the overwhelming majority of British hospitals, we were astonished at the warm welcome given by the staff of the Rechts der Isar Hospital."

The council issued its statement in April. It had discovered that the "horde" of British photographers consisted of six, although cameramen of other nationalities were present, including German, French, Italian, and Hungarian. It did not believe that any British photographer forced his way into the wards, and though there were sharp differences of evidence, accepted that the photographers were invited into the wards. The general charge of intrusion therefore failed. "We believe Mr. Anthony Milward . . . was not aware of all the facts and has given a wrong impression." "The Press Council deplores that so many people assumed that Mr. Milward's complaint in *The Times* was unanswerable and joined at once in blaming the Press, making no distinction between indictment and conviction." Whether some of the photographs should have been printed was a matter of taste but the council thought that, as a general principle, a photograph of a seriously injured person likely to cause needless distress and pain to relatives should not be printed.

In spite of this verdict Mr. Milward declined to change his views, but the council saw no reason to alter a word of its findings.

No inquiry within the circumscribed limits of the council's authority and resources could have been more thorough, yet for long afterwards critics of the press refused to accept it as honest or impartial. When, two years later, the Labour party complained about press intrusion on Mr. Aneurin Bevan, who lay seriously ill in the hospital, a Labour M.P. wrote to the *Times:* "Is there no limit to this ghoulishness?" and referred back to the Munich case as "the whitewashing by the Press Council which convinced no one."

But it did convince more than a few. The *Observer* thought the findings were "a handsome vindication of the Press" and reflected that it had shown many people ready to believe accusations against journalists. "It does not explain why this deep prejudice exists. Yet that is surely a matter of great concern." Similarly the *Guardian:* "Although the good name of the Press has been vindicated it remains disturbing that so many people in all ranks of life should have been so willing—indeed so anxious—to believe the worst." The *Daily Mail* said such attacks on the press "are as old as newspapers. . . . In every age there are people who fear and dislike the Press and will do all they can to discredit it." The *News-Chronicle* said Mr. Milward was entitled to stick to his opinion even if it was one man's word against the findings of an inquiry. "But this leaves unsettled the unctuous joy with which the popular Press is attacked whatever the weight of the evidence."

The charges in the Bevan case proved as flimsy as in the other two.

Mr. Bevan underwent an operation in the hospital at the end of December 1959, but suffered a relapse on January 21, 1960. Four days later the Labour Party announced that, owing to pressure of press inquiries at the hospital, they would issue future information from their own headquarters. Their statement continued: "The conduct of Press representatives has been generally considerate despite the difficult conditions of their work, but recently there have been unauthorised attempts to gain entry to Mr. Bevan's room." The next day they said they would put the facts before the Press Council at the proper time showing that a small minority of journalists had done a disservice to the profession.

The council did not wait for a formal complaint to be made, but at once asked for details of what had occurred. Owing to the long delays on the part of the Labour party it was not until June that the evidence was received and September before the adjudication could be issued. Once again the council went deeply into the affair, even to the extent of preparing and circulating a sketch of that part of the hospital where Mr. Bevan had lain. It was found that the rush of newspaper inquiries from January 21 onwards had seriously interfered with the routine of the hospital because inadequate arrangements had been made to deal with them. One statement referred to the "failure to understand the justifiable interest of the Press in ascertaining facts about the welfare of an important public figure."

It was discovered that on a Sunday when there were no officials available to give information, some reporters had gone upstairs to the ward adjoining Mr. Bevan's room to try to get something from a nurse, and on another occasion reporters went up to the deputy matron's room, with permission, to get what news they could. In all instances when these journalists were asked to leave they did so without demur. The Press Council regretted that some reporters visited the upstairs ward, and were undoubtedly at fault in doing so. But the Labour party's allegation that there had been unauthorised attempts to get into Mr. Bevan's room were misleading, and not borne out by the evidence.

For a reporter to burst into the room of a dying man to get news would be inexcusably callous and deserving of the severest censure, but to the press in some other countries it may appear strange that any objection could be made to the methods, far short of heartless intrusion, which were actually adopted. American newspapermen, in particular, may look almost with disbelief upon some of the handicaps which normally restrict the British journalist in his daily work, and which arise from the ingrained inhibitions of British citizens. These differences have been nowhere better described than in an article written for the *Guardian* in 1958 by Mr. Joseph Harsch, then the senior European correspondent for the N.B.C. and columnist for the *Christian Science Monitor*. His reflections do help to explain why a Press Council was appointed in Britain, and are therefore worth quoting at length. He wrote:

"The American Press of to-day, leaving aside its past record, is less frequently accused by individuals of undue intrusion into privacy than is your Press. . . . The American reporter is quite as ingenious and imaginative in getting information he wants but he probably is less ruthless partly because the obstacles to the pursuit of information are less. . . . There is intrusion on private grief. There is also a difference in public attitude towards publication of news. The American people are less jealous of privacy, taking the appearance of their names in the public Press more or less for granted. . . . The public is extremely active in helping a newspaper get the story it wants. . . . The reporter does not really have to resort to ruthlessness or intrude objectionably on personal privacy. . . . He seldom faces a serious problem of how to get through a door which is closed to him. He is more concerned with how to avoid getting dragged through the door by an eager Press agent with something to sell. . . . If American practice were applied to your Press it would be given greater freedom than it now enjoys, not made subject to greater restraint. And I would at least be willing to contend that the result would reduce, not increase, the incidence and validity of complaints."

An article on "Intrusion" in the Press Council's fifth annual report showed the rather different attitude prevailing in Britain. Having remarked that though many charges of intrusion were made against the press few specific cases came to the council, it said that every trained reporter would be polite, sympathetic and eager to be accurate in his quest for information. Those who resented polite inquiries often had something to hide and it might be a danger to the public to wrench from the press the powers of investigation which had made it a watchdog of the public safety.

The article mentioned the two Foreign Office officials (Burgess and Maclean) who defected to Russia in 1952 and recalled that when the newspapers made inevitable inquiries among the families of the two diplomats they were accused of distressing intrusion into privacy. In particular, some people rushed to defend the privacy of Mrs. Maclean when reporters sought to interview her. It was not long, however, before she, too, disappeared, and turned up in Moscow.

The sixth annual report, of 1959, recorded "with genuine dismay" the resignation of Sir Linton Andrews from the chairmanship of the council owing to pressure of other work. "He has become so identified with the Council, as vice-chairman and then as chairman for four years, that it will be hard to think of it without him," it said.

"Dealing, as it does, with vague and shifting standards of taste and opinion the Council needed, above all else, the support of precedents and definitions if it was to gain confidence and assert its authority. These have been abundantly forthcoming under Sir Linton's direction. The Council has been greatly assisted not only by his lifelong experience as a journalist, as the distinguished editor of the *Yorkshire Post* and a well-known public figure, but also by his erudition and his knowledge of men and affairs."

The minutes record that at the meeting of April 14, 1959, members of the council paid tribute to their retiring chairman. "They thanked him for the wonderful work he had done for journalism in general and the Press Council in particular."

In a "looking-back and looking-forward" piece, Sir Linton said the council had never moderated its verdicts and reprimands from a motive of expediency. They had been based on facts investigated and stated without malice but, he added somewhat wistfully, "If we had had more money at our disposal we might have made fuller investigation into some alleged scandals and relied a little less on written statements."

In 1960, Mr. Alan Pitt Robbins retired from the secretaryship and was succeeded by Colonel Willie C. Clissitt, who had seen active service in both world wars. These interruptions apart, he had been a lifelong journalist and editor of regional newspapers for thirty years, including twenty-five years as editor of the Liverpool *Evening Express*. He was a founder-member of the Editors' Guild, and an examiner for the journalists' training scheme. When he applied for the council post at the age of sixty-two, he said it was because he believed in what the Press Council stood for. Many men make such statements as a matter of form, but Willie Clissitt meant it wholeheartedly. Never was a man more dedicated to his work, and the Press Council owes him more than most of its members knew. In a short time he transformed the office and put its somewhat exiguous organisation on to a businesslike footing. He refused to take personal expenses, even travelling expenses, from its limited funds, and was with difficulty persuaded to take short holidays. When the council moved from its attic rooms in Bell Yard to an office in Fleet-street, he spent some of his free time scouring secondhand shops to buy furniture for it, securing some handsome chairs for the committee room, and a magnificent table for which he paid five pounds. The wealthy newspaper industry was well served by Willie Clissitt.

When Sir Linton Andrews retired in June 1959, his place was taken as acting chairman by the present writer, a nominee of the Institute of Journalists on the Council, then chief leader writer of the *Daily Mail,* and a director of Associated Newspapers, who, six months later, was elected to the chair. Mr. Henry Bate, another founder-member, nominated by the N.U.J., and on the editorial staff of the *Daily Telegraph,* was elected vice-chairman.

The council was now increasingly being asked for its judgment on matters of journalistic ethics, on standards of reporting and matters of that kind. The new chairman in his foreword to the seventh annual report noted that "as its purpose and function have become better appreciated it has moved from the shallows of everyday practice into the deeper waters of basic principle."

In June 1960, there had been a debate on the press in the House of Lords, in which several speakers regretted that the council did not have the power to punish. The archbishop of Canterbury said it could not rely on the force of public opinion. An article in the 1960 annual report on the "Power of the Press Council" pointed out that the House of Lords itself had little power beyond that of persuasion and that the debate itself was merely an appeal to public opinion. "It was disconcerting to find speakers underestimating the force upon which they have to rely. . . . Nevertheless public opinion is, in the end, decisive."

Some peers in the debate had suggested a body to license, register, and control journalists on the lines of the General Medical Council or the Law Society and the article explained why this could not be done. "Medicine and the law are so different from journalism that there is hardly any ground upon which a true comparison can be made," it said. "In both the learned professions unorthodoxy is an offence and self-advertisement a crime. In journalism these are virtues. In medicine and the law there is a body of fixed knowledge and general practice which can be tested by examination. The entrant into journalism learns mainly from practical experience and from contact with his fellow men. Human nature, inconstant, volatile, unpredictable is the raw material of the journalist, and the world is his parish.

"One speaker in the House of Lords gave as an example of journalistic irresponsibility a man who had written articles on two entirely different subjects in consecutive editions of an evening paper. The speaker said that 'anything said in the one field could not possibly have qualified the writer to have written anything in the other field.' That remark illustrates the profound misunderstanding of what journalism is. The art of the journalist is to be able to write on different subjects in an interesting way, and that is why journalism is not, and cannot be, an academic profession. It is less important for a newspaper writer to know the facts himself than to know where to get them, and to be able to present them clearly and accurately."

"One imagines," said the article, "that members of both Houses of Parliament discuss topics on which they are not specially well-informed. This very debate in the Lords contained a good deal of erroneous and inaccurate information about the Press."

Having thus put their lordships in their places, the article wagged a finger at the "quality" newspapers who (perhaps to the surprise of Mr. Cecil King) were not taking enough part in the work of the Press Council. After the resignation of Lord Astor neither the editorial nor the managerial departments of the *Times* had been represented. Nor had those of the *Guardian, Observer,* or *Sunday Times.* Some of these newspapers had been critical of the council, which was their right. But when the organisation attacked was so intimately concerned with the press, collaboration could be more helpful than criticism and do more good to the newspapers and the council.

The quality papers, though often critical of others, nearly always showed themselves extremely sensitive to criticism of themselves, whereas the popular press normally "took it on the chin" without crying—a contrast in attitudes soon to be illustrated. In 1960, three Sunday newspapers began to run the memoirs of the film star, Diana Dors and her husband Dennis Hamilton, and of another film star, Errol Flynn. Affronted by these revelations many people wrote to the Press Council which, in a circulated statement, recalled its deep concern of 1953 in the unwholesome exploitation of sex, and its intention to keep the matter under review. The statement went on: "The Council has considered (a) Recent articles in the *News of the World* and the *Sunday Pictorial* giving accounts of the sexual adventures of Diana Dors and Dennis Hamilton, and; (b) Articles in the *People* on the sex experiences of Errol Flynn. In the opinion of the Council these articles sank below the accepted standards of decency and the Dors and Hamilton articles, in particular, contained material that was grossly lewd and salacious. When it first expressed its views on the treatment of sex in the Press, the Council declared that its unwholesome exploitation was calculated to injure public morals especially because newspapers and periodicals are seen and read by young persons. It has noted that, over the ensuing years, a general improvement has been registered. It is all the more to be deplored, therefore, that the newspapers named should now have permitted their standards to be debased to a level which is a disgrace to British journalism."

This was strong meat—much more highly flavoured than the mild portion doled out some months afterwards to three quality papers which had printed words regarded in law as obscene but which had figured prominently in the case (which failed) brought against publication of D. H. Lawrence's *Lady Chatterley's Lover*. The council received no complaints from the public but, acting on its own initiative, issued the following statement after its meeting in February 1961:

"The Press Council has considered the action of the *Spectator,* the *Guardian* and the *Observer* in publishing certain 'four-letter' words mentioned in the *Lady Chatterley's Lover* trial. In the opinion of the Council this was both objectionable and unnecessary. The Press, in general, demonstrated how a court case of this kind can be adequately and broadmindedly covered without debasing standards of decency."

All three hooted back in sorrow or in fury, or both; leading articles were written in protest and the chairman was involved in published correspondence with the three. For some time thereafter the *Guardian* ceased to publish the council's quarterly bulletins, mentioning merely the headings of each case, a practice which gave no real information to anybody and must have puzzled its readers. It seemed an odd interpretation of the "facts are sacred" formula upon which the reputation of the *Guardian* had been built.

One matter of principle did arise from this brush with the quality. The three papers attacked the Press Council for its "discourtesy" in failing to inform them that their cases were to be considered and pronounced upon without giving them any opportunity to submit evidence and defend themselves. This was certainly a valid point. It was discussed by the council which then declared that the issue had been debated as a matter that affected press standards, and that no specific complaints had been lodged. No issue of fact had arisen since there was no dispute that the words had been published. In these circumstances there was no need, in the council's opinion, to call evidence.

Nevertheless, an important question had been raised, and the chairman returned to it in his foreword to the next annual report. He said that such a complaint came strangely from newspapers which criticised persons, policies, and institutions without preliminary warning. This form of "discourtesy" was a right which the press must constantly employ if it was to be effective. The Press Council claimed a similar right. It could, and did, take the initiative when in its view, newspapers by some general act of policy fell short of the standards expected of them. The "four-letter words" constituted such a case. Their publication could only have been the result of a deliberate act of editorial decision and in the council's opinion it was a wrong decision. Sometimes rebukes had been passed by emergency resolution and in such cases it was obviously impossible to give previous notice to the "accused." "Any newspaper," said the foreword, "at any time is liable to be denounced in Parliament or from platform or pulpit without expecting, or receiving, notice of any kind. To deny the Press Council a similar freedom would be to rob it of one of its sharpest weapons. To suggest that this should be done comes ill from some of those who simultaneously complain that the Council lacks strong teeth."

The *Guardian* agreed that newspapers and journalists who criticised others should not complain when they themselves were criticised. "The Press Council has, however, an important job to do in helping to raise the standards of the British Press. Its words need to carry weight. They will not do so while it condemns people, in their absence, behind closed doors and by minority votes."

The *Guardian* reacted with a similar air of shocked rectitude when the council had occasion to admonish it in 1969. A hospital management committee had complained of distortion in an article by a woman reporter, Ann Shearer, describing the allegedly foul conditions in a children's ward of Harperbury Hospital, a mental hospital in Hertfordshire.

The accuracy of certain descriptions was disputed by the hospital group secretary. He said the reporter had visited the hospital by appointment in connection with her article. This followed a private visit she had made, apparently without knowledge and authority. At that time the ward was in isolation because of an outbreak of dysentery. On the day the article appeared, said the secretary, an immediate investigation was carried out, and grave concern was expressed "at this type of irresponsible article and the effect it would have on the parents and relatives of patients, and nursing staff."

Mr. Alastair Hetherington, the editor of the *Guardian,* told the council that the reporter had substantial knowledge and experience of hospitals. He submitted to the council a statement from the mother of a child patient endorsing the article.

Nevertheless the council's verdict, after a recital of the facts, was: "While the subject of the article in the *Guardian* is one with which the Press has a right to deal within the discretion of an Editor, when the Press does deal with a subject of this type it must be careful to do so with the utmost objectivity and accuracy. The article in the *Guardian* does not conform to those standards. The complaint is therefore upheld."

When this adjudication was issued, Mr. Hetherington took the unusual step of reprinting the article in his paper with the following comment: "Since the Press Council does not say where the article lacked objectivity or accuracy, since the article was one whose publication the *Guardian* regarded as important, and since the article took care to explain the background of staffing difficulties, we reprint it in full below the adjudication. Readers may wish to form their own judgment."

Then followed an exchange of letters between the editor and the council. These are of interest as showing the typical point of view of an Editor in conflict with the council's interpretation of its function and duty.

Mr. Hetherington to Lord Devlin: "I know that on Press Council adjudications one ought to take the rough with the smooth. But this morning's on the Harperbury case is so eccentric as to be beyond understanding.

"It says that the *Guardian's* article did not conform to the proper standards of objectivity and accuracy. It fails to say in any particular where the article fell short. By implication it appears to sustain the complaint about particular phrases such as 'these then are mad children,' but it does so without reference to the context in which they were used. The only inaccuracies of which we are aware are on trivial points such as the floor covering being of vinyl tiles, not linoleum.

"Secondly, the adjudication repeats the Hospital Group Secretary's complaint that Miss Shearer first visited the hospital 'apparently without knowledge and authority.' Although the adjudication later mentions my comment on the circumstances in which Miss Shearer went to the hospital, by implication it appears to accept the Hospital Group Secretary's contention. Are we then to assume that the Press Council believes that journalists should make visits only with prior authority from officials? If so, this seems an extraordinary way for the Council to interpret its first objective, namely to preserve the freedom of the British Press.

"Thirdly, although the adjudication mentions the evidence both of the women who first asked Miss Shearer to visit the hospital and of the mother of another child patient, it appears to place no weight on this corroboration of what Ann Shearer said. Of course you have had the benefit of listening to members of the hospital staff, but does that make any less truthful Ann Shearer's account of what she saw?

"Finally, the adjudication seems to ignore the fact that a large part of the article was devoted to describing the difficulties of staffing which such hospitals encounter.

"May I assure you that my decision last night to reprint the article was not taken lightly? Had any adequate reasons been given for your Council's judgment, that decision would not have been taken."

Lord Devlin to Mr. Hetherington: "The Complaints Committee of the Press Council considered at its meeting yesterday your letter to me on this case and the circumstances in which you reprinted in the *Guardian* the article with which the Council had found fault.

"It is, of course, accepted that if an Editor thinks it necessary and right to do so, he is at liberty to express his dissent from an adverse finding against his newspaper. Obviously he would not do so without grave reasons. Even without your express assurance, the Council would have known that you would have given the most careful consideration to this matter before taking the action you did.

"The Committee feels that the way in which the *Guardian* expressed its dissent is, if I may use your word, 'eccentric.' But the reprinting of an article, when accompanied by a statement that the Press Council has found it lacking in objectivity and accuracy, is not likely to do any further harm. The Committee considers that the way in which the

Guardian expressed its dissent was a matter within the Editor's discretion.

"This being so, the Committee would not normally comment on the way in which the discretion was exercised. But since you were kind enough to give me your reasons for acting as you did and since in the Committee's view they show a misunderstanding of the nature of an adjudication generally and of this one in particular, the Committee felt that you might wish to have its comment.

"You say in your letter you would not have taken the decision you did if the Council had given reasons for its adjudication. An adjudication of the Council is expressed as a conclusion. It is not intended to contain reasons and cannot be expected to do so. A single judge can easily express his reasons in his judgment. The same is true of a judgment given by a small body of judges so long as they have unlimited time for discussion and drafting. But the judgment of a large body, such as the Press Council, can be expressed only as a conclusion, since different members may have different reasons for reaching the same conclusion. An adjudication of the Press Council must be regarded as much closer to a verdict of a jury than to a judgment. It derives its force from the fact that it is a conclusion approved for one reason or another by a wide spread of experienced professional opinion.

"Your comments on the adjudication seem to take it for granted that the only inaccuracies in the article were trivial. But, as you know, there was an acute conflict of evidence about conditions in the hospital, not only generally but also on the day Miss Shearer visited it. Where there is a conflict of evidence of this sort, a common explanation is that each side is seeing only what it wants to see. I think it is plain from the adjudication that the preponderant view on the Council was that the discrepancy must be accounted for, at least in part, by some lack of objectivity on the part of Miss Shearer. But it is unlikely that everyone resolved the conflict in precisely the same way. There must also be taken into account the possibility—which I think also emerges from the adjudication—that some members thought that the article ought not to have been published at all; in their view it could only be calculated to make the performance of a difficult but essential social service more difficult still. Such members would naturally be disposed to think that, if such an article was to be published, the standard of objectivity must be put very high.

"The course you took in reprinting the article in order that your readers might form a judgment upon it is in the Committee's view based on the erroneous assumption that it is possible to decide what is or what is not objective reporting in a case such as this simply by reading the article and without hearing the witnesses or considering their evidence.

"The Committee wishes me to add that the Council did not, as you think, form the opinion that Miss Shearer ought not to have visited the hospital 'without knowledge or appropriate authority.' Certainly the words quoted were used in the recital of facts in the letter of complaint but this fact was not made the subject of any specific complaint or, indeed, so far as I recollect, of any express criticism. So no adjudication was called for. I cannot understand how you can read into a finding that Miss Shearer's article was not sufficiently objective an additional finding that she ought not to have gone to the hospital without the knowledge of the authorities.

"If the *Guardian* wishes to publish your letter to me and this reply, I am very happy that it should do so."

The letters were duly published.

8 A Year of Crisis

THE year 1960–61 was the most cataclysmic in the history of British newspapers. Its events were critical not only for the press and the Press Council but also, it could be said without exaggeration, for the British democracy. They brought into question, once more, the whole relationship between the press and the people, the dangers to freedom of expression from concentration of newspaper ownership, and the competence and authority of the Press Council. When the dust had settled the scope and structure of the council had changed (though not radically) and the press was given a special place within the authority of the Monopolies Commission.

Three Sunday newspapers disappeared during the year – the century-old *Sunday Dispatch,* the *Empire News* (which had absorbed the *Sunday Chronicle*), and the *Sunday Graphic.* Although the first two had circulations around the two million mark, they were unable to pay their way. These extinctions caused comparatively little comment. The uproar came when the *News-Chronicle* and *Star* were merged with the *Daily Mail* and the *Evening News* respectively on October 18, 1960.

The *News-Chronicle* had begun life as the *Daily News* in 1846, with Charles Dickens as its first editor, and throughout its existence was a great popular organ of liberal and radical opinion. Since the turn of the century it had passed through several difficult periods – largely because it sacrificed profitability to principle – and was kept going, as already mentioned, by infusions of other circulations. The *Star* was founded by T. P. O'Connor, a journalist M.P., in 1888, and had twinkled saucily in the London evening sky. At one time it could boast the most brilliant band of contributors ever assembled on an evening newspaper, including George Bernard Shaw as its irreverent music critic.

By 1960 the *News-Chronicle's* circulation was about 1,250,000, and that of the *Star* something in excess of 800,000 – large enough, it might be thought, to ensure continuance, if not prosperity. But though the *Star* might have been viable the *News-Chronicle* was in very low water. It had striven to give its readers not so much what they wanted as what it thought they ought to have and had fallen somewhere between the popular and the quality market. It was preeminently a newspaper of that "intermediate type" whose numbers, said the Press Commission, were too small. Now they were smaller still.

The *News-Chronicle* was not popular enough to attract the mass advertising needed to keep it afloat, nor sufficiently in the quality range to attract the "class" advertising which might have saved it. Since the selling price of national newspapers had risen from 2d. to 2½d. in 1957, the *News-Chronicle's* circulation had fallen by 232,000 and that of the *Star* by 172,000. In the first nine months of 1960 the two papers had lost £300,000 – a figure which would not immediately have overwhelmed some other national newspapers which at that time, or soon afterwards, were carrying on with losses of more than £1 million a year. By the violence of its opposition to the Suez adventure of 1956 – which a majority of the populace upheld – the *News-Chronicle* had alienated a sizeable portion of its readership, dropping as much as 100,000 circulation which it could not possibly afford.

So it had to go. What shocked many people was the secrecy and suddenness with which the operation was performed, and the absorption of this newspaper by, of all possible rivals, the *Daily Mail*. In years gone by, no two journals could have been more antipathetic. In politics, principle, practice, they were far apart, with the *Mail* well to the Right and the *News* far to the radical Left. In Northcliffe's time, when A. G. Gardiner edited the *Daily News,* there had been bitter hostility. By 1960, however, that was a closed chapter, though, as ever, diehards of the two persuasions, living in the past, had not realised that the two papers had each in recent years tended towards the centre.

However that may be, the crash came and the fat was in the fire. Everyone was blamed – the management for incompetence, the trade unions for making excessive demands on an ailing concern, and the journalists for producing a poor newspaper. In particular abuse was hurled at Mr. L. J. Cadbury, the chairman of the *News-Chronicle,* for selling the paper to the *Daily Mail;* at Lord Rothermere, the chairman of the *Daily Mail,* for buying it; and at both for the stealthiness of the deal. The agreed price was about £1.9 million of which £1.2 million was set aside as compensation to the displaced staff. This allotment was, however, stopped by the High Court on the application of a *News-Chronicle* shareholder, who objected to it. Later the capital of the company was reduced to £1,140,000 and distributed to the Ordinary shareholders, who were invited to transfer their share to a compensation fund for the staff.

Whatever the outcome of these financial arrangements the fact is that the first thought throughout was for the thirty-five hundred employees who had lost their jobs, though most of them were quickly absorbed elsewhere. As someone asked when recriminations against Mr. Cadbury were at their height: "How many proprietors of large-scale enterprises had devoted nearly all the purchase price of their business to the benefit of the employees?" There is another thought, too. It is that in spite of the God-fearing trust drawn up by an earlier Cadbury, it was the money of the "hard-faced" *Daily Mail* which was used to cushion the blow to the workers.

Lord Rothermere disclosed that, some time before the actual transference he had been asked whether he would buy the *News-Chronicle* and *Star* for enough money to see that everyone was properly compensated. He had promised to do so, but only if they could get no one else to carry on the newspapers alive. His company, Associated Newspapers, was to be the last resort. Other approaches were made during the *News-Chronicle*'s last few years but no offer was backed by sufficient money to pay the large sums needed for the staff, nor to revive the paper. To bring it to the equivalent size of its rivals would have taken £4 million over two years, and that would have been no more than a first step towards recovery. Finally the whole thing had to be put through in secrecy to prevent other newspapers snatching at the circulation now to go a-begging, and to guarantee the *Daily Mail* the full fruits of its expenditure. The trade union leaders had been told a few weeks before of the inevitability of what was to happen, and not one of them betrayed the confidence.

The truth about the *News-Chronicle* is that, having withstood the conditions of the twentieth century for two generations, it finally broke under the strain. It was the old story of rising costs and falling revenue. But what caused these adverse tendencies? Lord Layton and Sir Geoffrey (afterwards Lord) Crowther (the one vice-chairman and the other a trustee of the *News-Chronicle*), in a letter to the *Times,* said: "The economics of the newspaper industry are very cruel to a popular paper with a relatively small circulation. It can sell less advertising space than its rivals and therefore can give its readers less editorial matter to read. Inevitably it appears to offer less value for the money. So its circulation ebbs away and advertisements are still harder to get."

A subsequent letter from members of the staff blamed the crash on the management. "Thrice since 1957," it said, "meetings of the N.U.J. have sent deputations to the board to express concern at the lethargic drift percolating from the top. The deputations met indifference. They were treated almost as agitators, even though they included distinguished and respected journalists, honoured in their profession and well known to the public." It is also a fact that the *News-Chronicle* was reported only once to the Press Council, and for a very minor offence. This may have been a tribute to its respectability – or an indication of its lack of vitality.

The greatest weight of censure fell on the trade unions. A book called *The Murder of the "News-Chronicle"* by Edward Martell and Ewan Butler said that "restrictive practices exercised by the trade unions have assassinated, in broad daylight, and in the presence of many witnesses, two newspapers whose names were familiar to most Britons." It also said that in ten years ninety-seven newspapers and magazines had been "killed by the same hands." It accused the dozen or so trade unions whose members staffed the two newspapers of regarding them not as a business which had to pay its way but solely as a source of income for as many of their members as the management could be cajoled or threatened into employing.

While the staff of the *News-Chronicle* amounted to about thirty-five hundred people, said the book, that of the *Guardian* and *Manchester Evening News* (who are stable companions) was about seventeen hundred – "positive proof that the number of staff really necessary for the production of the *News-Chronicle* was prodigally excessive." The payroll amounted to seventy thousand pounds a week, whereas the papers could have been run efficiently on twenty-five thousand pounds a week. Three defendants stood in the dock, the authors of the book said. These were the trade unions and after them the newspapers and the government who had allowed "spineless expediency and abject subjection to blackmail to place the whole future of newspapers in this country, and with it the freedom of the Press, in jeopardy."

The *Times* also wagged a minatory finger at the trade unions. It said: "The idea of some trade unionists that no matter how hard they may have pressed the industry in the past, and no matter how uneconomic they may have helped to make some of its activities, they nevertheless have the invulnerable right to maintain exactly the same volume of employment in that industry, is wholly unreal."

But Mr. Robert Willis, general secretary of the London Typographical Society, denied that the wages paid in the industry and labour costs generally were the cause of newspaper close-downs. He blamed it largely on the high cost of newsprint which had advanced in price from ten pounds a ton in 1939 to fifty-eight or sixty pounds a ton in 1960. Thus the argument about paying labour too much for doing too little owing to the rapacity of the unions raged, and was destined to rage even more before the year was out.

In the meantime, Parliament weighed in and, as usual, managed to split the argument neatly down party lines. While Labour M.P.'s called for a new Royal Commission to inquire into "monopolistic control," Conservative M.P.'s deplored the "restrictive practices of printing and journalistic trade unions which were mainly responsible for the closing down of the *News-Chronicle* and *Star*." The Spirit Ironic may allow us a peep at Mr. Harold Wilson, who was to be Labour prime minister from 1964 onwards and who now criticised the government for holding that amalgamations between private enterprise competitors produced economies and a more balanced outlook and were of advantage to the consumer. A few years later Mr. Wilson's own government formed the Industrial Reorganisation Corporation, backed with public money, to promote mergers between private industrial concerns.

The government refused to refer the *News-Chronicle-Daily Mail* merger to the Monopolies Commission or to appoint another Royal Commission on the Press. "The intervention of the Government in the affairs of the Press is not a thing to be undertaken lightly," said Mr. R. A. (afterwards Lord) Butler, the Home Secretary.

The Press Council had already expressed its deep concern at the closure of the two papers, and others as well. "The loss of these journals . . . further restricted the variety of opinion and information available to the nation through the Press, a tendency which the Royal Commission on the Press in 1949 stated was undesirable. The Press Council greatly regrets that economic circumstances have given impetus to this tendency in recent years."

That did not amount to much either.

Some M.P.'s were far from satisfied and the Labour Opposition initiated a debate calling for an inquiry. This was again resisted by the government, and Mr. Vosper, the minister of state for Home Affairs, said that if there was any evidence to suggest excessive concentration of press ownership it was open to the Press Council to investigate the facts and make any recommendations they saw fit. The council had already commented on the failure of the two newspapers, and it remained to be seen whether it would institute a wider inquiry.

He added: "I find it difficult to see what a committee of inquiry could achieve that the Royal Commission did not recommend in their report ten years ago." When he was asked whether he thought it desirable that the Press Council should begin an inquiry he said: "The Government have never made any comment on the activities of the Press Council. Following this debate action may well happen on some or other of the lines indicated. Something may happen."

In other words he was saying in one breath that nothing could be done, while in the next breath he was inviting the Press Council to do something. This contradiction was not merely a perfect example of passing the buck, but also typified the attitude of the public and some newspapers towards the Press Council which, with little money and less power, was expected to perform miracles. It drove the council's annual report for 1961 to reply somewhat bitterly, and to examine the council's functions and limitations in a way worth extensive quotation. In an article on "The Functions of the Press Council" it said:

"As many people have pointed out, Article 2 (vii) of the Constitution states that one of the Council's objects shall be to 'study developments in the Press which may tend towards greater concentration or monopoly.' Clearly, some kind of duty has been laid on the Council in this matter, but what is it? What does 'to study' mean? Does it imply the collection and collation of economic statistics, the holding of inquiries into the deaths of newspapers, or the ability to command foreknowledge of pending mergers or take-overs? If it means any or all of these things the task is obviously beyond the reach of the Press Council as it is at present constituted.

"Its activities are limited and confined within a total income of £4,100 a year—a sum insufficient to maintain anything beyond the present exiguous organisation. The Council is well aware of the restrictions imposed on its activities by a thin purse. Before this report was compiled it had instructed the General Purposes Committee to review the Council's financial resources and to make recommendations. The Secretary and his assistant, who are already hard-pressed, have neither the means nor the time to act as a clearing-house for the constantly-fluctuating and infinitely-varied economic fortunes of the British Press. Such work would need the services of a highly-paid specialist staff. So, also, would the duty of inquiring into the closing of newspapers. It was the size and impact of the *News-Chronicle* disaster which led to calls for a thorough investigation into the events which led up to it. But the end of every newspaper means a loss to the community it serves and to the people who produce it.

"Since the Press Council was formed in 1953, many morning, evening, weekly and Sunday newspapers have ceased to exist. Did none of these deserve an inquiry except the largest? If there is to be an inquest on one there should surely be inquests on all. Who is to conduct them? The Press Council is composed of busy men who give voluntary service. It is, in fact, a condition that 'membership shall be restricted to . . . full-time directors or employees on the editorial or managerial staffs of newspapers, periodicals or news-agencies . . . or full-time professional free-lance journalists.' It would be impossible for them to probe the circumstances of even one closure, to say nothing of all. The Press Council (unlike a Royal Commission) has no authority to demand the production of information or the attendance of witnesses. Unless it were armed with statutory powers of the most far-reaching kind it could never obtain details of contemplated mergers, upon which close secrecy is normally maintained by the principals concerned.

"A few years ago the Council, at the instance of one of its constituent bodies, did attempt to elicit particulars of newspaper finance and other details of Press production by means of a questionnaire, but another constituent body declined to circulate it. In short, the Council had been compelled to interpret Article 2 (vii) of its Constitution in the terms of Article 2 (viii). This enjoins it 'to publish periodical reports recording its own work and reviewing from time to time the various developments in the Press and the factors affecting them.' But this restricted form of 'study' has itself been criticized because the Council has failed to review such 'developments' as the newspaper strike of 1955, and the 1959 stoppage in the printing industry. The inclusion of these momentous episodes was vigorously debated, but on each occasion it was decided, by a majority vote, to exclude them.

"Such decisions, it must be pointed out, arise from the nature of the Council. Its primary function is to consider ethical questions concerning the newspaper Press and this it performs as a homogeneous body. But when it comes to economic questions there is, naturally, a division of opinion among constituent bodies representing varied interests. It would be almost impossible to present a unanimous report on, for example, an industrial dispute within the industry.

"Let it now be supposed that the Council had been equipped to conduct an inquiry into the merger of the *News-Chronicle* and *Star* with the *Daily Mail* and *Evening News*. The question then arises: What purpose would such an investigation have served? For answer, some statements made by Mr. Vosper in the Parliamentary debate may be recalled. He said that any committee or commission set up for this purpose would have two inter-related functions. The first would be to attempt to uncover relevant facts not contained in the Report of the Royal Commission of 1947–1949. The second would be to recommend legislation or other remedies. He went on: 'It would be difficult to see what, if anything, could be proposed. Hon. members who are familiar with the Royal Commission's report will recognize that with two possible exceptions the Commission came firmly to the conclusion that there was no possible reform which could be undertaken. Despite recent developments, despite the advent of commercial television, it is difficult to find any reason for believing that any other commission or committee of inquiry could today come to a different conclusion.'

"At least four times the Minister repeated his belief that no committee of inquiry could achieve anything of value. It is hard to understand why he should then have seemed to suggest that the Press Council should 'investigate the facts and make recommendations' when, in his own emphatic view, no useful recommendations could have been made.

"If a new inquiry had to be made, a Royal Commission was undoubtedly the best way of doing it. Had it been undertaken by the Press Council, the objection that this was an interested body would at once have been raised, and, indeed, would have been justified. It is of the essence of such tribunals that most of their members shall approach their task with open minds and little, if any, expert knowledge of the matter in hand. The Royal Commission on the Police is not manned by police-men, nor an inquiry into doctors' pay by members of the medical pro-fession. Those who have demanded an inquiry into Press closures by the Press Council appear to have given small thought to what they were asking.

"If the Council, in addition to its existing duties, is to be expected to handle the kind of business under notice, it is obvious that its constitution must be radically changed and its scope, functions and finances vastly enlarged."

As it happened, that last sentence proved to be a flash of prevision as the result of an even greater sensation which convulsed press, Parlia-ment, and public a few weeks after the death of the *News-Chronicle.* This was the taking over of Odhams, a large newspaper and periodical publishing house by the *Daily Mirror* interests. Odhams, with total assets of forty million pounds published the *Daily Herald,* the Sunday *People,* the *Sporting Life,* and many magazines. It controlled Newnes, the Long Acre Press, Hulton Publications, and the Temple Press, all considerable publishers of magazines and trade papers. The *Daily Mirror* group published the *Daily Mirror,* the *Sunday Pictorial,* the Scottish *Daily Record,* and the *Sunday Mail.* It controlled Fleetway Publications, the largest magazine firm in the country, the Iliffe Press, and West Afri-can Newspapers; and it had vast paper and commercial printing invest-ments.

As 1960 faded into 1961 Mr. Roy (afterwards Lord) Thomson, the Canadian-born owner of more newspapers than anyone else in the world, was negotiating with Odhams for a merger. He and Sir Christopher Chancellor, the chairman of Odhams, had appeared on television to-gether in January 1961 to announce the deal, though it had not then been completed. Mr. Hugh Cudlipp, the joint managing director of the *Daily Mirror* group (who was later to displace Mr. Cecil King as chairman), wrote of the new partners-to-be as "beaming into the cameras in antici-pation of a harmonious union." The interests Mr. Cudlipp represented were, however, determined to have Odhams, even though it might mean making a bid for Thomson-Odhams.

For weeks Fleet-street watched with fascinated interest while the mastodons manoeuvered. The outcome was the withdrawal of Thomson and the triumphant emergence of King and Cudlipp as the heads of what was to become the International Publishing Corporation—by far the biggest empire of its kind in the world, controlling, besides its newspapers, some 220 magazines and periodicals.

Again the government were asked to order an official inquiry, and again they refused. The prime minister pointed to the changing nature of newspaper control—from editors to proprietors. "Nowadays newspaper organisations are concerned not so much with power as with profit. . . . We must take a balanced view of all this. After all, we still have something like 150 daily and Sunday newspapers with considerable diversity of ownership, and there is now the prospect of a new Sunday newspaper" (the *Sunday Telegraph,* which duly appeared). Mr. Macmillan even hinted once more at intervention by the Press Council when he said he doubted whether there was scope for government action but "there might be more value if . . . the component parts of the industry itself were to undertake a review of its current problems and future development."

It was of no use. Not only was public opinion seriously aroused, but there were threats of strike action among newspaper workers if it was found that their interests were adversely affected. So the government had at last to give in. On February 9, even before the takeover had been completed, Mr. Macmillan announced that another Royal Commission on the Press would be appointed. Though the government declined to interfere in any way with the Mirror-Odhams transaction, the Prime Minister thought it was "symptomatic of some general unease in the industry." He also conceded that "the recent closure, through inability to pay its way, of a national daily newspaper with a circulation exceeding a million clearly came as a shock to the public."

So the *News-Chronicle* had edged into the picture after all.

9 The Toils of the Press

THE chairman of the new commission was Lord Shawcross who, as Sir Hartley Shawcross, had been Britain's chief prosecutor at the Nuremberg Tribunal, and was later attorney general and president of the Board of Trade in the postwar Labour government. Lord Shawcross had won a reputation as a brilliant cross-examiner and his abilities in that direction were brought home to more than one witness in the forthcoming inquiry. The other members of the commission were: Sir Graham Cunningham, Mr. Robert Browning, Mr. W. B. Reddaway, and Mr. W. J. P. Webber.

The emphasis, this time, was not to be on the professional but the industrial aspects of the press, for the commission was required: "To examine the economic and special factors affecting the production and sale of newspapers, magazines and other periodicals in the United Kingdom, including (a) manufacturing, printing, distribution and other costs; (b) the efficiency of production; (c) advertising and other revenue, including any revenue derived from interests in television; to consider whether these factors tend to diminish diversity of ownership and control or the number and variety of such publications, having regard to the importance, in the public interest, of the accurate presentation of news and the free expression of opinion."

The commission noted that they were not appointed to consider the rights and wrongs of the *News-Chronicle* and Odhams affairs, but to inquire into the economic factors affecting the press in general. They were not to be concerned with the performance of the press, or ethical questions. When they came to write their report they remarked (like others before them) how much easier it was to diagnose the disease than to prescribe a cure. And, indeed, at the end of their labours in 1961–62, they came up with little or nothing more than had been pro-

117

posed by their predecessors of fifteen years before. But many words had to be written and spoken, and many witnesses examined before that conclusion was reached. In general, they said, there was no difficulty in obtaining information, "though one or two undertakings, notably Tribune Publications Ltd., failed even to render the courtesy of a reply to repeated requests for information [although *Tribune* contained articles relevant to our terms of reference]."

To the public the most startling revelation was that of the crazy economics of the press. Witness after witness spoke of high wages and low hours; of overstaffing; of the most absurd demarcations and restrictive practices. The truth, as it emerged, was that this industry, sheltered from overseas competition, had been so prosperous in the past that it had become bloated and overweighted. Through the years demand after demand by its labour force had been conceded, not only because the money was there but also because the nature of the business made it expedient for the employers to give in rather than risk abrupt stoppages in publication. More than one witness, when questioned about some wage rate or practice which seemed rooted in economic absurdity, said it originated perhaps fifty years before, no one knew quite how or why, and had become traditional.

One of the first witnesses, Sir Geoffrey (afterwards Lord) Crowther, a former editor of the *Economist,* said that the first aggravating factor in the concentration of the press was the rampant restrictionism of the printing industry. "There is an appalling state of affairs in the deliberate cutting down of the amount of work that can be done," he said, "in demarcation disputes between unions; in restriction of entry to the trade, and in general quarrelsomeness." When he first became editor of the *Economist,* before the war, it was produced with a total writing staff of five. "Now we have more than 30, but I do not think it is five times as good."

Mr. Cecil King, of the *Daily Mirror,* who appeared as chairman of the N.P.A. with Mr. Wade, and the Association's secretary, Mr. Bernard Alton, said it had taken four years of negotiations with the unions to get the introduction of a string-tying machine to replace manual tyers. This machine was of a type which had been in standard use in the U.S. for thirty years. Asked if labour had been cut down to an efficient number, he replied: "You are hardly serious, are you?" and said the labour force in the parcel-tying department would be run down by natural attrition – death, retirement, resignation. Even after eight years of this process they would be using much more labour than would be necessary.

On the subject of extra remuneration, Mr. King said there were offices in which stereotypers were paid fifteen pounds basic wage but took home more than forty pounds. Mr. Wade said these men had a thirty-hour week, but worked an average of fifty hours and earned overtime at time and a half. When the chairman wanted to know why, when a forty-two or forty-four-hour week was generally worked in industry, a thirty-hour week was worked in London newspaper offices, Mr. Alton said the agreement went back forty years at least, when the men's services may not have been wanted for more than thirty hours.

Asked whether it was true that the stronger newspapers were using restrictive practices, high costs, and low prices to drive weaker rivals to the wall, Mr. King said it had been true of Northcliffe years before but today he would regard his position, as the paper with the largest circulation, as stronger if there were lots of others than if there were few others. "If we go on as we are we will end up with three morning newspapers in London, and I would regard that as highly alarming, although I will have at least one of the three." Speaking of papers which had failed or were failing, Mr. King said: "If you flick over the pages of the *Daily Sketch* (the rival tabloid of his *Daily Mirror*) you will see the reason for its impending demise was in the nature of the paper." (Ironically, seven years later the *Daily Sketch* was still very much alive and kicking while Mr. King had been ousted from the *Daily Mirror*.)

The N.P.A., like other organisations, had put in a written memorandum which was not particularly helpful. It said that restrictive practices and high earnings were matters for individual newspaper offices. The vital factor was not costs of production and distribution but revenue. Another important factor, it said, was the necessity for smooth labour relations between managements and staffs.

Mr. King remarked that he had no admiration for this document, as he had already said to his council, but it was the maximum that could secure general agreement—"believe me, when you sit round that table the measure of agreement on any single subject is extremely small."

CHAIRMAN: Of course, that is one of the weaknesses of your organisation? MR. KING: When you say "What does the N.P.A. think?" I am afraid the N.P.A. thinks very little about very little.

Q.: Do not expect me to say that the rest of your memorandum added much to the fund of human knowledge? A.: I told the Council I was ashamed of it. That was all we could do.

Mr. King added that the whole relationship between N.P.A. members and unions was based on the fact that at the last moment one of the members would run away.

The chairman reminded Mr. King that he had described the N.P.A. as "the most spineless organisation which had ever been invented," to which Mr. King replied: "I was quoted as saying that it had all the initiative and courage of a stranded jellyfish." Mr. Alton, however, put in that the N.P.A. did a great deal of valuable administrative work, particularly in the fields of distribution, advertising, and photographic coverage.

It was stated that the council of the N.P.A. had set up a special committee "with a sense of urgency to consider and report generally on the efficiency of production in N.P.A. offices in relation to numbers and redundancy of staff."

CHAIRMAN: What did the Council do as a council, having described this sense of urgency, to bring to bear on its members the fact that they were inefficient and that something ought to be done to improve their arrangements? MR. WADE: It must be said that at that stage, and immediately, nothing was done. There have since been discussions and consultations but without any definite outcome.

Mr. King, when asked if there was standard staffing for a particular machine, as in most other industries, said "No."

MR. WEBBER: Are you trying, as the N.P.A., to get it? MR. KING: No.

Speaking as chairman of the *Daily Mirror* Mr. King said he did not object to high labour costs. He believed in high pay. "Mr. Thomson gets up and says, 'I am only interested in making money out of newspapers.' If the proprietors say this, why should not the man who sweeps the floor in the machine room say so? I do not criticise it at all." He agreed that the newspaper proprietors had not been very good on the labour side—"and in that we should be included. . . . We have been weak for all sorts of reasons I need not go into, as other people have been. I do not want to give the impression that other people have behaved badly and we are the blue-eyed boys, which is not true."

As a comparative newcomer to British newspapers, Mr. Thomson appeared for Thomson Newspapers Ltd., with Messrs. E. W. Cheadle,

C. D. Hamilton, A. M. Burnett-Stuart, and F. W. Wallace. He confirmed that he was in the industry to make money and that he had a very substantial ownership of his business so that he could keep control. "I like to sleep at night. I do not want to come down in the morning and find that someone has taken me over." He said that 80 percent of Thomson Scottish Associates was owned by British Thomson Publications Ltd., which was owned by Thomson International Ltd. of Toronto, Canada. That was owned 100 percent by his family. In addition there were fifteen subsidiary companies.

He was forthright on the subject of union pressures and demands, and mentioned a union strike which had stopped the Vancouver *Province* for six weeks. "When that strike came I suppose the *Province* was worth 10 million dollars. . . . When it started up again everybody had got used to buying the *Sun* which then had a two-to-one circulation advantage on the *Province*. The *Province* has never recovered, and never will, and I would say its value dropped from 10 million to maybe 3 million dollars. . . . The only way you can resist chapel and union pressure, or anything you like to call it, is by a united front of the proprietors. . . . What the unions or chapels do is against the public interest. . . . It is very difficult to resist even the most impossible demands—and I think I have got as much guts as anyone."

He had always found that newspaper workers had a regard for their paper. They will damn the proprietor up hill and down dale, but they will get the paper out and argue about it afterwards. "That is almost always the situation in Canada and America. But it is not the situation here and we cannot fight—no one can fight—that sort of thing. . . . You have seen those figures; basic wages of £15 and a man takes home £40. I ask you, what relationship is there in that? All it is, is that the basic wage is something to peg the extras on. . . . It is this leapfrog business that causes most of the trouble." He thought the management should, as a matter of principle, have the right to fix the staffing.

CHAIRMAN: And the reason you do not do it in your industry is that which you have explained to us, that you might be stopped? MR. THOMSON: We not only might be. We are told what the staff is to be. We are told how many men are to work.

SIR GRAHAM CUNNINGHAM: Is it true that often half-an-hour before you are due to go into production they come along with some demand and you have to make up your mind quickly, or else the newspaper will stop? MR. CHEADLE: Not always half-an-hour before; sometimes when we are actually running.

Mr. Thomson said there was not a newspaper in North America which was not printed in two sections, but when they introduced this on the *Sunday Times* they were immediately faced with a demand for more money. Mr. Burnett-Stuart added that far from involving extra work this operation made the job easier; and Mr. Cheadle said there was absolutely no justification for any extra all-round payment, but they had to pay. Mr. Thomson added that when there was talk about colour printing in newspapers, the packers – the people who bundled the papers – wanted an extra payment if they were in colour. "Is that not ridiculous. How could that possibly affect them in their work?" he asked.

"I used to worry about these things on the *Scotsman*," he went on, "but as I see them now they are negligible. But in London and Manchester it is a jungle. I never saw anything like it. . . . All I want is a peaceful, happy, quiet existence, and I am sure not getting it. I often think there must be easier ways of getting a living. I am doing all right – this business is good enough that everybody in it can be contented and fairly paid. What I object to are these fabulous amounts that are demanded and the constant pistol at your head. . . . If I could start a national daily on a realistic basis of wages and staffing I would be inclined to take a crack at it, but with these present practices and costs it would be quite impossible."

The Times Publishing Company was represented by the Hon. Gavin Astor (chairman of directors), Sir William Haley (editor of the *Times*), Messrs. F. Mathew, and G. R. (afterwards Sir George) Pope. Mr. Astor said he thought the production costs of the *Times* would compare remarkably well with those of other newspapers because they were the most efficient newspaper, not only editorially but from the production point of view as well. Mr. Mathew said the most important thing they did was to give their employees self-respect. In 1960 their profit had been £591,000 and in 1959, £501,000.

MR. BROWNING: Would it be fair to say that the general policy is to have a proper dissemination of news and opinion with priority over making a profit? MR. MATHEW: Yes.

SIR WILLIAM HALEY: It has always been the decision of the proprietors that, if we are faced with an emergency and the editor says
that he must have so much space to do the *Times* job, then, whatever
the financial consequences, he has what he wants.

(However, four or five years later, when the profit on the *Times*
group had turned into a loss of £65,000, it was sold to the Thomson
organisation.)

Some intriguing sidelights on practices in the printing trade, though
not necessarily in newspaper offices, came from the British Federation
of Master Printers (Messrs. J. F. Morris, B. I. Bartlett, G. D. Ash-
croft, N. C. B. Harrison, L. E. Kenyon, and C. W. D. Alister).

Mr. Bartlett said the Sun Printers of Watford had told him that on
a Seybold 4 V8 trimmer, a machine cutting three edges of periodicals
after they had been completed, their normal crew was eleven people—
"They tell us that a similar machine is operated in the U.S. with three
men running at the same speed. The thing is almost a joke at Watford.
The men can hardly get near the machine."

He also told of another, specialist machine, not in general use,
with a crew of twelve, agreed with the union. This machine began by
printing between 80 and 120 pages. The number of pages grew steadily
until it reached 160 pages. Then the unions insisted on a crew of nine-
teen. Later the firm reverted to less than the original number of pages,
but the union insisted on maintaining eighteen men—an increase of
50 percent over and above the original number, twice the number
commonly employed on the Continent on this machine.

Mr. Morris mentioned the firm of Hazell, Watson, and Viney at
Aylesbury where they printed the *Reader's Digest* on a letterpress
rotary machine which was run in the U.S. with two skilled minders and
three assistants—five in all. "When it was installed at Aylesbury the
Typographical Association claimed four skilled minders and three
assistants, or double the number of skilled men. . . . It is all very
well to say: 'Why don't you fight them?' But Hazell, Watson, and
Viney would say: 'It is more important from our point of view and
from the *Reader's Digest* point of view to get the publication out on time
rather than worry about an extra body on the machine. But, of course,
all these extra bodies mount up, and when you give way in one place
you give way in another and another."

Mr. Livermore of the Printers' Managers and Overseers Association (Messrs. H. J. Harcourt, A. G. Lathrope, H. L. Livermore, H. Hill, B. Morgan, and R. F. Hillier) said the exigencies of printing, say, three periodicals on one day of the week, but not on others, meant the employment of casual staff. These were engaged through the Father of the Chapel (corresponding to a shop steward in other industries) who would ring up the branch secretary of the union, who would round up the men and send them in. "If the staffing for a rotary machine was eight and only six turned up, the paper would come out in exactly the same time and nobody would have to work any harder. But you paid the same amount of money into the chapel so that these people, instead of getting one amount of pay, got their own plus that of the two ghosts." MR. HILLIER: It is called blood money.

This association mentioned the case of an apprentice who did very well as a compositor and won a grant to the London School of Printing. Later his firm wanted to employ him in their order office, but there was an interunion dispute over the proposed appointment. One union said they would stop work if he did not take up the position, while another union said they would stop work if he did. The man, in the end, found work with another company.

The commission asked the unions for their written observation on the suggestion that managements were reluctant to incur expenditure on new plant, processes, and techniques because they could not agree with the unions in advance on manning standards.

The London Typographical Society said that as far as they were concerned no difficulties had been placed in the way of managements in these matters. The Monotype Casters' and Typefounders' Society said they had no direct knowledge of it. The National Society of Electrotypers and Stereotypers had never had any difficulties about manning. The National Society of Operative Printers and Assistants (NATSOPA) said if there had been failure to agree on manning it was as much the fault of the managements as the unions. They had no solid evidence that their society was opposed to change. What worried the unions and their members were assurances about their share of the advantages coming from new processes and installations, and also their wariness with regard to unemployment. They claimed to have taken "a most progressive attitude" with regard to the string-tying machines.

The National Union of Bookbinding and Paper Workers said they had discussed the matter of the packing machine with representatives of newspaper firms, "the employers clearly hiding from us their real intention—as we saw it—of reducing the labour force by possibly 75 percent if they could, and we being told their intentions were much more moderate. . . . We were not prepared to see our workers thrown out of work in hundreds and felt it necessary to make that quite clear to the employers. We used the words at the time 'No guarantees, no machines.' We got our guarantees and they got their machines."

The Typographical Association said they welcomed new processes and techniques because they recognised that innovations would strengthen the economy of the industry. They had made two provisos—
1. That their members should not be harmed by such innovations;
2. They would enjoy some of the benefits these would bring.

The commission asked: "Is there anything in the industrial practices of employers that is harmful to the wellbeing of the industry?"

The Association of Correctors of the Press; the London Typographical Society; the National Union of Journalists; the Society of Lithographic Artists, Designers, Engravers, and Process Workers; and the Typographical Association did not answer the question, either at all, or at that stage. The Bookbinders and Paper Workers said: "We do not seek to use the Commission for the ventilation of grievances."

The Amalgamated Society of Lithographic Printers listed five main grievances: 1. Gentlemen's agreements between employers relating to the nonacceptance of men from other shops in the area; 2. Family relatives in management positions; 3. Almost total absence of craftsmen from boards of directors; 4. Preference shown to office as opposed to practical personnel in advancements; 5. Growth of management consultant firms to assist managements.

NATSOPA somewhat obscurely argued that "employers tended to encourage an outmoded traditional position and are basically responsible for many of the organisational difficulties which subsequently arise." They criticised the N.P.A. "closed shop" which resulted in the shutting down of all London national newspapers if one was involved in a stoppage.

The National Union of Press Telegraphists alleged that employers, while pleading for greater efficiency, production and cooperation from the unions, did everything possible to make such cooperation as difficult as possible. They had themselves adopted new techniques in the past fifty years but their basic rates were the lowest craft rates paid by the N.P.A.

The Scottish Typographical Association—"As a result of the continued policy of the newspaper proprietors to reduce the differential between the newspaper and the commercial sections of the industry, dissatisfaction exists."

None of this seemed very convincing, and what followed was even less so. In the face of factual evidence the unions were almost unanimous in denying that demarcation existed between different unions and different operations in the same craft. The Lithographic Printers replied: "Demarcation lines are becoming a trifle obscure"; Correctors of the Press: "For many years we have been free of demarcation difficulties"; London Typographical Society: "We do not accept the suggestion that there is excessive demarcation"; Electrotypers and Stereotypers: "There is no limit to the operations performed in the foundry by stereotypers"; NATSOPA: "Some problems arise from traditional trade union and jurisdictional procedures and structures"; Press Telegraphists: "It is the policy of this union that its members should be allowed to take part in all aspects of telecommunications"; Bookbinders and Paper Workers: "On demarcation we have very little difficulty between ourselves and other unions"; Lithographic Artists: "We have no evidence of serious demarcation difficulties"; Typographical Association: "We have no idea what 'excessive demarcation' means." Almost alone, the Monocasters and Typefounders said, bleakly: "Demarcation does exist."

Vague and evasive answers were given to questions about manning and comparisons with similar plant abroad. The Master Printers gave details of three machines: 1. A collating, stitching and inserting machine run by five women here, but by only two women on a similar one in Brussels with a higher output; 2. Bundling machines operated by four men here, but two women on the Continent; 3. Knifetrimmers with a crew of three men and two women here, against two women on the Continent. Unions either sidestepped or made no reply to questions on this matter, and on whether they required certain unskilled tasks to be performed by skilled men.

Oral replies to questions were more specific and illuminating. Mr. R. Willis, for the London Typographical Society (also represented by Messrs. H. J. Griffin, W. T. Booroff, and J. Clifford), said they should be careful in making comparisons between British and Continental manning standards. "We are printing in millions—two million, four million, six million—whereas on the Continent they are printing almost in hundreds of thousands. It makes a vast difference to your manning." The chairman asked why there should be any difference between the manning of, say, the New York *Times,* with its comparatively small circulation, and that of the *Daily Express,* because it has a larger circulation. Mr. Booroff said that the large circulation had also a terrific handling problem. There were also several edition changes throughout the night. In view of size of circulation and speed of production he thought British manning was not in any way extravagant.

Mr. Clifford said their members were free to work for two papers in the same house: i.e., the *Daily Mirror* and the *Sunday Pictorial,* but only for extra payment. The chairman pointed out that the man was employed to work thirty-five hours a week and he worked thirty-five hours a week. It surely did not matter whether the stuff he was composing turned up in any of the company's papers. But Mr. Clifford answered that when a *Daily Mirror* compositor worked for the *Sunday Pictorial* he had to have extra knowledge of the style of the house, for the style of the one was certainly not the style of the other. Mr. Willis said there was also the question of concentration, the degree of vigilance, to make sure that the wrong stuff did not get into the wrong place.

CHAIRMAN: What may seem strange to outside people, and what I am anxious to have you justify, is that an employer who employs a man at a given rate of wages for a given number of hours a week is not allowed to say: "I want you to print this," or "I want you to print that," the work itself being identical. MR. WILLIS: The point is that the man is employed by the paper . . . he is not employed by the firm.

Mr. C. W. Wallace, for the Correctors of the Press (also Mr. O. McCarthy) said that if during his thirty-five-hour week a reader corrected a proof for the daily as well as the Sunday paper he got extra payment. Asked why, he said: "There is a provision in the agreement . . . there is a payment of one guinea a week extra covering the reading of Sunday paper proofs by morning paper staff."

MR. WEBBER: Does it not imply that a reader has not sufficient work to occupy his thirty-five hours on his basic wage? MR. WALLACE: There is a point there. [He agreed that it was possible for a man to work hard on one paper for no extra pay and to work less hard for two papers and get more for doing it.]

The Lithographic Artists, Designers, Engravers, and Process Workers (Messrs. D. A. Anderson, H. G. Bellingham, and L. Knapp) were questioned on the same matter. Why, it was asked, did a man making blocks get more for a dual paper than a single paper. Mr. Knapp said it was a recognition of higher productivity.

CHAIRMAN: How is higher productivity involved in the fact that he is making blocks for two titles instead of one? MR. KNAPP: Because he is working constantly.

Q.: He would be if he was working efficiently? A.: You cannot treat newspaper production like the manufacture of motor-cars.

Mr. Bellingham, expanding on this theme, said that on one paper a man had to work "like the very devil," and this could not be maintained throughout the shift. There were certain "blow times" when a worker could rest. If he was working for two papers the tempo of production at the peak of one paper had to be maintained throughout the day. This justified the extra payment.

There were several sharp exchanges between the commission and the Printers, Bookbinders, and Paper Workers (Messrs. J. Mackenzie, T. J. Smith, S. A. Axtell, and W. Keys). Mr. Smith (the general secretary) said the talks with the proprietors on the packing, or tying, machines had gone on for three years. It was learned that the *Daily Mirror* would be able to dispense with 80 percent of their staff if they introduced these machines, and "our duty was to protect the very large membership we had on this hand-tying operation by some agreement and assurances in regard to redundancy, so that they would not be thrown out into the gutter." To ask for no redundancy, he thought, was not asking a lot from a wealthy industry.

CHAIRMAN: To say there would be no redundancy would mean they were engaged in considerable capital investment for new machinery and continuing to pay the same labour cost. Did you really expect they would agree? MR. SMITH: Why should they not agree?

Q.: All right—is that your answer? A.: If I may qualify that a trifle; if new machinery is introduced . . . why should working people be thrown into the gutter? [The witness added that it was agreed the liquidation of the number employed would take place by attrition.]

MR. WEBBER: Is it a fact that under this arrangement people could stay on and draw their pay as long as they liked to do so? A.: As long as they did their work.

Q.: But there was no work for them to do because the machines were doing their work. They were above establishment but were being kept on? A.: We have no understanding with the employers that people shall retire by a certain age.

MR. REDDAWAY: You did not guarantee the number to be kept on would be reduced by, say, 2½ percent every year or something of that sort? A.: Why should I? It was my duty to protect my members.

SIR GRAHAM CUNNINGHAM: If those machines were manned on an economic basis would redundancies arise? A.: I should say, yes.

Q.: Therefore the men are being occupied on these machines un-necessarily? A.: What do you suggest we do with them—just throw them out?

Mr. Smith said that some of the men were skilled, some semi-skilled.

CHAIRMAN: What is the skill in tying a knot? A.: That is not the only skilled requirement and you know it.

Q.: I am asking you. A.: The skill . . . is not only in tying a knot but knowing in many cases the route where, for example, the parcels have to go; and all those things combine to make good newspaper workers.

SIR GRAHAM CUNNINGHAM: Do not a lot of them just push a bundle a bit further along? A.: Some do, but they have to know where to push it.

Mr. Smith said the demand for more money for handling papers containing coloured advertisements was being discussed. He said it would make a lot of difference to his men if there was a picture in colour on an inside page. When the chairman asked: "What differ-ence?" he replied: "You are addressing to me a hypothetical question about something that has not yet arisen."

CHAIRMAN: Can you give any conceivable reason why, in the pub-lishing room, you should ask for extra pay? A.: I have not had occasion to give thought to it.

Q.: Give thought to it now. It is a simple question. A.: I would have to see the situation and see what it involved. [He had nothing more to add.]

Mr. Smith and Mr. Keys stated that the working day was one of seven hours, of which one hour was for mealtime. Sometimes men did not work the full seven hours and could then be released. If they came in, say, ten minutes before the hour of starting they would get an hour's overtime. After discussion of the somewhat complicated wage arrangements, Mr. Smith agreed that it would be possible for a man to be paid five hours' wages for two hours' work. He also agreed that it could sometimes happen that the full staff necessary in some publishing rooms could not be employed because there was not room enough for them. There might be three hundred men employed on a small-sized paper (tying up the parcels) but if the size suddenly went up, another one hundred might be necessary.

CHAIRMAN: We have figures suggesting that . . . the number of copies per man hour is in almost every case steadily getting worse. What is your opinion of that? MR. SMITH: A fair answer is that I am an old newspaperman and before the war I had to work very much harder than I would ever see my members work today.

NATSOPA, many of whose members are unskilled workers, gave evidence through Mr. R. W. Briginshaw (general secretary), H. S. Lloyd, J. A. Harley, S. Butler, C. S. King, and A. W. Mattingly.

Mr. Briginshaw said it was not true that an office chapel would raise some dispute and threaten to hold up production of a newspaper at a critical time. He suggested that some of these allegations came from people who did not know the business. He did admit, however, that it was possible for some unbalanced or irresponsible person to take advantage of a situation and stop a paper. "It seems to me it would stop a car factory as well." But because this could happen was no reason why the N.P.A. should bring the whole national press to a standstill because of the closure of one paper.

Harking back to the question of extra payments just because part of a paper was printed in colour:

CHAIRMAN: The man who is making up a parcel does not know whether there is a coloured picture inside it or not. It does not weigh any more; it does not smell any different; it is the same size; as far as making up a parcel is concerned it is no more important to him than the subject matter of the editorial. Why should he get extra pay because there is a colour picture in it? MR. BRIGINSHAW: One of the contentions of our people in some houses has been the production of colour itself enhances the position of the publication as a business, and we want to share in it.

Q.: Might it not be the last effort to save their lives? A.: In those circumstances, and it usually seems that the management say that to those making application on those lines, they do not get paid.

Q.: It does seem a curious arrangement? A.: It is curious, yes.

In the opinion of the Typographical Association (Messrs. J. M. Bondfield, F. Simmons, W. G. R. Hutchings, and J. F. Wade) if the introduction of new machinery were properly planned, there need be no redundancy. They would expect the employers to find the displaced men employment for the time being.

CHAIRMAN: If he introduced a machine which he says is going to save labour, you say "By all means introduce it but you cannot save any labour; you must employ the labour elsewhere?" MR. BONDFIELD: That is a hypothetical question.

Q.: Many questions have to be. This is a point the employers put to us. They say: "We are afraid to introduce new machinery," or "It is not worth our while because if we do we shall still have to employ the same number of men." A.: It is not for me to interpret what they are saying.

Q.: It seems to me you confirm what they are saying? A.: I take the view that they mean something quite different from what you suggest.

After more questions Mr. Bondfield said they did not regard industrial activity as purely an economic activity but a social one as well, with obligations. They had told their members they must co-operate in the introduction of new machinery but "we shall insist that there be no redundancy from the introduction of these new things, and in due season we shall want our share of the benefits from them."

When the chairman raised the point about the *Reader's Digest* machine which in England took seven workers and double the number of skilled men that were necessary in the U.S., Mr. Hutchings said: "In America they are taken as a machine crew and therefore you cannot apply American standards in England because our measurement is different."

So the probe continued, disclosing what must have looked at times like a deadlock between proprietors who wanted to introduce improved methods to raise productivity and cut labour costs, and certain unions who refused to admit new machinery if it meant the laying-off of even one man. It may appear to be remote from any question likely to come before the Press Council but, as will be seen, Lord Shawcross contended that it was exactly such matters that the council should have been examining. They were certainly relevant to the death of the *News-Chronicle.* One significant factor in that newspaper's disappearance was undoubtedly the number of people it employed. It had, for example, 79 process engravers, compared with 55 on the *Daily Express* and *Sunday Express* and 32 on the *Evening Standard.* Those three Beaverbrook papers, employing 87 among them, had a combined circulation of about 10 million, whereas the sale of the *News-Chronicle* was 1,250,000.

Evidence was given by Associated Newspapers (Lord Rothermere, chairman; Sir Geoffrey Harmsworth Bart.; Messrs. R. A. Redhead, managing director; R. F. Hammond; G. L. Howell; and J. Thomson, managing director, Northcliffe Newspapers).

Lord Rothermere said the management of the *News-Chronicle* had made a lot of mistakes, especially one; they had a lot of money at the end of the war but did not spend it wisely.

CHAIRMAN: What did they spend it on? LORD ROTHERMERE: Mainly on new machines, and when they were delivered there was not the sale to print the paper. They were overoptimistic of their future at the end of the war. Of the £2 million I think they spent they would have been happy to have had one of those in the bank when they got into trouble.

He disclosed that when the *Mail* took over the *News-Chronicle,* it printed the whole of that paper's circulation for some months and also, for a few weeks, printed all the *News-Chronicle*'s advertisements at that paper's rate. "We felt it was unfair to make any alteration at least for a few weeks. . . . It is, of course, a very expensive operation. If you are asking the sort of cost one is involved in immediately, just as an example we took on the whole of the staff of the *Chronicle* for one week. We authorised the *Chronicle* to pay and we footed the bill so as to avoid the staff coming in and finding themselves without a job on the night."

Soon after the *News-Chronicle* closed, the prices of the other national newspapers had been raised, and it had been suggested that they had held back in order to drive that paper out of business and pick up the circulation. This idea was refuted, among others, by Sir Geoffrey Crowther, who said: "Though it is a ruthless industry it is not as directly ruthless as that." He thought it would have taken five or six million pounds to get the paper out of the red and that "the supreme blame for its failure must rest with the management."

CHAIRMAN: If you had started publishing pictures of pin-up girls and so on, gone in for a little more pornography, your circulation, I suppose, might have gone up? SIR GEOFFREY: I suspect had we chosen to go in for pin-up girls they would not have been very good pin-up girls.

When the chairman asked a hypothetical question—if Beaverbrook Newspapers were to be taken over by an American group of publishers, what he would think of it, Sir Geoffrey replied: "I do not myself think that there would necessarily be anything wrong in that. . . . I can imagine a good American proprietor being much better than a bad English proprietor, and vice versa. . . . So far as the public is concerned there would be such a furore that he would be a very bold American who ventured his money in that way. . . . Why should we object to Americans when we manifestly do not mind Canadians owning newspapers?"

Mr. Reddaway asked him why newspaper companies wanted to take over other newspaper companies. He said: "Very largely, to be blunt, it is pure megalomania and empire building . . . but there are some real reasons also. For example, there are obvious economies for a morning and evening paper being in the same ownership. . . . Papers are born; they die. It is impossible to conceive circumstances in this country where a new national daily could be started with any chance of success without the necessary capital running into seven figures."

Sir Christopher Chancellor had something to say about this, too. He told how Hultons was "being hawked around," and Odhams bought it. How the *News of the World* was after Newnes, who offered themselves to Odhams and were taken, and how, by buying both these concerns, Odhams set the stage for the *Mirror* at one stroke to stabilise a monopoly in the mass circulation women's magazine field—"and that was the avowed purpose of the take-over of Odhams."

Sir Christopher thought a merger might well prolong the life of a publication which was unprofitable, but might turn the corner in the long run. He said the *Daily Herald,* having made a profit in only six of its thirty-four years of life, seemed to be dying, but the prospect of a two-million-pound profit from Newnes made the Odhams directors resolve to spend a lot of money on the paper in an attempt to save it.

The attempt failed, and at this point we may break off from the commission to consider the *Sun,* hailed as the first new national British morning newspaper to appear for thirty-four years. It was not quite new, for it replaced the *Daily Herald* by the same publishers on the same presses overnight. When the *Mirror* interests took over Odhams, Mr. Cecil King gave a guarantee to the trade unions that the *Herald* would be carried on for seven years, win, lose, or draw, whereupon in 1961 the unions sold their interest in the paper for seventy-five thousand pounds. But the *Herald* could not be made to pay and in 1964 the *Mirror* interests (now the International Publishing Company, or I.P.C.) killed it. The seven-year pledge was to be maintained by the *Sun,* which succeeded it.

There never was such a ballyhoo as preceded the birth of the *Sun.* It was to be "a newspaper born of the age we live in." It was "the greatest and most exciting newspaper revolution of our time. . . . What a terrific story it will be when the *Sun* sets out to fulfill in the next 34 years the tremendous role of the *Daily Herald* in the past 34 years." Its stable companion, the *Mirror,* published several scarcely disinterested articles on the coming phenomenon. In one it said that, "already 17 days before publication date, the *Sun* is the focal point of controversy and speculation. Even of anger. And envy. And fear. The uneasy newspapers in the Petrified Forest are the *Daily Mail* [Britain's third most popular newspaper] and the *Daily Express* [Britain's second most popular newspaper]."

Hardly heard was the dissenting voice of Lord Thomson, who said of Mr. King's decision to start the *Sun:* "I admire his courage more than I admire his discretion." And Mr. Hugh Cudlipp, the editorial director of I.P.C., in one quiet pause amid his fanfares, reflected that it was "a very dangerous experiment. If we fail this will be the last new daily paper any of us will see in our lifetime."

Fleet-street held its breath and wondered what sort of heavenly body was about to strike it and perhaps shrivel it up on September 15, 1964, the day the *Sun* was due to be launched into orbit. But rival editors need not have worried. When it appeared their sigh of relief mounted to the empyrean, for the *Sun* was so ordinary, so pedestrian a compilation that everyone began to wonder what the fuss had been about. The *Guardian* said the *Daily Herald* staff could have produced it with one hand tied behind their backs, and the *Observer* observed that it was short of its most crucial commodity—news. The *Sun* did improve, and became even brilliant. But, too late to recover, for it had lost that vital first impetus.

To many it seemed that the *Sun* was making the same mistake as the *News-Chronicle* in trying to be serious and popular at the same time. Its first day's sales were 3.5 million; its second, 2.5 million; its third, 2 million; its fourth, 1,750,000. By the following month the sales were down to something over 1.4 million. This was little more than the *Herald* had sold, and soon they were to dip below even that—tragically below as the years passed. In 1965 Mr. King said "a tough struggle lies ahead." In April 1967, however, he said the *Sun* was off the danger list and would be with us in the 1970s. There was no question of its ceasing publication at the end of its guaranteed seven years, which ended in January 1968. Nor did it cease at that date, even though in July 1967 Mr. King, reversing his earlier optimism, said that the *Sun* was by no means off the danger list. "The paper is a source of great anxiety to us," he said—as well he might. In 1969 Mr. Hugh Cudlipp, announcing that the paper had lost £12 million in eight years, said it would be closed down at the end of the year.

Long before that, the scholars of Fleet-street were recalling the ancient Greeks who believed that *hubris* was followed, inevitably, by *nemesis*.

But in that month of October 1969 the *Sun* was acquired by another newcomer to Fleet-street—this time the young Australian newspaper proprietor, Mr. Rupert Murdoch, who, some months before, had acquired a controlling interest in the *News of the World*. By the middle of 1970 he was claiming a circulation of 1.5 million for the *Sun*.

To return to the commission, it was obvious that much of the questioning by its members was directed towards the search for some remedy for newspaper concentration, some useful conclusion which they could recommend to the government. But such a thing was hard to find. One possibility was the formation of an antitrust tribunal to examine future press mergers or take-overs, and some witnesses were asked for their opinion.

Lord Thomson thought the press should not be subjected to any more or less control than other businesses. The danger, put to him, that all the evening papers might one day be owned by one man was "stretching things pretty far." But supposing it did happen, he asked, "what predictable harm would be done if the papers are operated the way I operate them?" In appointing an editor he had never had any consideration for his political views. He believed in a complete delegation of editorial responsibility. When asked if he thought there would be a great switch in advertisements from newspapers to television, he said there was a limit to TV advertising. "Newspapers are, I would say, as prosperous in the U.S. as they have ever been, and, for goodness sake, if you take television coverage in the U.S., it is nearly 100 percent." Referring to his potential power as owner of newspapers and television stations, Lord Thomson said: "I think I have got a lot of potential power so long as I don't use it, and I think if I tried to use it I would find I did not have it."

About a possible antitrust tribunal, Lord Rothermere said it sounded very good in theory but "you never know when you put something in theory what on earth is going to happen when it gets put into practice."

Mr. Cecil King saw no real harm in the idea of a tribunal, but he was less enthusiastic, to say the least, about the Press Council. Asked if the N.P.A. had considered whether the council could run effectively on forty-five hundred pounds, he said that any attempt to increase its contribution would meet with opposition from five members. (As chairman of the *Daily Mirror* organisation he commanded five votes out of the twenty-one.)

MR. WEBBER: Would I be right in assuming that you do not want it to be an effective organisation? MR. KING: No, I think it is completely futile and an utter waste of time, and I do not think it is worth paying a penny for the job it does. When it was set up he said it should have an independent chairman and without that he was not prepared to support it.]

Later it was Mr. King who was instrumental in securing the services of the council's first lay chairman. The piquancy of the situation lay in the fact that had it not been for his take-over of Odhams there would have been no second Royal Commission and, without doubt, no change in the structure of the Press Council.

One curious development emerging from the inquiry was that the two journalists' organisations, the N.U.J., and the institute, had each modified its opinion about monopolistic tendencies, in an opposite direction from its standpoint at the first Royal Commission. The institute (Major Alan Simpson, president; Messrs. S. R. Pawley; Brian Roberts; W. Rees-Mogg; H. A. Taylor; and Steward Nicholson, general secretary), which had tended to minimise the dangers in 1947–49, now appeared very much concerned. "We are convinced that the control of a number of newspapers by one individual, be he a personal proprietor or a chairman, does lead to a uniformity of opinion among the papers which would not exist if they were independently owned," said Mr. Taylor. "Editors are shrewd people. . . . Their minds are in tune with those of the proprietor or chairman; and without the chairman's intervention there is a certain harmony of opinion." But Mr. Rees-Mogg (later to become editor of the *Times*), who was the only Thomson journalist in the group, said he certainly had freedom of expression. He would not take any notice of Mr. Thomson's view because he did not think he would wish it, nor would there be any pressure to do so.

When it came to the turn of the N.U.J. (Messrs. T. Bartholomew; P. H. Benson; H. J. Bradley, general secretary; E. A. Lofts; P. G. Reid; G. Viner; and M. K. Williamson), Mr. Bradley did not think there had been any restriction on the free expression of opinion because there were fewer newspaper proprietors, and Mr. Williamson echoed Mr. Rees-Mogg's tribute to Mr. Thomson in that respect. Mr. Bradley added: "The last Royal Commission did a large amount of unbounded good. It was a noticeable thing that, while the Commission was sitting and after, this tendency to send stuff out from the centre and more or less advising the editor—if not exactly directing him—on policy, tended to come to a stop."

In their written memoranda the two organisations mauled one another as they had done fifteen years before. The institute, expressing "grave concern" at the threat to the "number and variety of voices" in the press, went on to say that the policy of the closed shop applied to editorial staffs imposed its own stifling restriction on the variety of voices. Members of the institute had been deprived of their employment or compelled to resign through the closed shop. Which was true.

In reply the N.U.J. wrote: "The Institute, having failed over many years to gain the support of the vast majority of journalists, habitually indulges in denigration of the Union." If a majority of editorial members in an office belong to the union, an institute member would be "urged" to join the union. "What is the choice of an Institute member in such circumstances? It is between an aging and ailing hybrid organisation of some 2,000 members and an expanding body, founded on trade union principles and numbering nearly 16,000 members.

"It is interesting to note that before the last war it was claimed in the U.S. that the existence of American Newspaper Guild 'closed shops' for journalists was a threat to the freedom of the Press. The Supreme Court declined to accept that view, which is nevertheless still propagated by the Institute and its employer members in Britain." And so the melancholy quarrel grumbled on.

The institute's memorandum was extremely critical of the Press Council. It said the condition of "unease" in the press which led to the Royal Commission might not have developed if the council had done its duty by its own constitution. It pointed out that nothing resembling the study demanded in Object 2 (vii) had taken place and the council's annual reports had given no review such as would provide a body of ascertained fact. "Of the Council's failure to perform its full duty there could hardly be more impressive evidence than its decision to make no comment upon the stoppage of newspaper production by industrial disputes." A good reply to this argument had already been given by Mr. Bradley of the N.U.J. when he said that such an event did not call for the council to exercise its duty to "keep under review developments in the Press" because the right to strike, or to lock out, was not a "development" but a very old right. Industrial conciliation was not the business of the Press Council.

An even better answer, which gave impressive evidence of the council's wisdom in steering clear of industrial relationships, has since been given by the experience of the Austrian Press Council. This was formed in 1961 by voluntary agreement between the Publishers' Association and the Union of Journalists. In 1962 it was split down the middle in the aftermath of an industrial dispute. There had been a strike of journalists, with tough and protracted negotiations over a wage claim. When these were over the publishers gave one account of the negotiations which was countered by a different version put out by the journalists. As a result the publishers withdrew from the Press Council. It was later reformed but, in the words of one commentator, "the dispute drove a deep wedge into the partnership which was the basis of the Council." Had this significant incident occurred before the

Shawcross Commission sat, its members might have had less to say about the British council's alleged weakness in failing to jump headlong into industrial controversy. The truth is that questions of newspaper ethics and matters concerning employer-employee relations are not compatible with one another, and it is asking too much of any one body to deal with both in the same harmonious spirit.

In any case, those who demanded so much of the council, including (as the institute did) an investigation into teletype setting and other advanced techniques, took too little account of the council's lack of financial resources—a condition which one might have expected the institute to view with sympathy in view of its own far from fat purse. This organisation was, however, more active than any of the others in proposing duties for the Press Council. For example, it wrote to the prime minister suggesting that the council should undertake an inquiry into the *News-Chronicle* and Odhams take-overs, without first taking the trouble to inform the council of what it was doing.

10 The Council Grilled

Now the Press Council (Messrs. George Murray, chairman; Henry Bate, Gordon [afterwards Sir Gordon] Newton; Stuart Campbell; and Colonel Clissitt, secretary) took the stand, and did not step down from it without some rough handling.

In its written memorandum the council had stressed that its main function was to deal with ethical questions and that on economic and industrial matters it tended to divide into its constituent parts. The council's chairman opened by restating this oft-stated fact. As an example he quoted the closed-shop controversy between the N.U.J. and the institute in which the Press Council refused to intervene. Replying to Lord Shawcross he said the only way it fulfilled the requirement to keep monopolistic tendencies under review was the record, in the annual report, of the changes in the press. Its income was £4,100 a year contributed by all the organisations on a share basis. It was quite inadequate.

CHAIRMAN: The actual resources of the members are such that they could contribute £40,000 without feeling it at all? – MR. BATE: Not all of them; I think the proprietors could, but the organisations of working journalists and editors could not contemplate very heavy contributions.

Q.: Would it be right to say that the council has never really considered or voted upon any of these economic factors that we have been discussing today? MR. MURRAY: No. It has considered matters like the printing strike and the newspaper strike, but on majority vote it has decided to make no statement on these matters or to include them in the annual report. . . . One attempt was made to find out what the costs and the economic background were in relation to the provincial newspapers, particularly the provincial daily newspapers.

No information was forthcoming from the various newspapers or the Newspaper Society.

Q.: They refused to cooperate? A.: They declined; the Press Council has no power to demand.

Q.: Of course, some people would say that is one of its great weaknesses. But when did that happen? A.: I would think four or five years ago. The institute had suggested such a questionnaire and it was put out as an exploratory proposal. Lacking the support of the Newspaper Society there was nothing to be gained from the idea, which was dropped.

CHAIRMAN: What were the circumstances which led to it? MR. NEWTON: One or two closures were going on in provincial newspapers.

CHAIRMAN: Did you look at Article 2 (vii) of your constitution and see that this required you to study developments in the press which might tend towards greater concentration or monopoly? MR. MURRAY: I do not think it was quite so firm as that. It really was not the council's initiative but rather a proposal from one of the constituent bodies.

Q.: There is very strong criticism of the Press Council. One has heard it from many sides. Is it true that it has done nothing at all in this particular matter? MR. MURRAY: Yes, quite true; Mr. Campbell: In mitigation I would like to point out that it is a very small body from a secretarial point of view; MR. BATE: Everyone serving on it is otherwise engaged; MR. MURRAY: We found that the basis on which we could get most agreement was the ethical side of newspapers. We have concentrated on that because there, at least, there is common ground for agreement and on all other issues it is quite impossible to get any common view.

CHAIRMAN: I am wondering whether you may not, none the less, be under serious criticism for not having considered these problems, because you are a body on which both the workers and the employers are represented. Surely the view in modern industry is not that these are opposite sides but that both sides ought to be equally concerned with the economic success of their newspapers? MR. MURRAY: The fact is that the unions exist to put forward one particular point of view and the employers' organisations exist to put forward another and often opposite point of view. I think it is quite impossible to expect to get unanimity on economic questions in a body of this kind. There have, I agree, been serious criticisms of the Press Council because we have not tackled these things. There were serious criticisms that we were not doing what you are doing now. We did not inquire into the death of the *News-Chronicle* but I think, in fairness, our limitations should really be emphasised. We cannot enter into these questions, we cannot handle these very difficult and complicated matters, because we have not got the resources. Whether or not we should have the resources is not within our present competence. It depends on the origin of the Press Council, how it was formed, the conditions thrown up, and all those other things. I think it is a little unfair to stress one side of this matter and not the other.

CHAIRMAN: Please do not think I am criticising you for a moment. I think the criticism is a criticism directed at your component members. It may be one of the difficulties is that when the Press Council was established in the early fifties they did not follow the advice in the recommendation of the Royal Commission in regard to its composition?
A.: It may well be.

At another stage of the inquiry, the commission questioned the Newspaper Society representatives (Messrs. J. T. L. Baxter, H. R. Davies, W. A. Hawkins, T. G. Moore, and W. G. Ridd) on the council's abortive attempt to inquire into the finances of provincial newspapers. Lord Shawcross said they had been told that the Council had tried to initiate the exercise but the Newspaper Society had refused to cooperate, "whereupon the Press Council had dropped the thing like a hot brick." Mr. Davies replied that this was perfectly true. It was the initiative of the Institute of Journalists who wanted the society, in effect, to hold an inquest on bodies which were at that time very dead indeed. The society's view was that the causes of the deaths of the newspapers concerned were so clear that no inquest was necessary.

Returning to the examination of the Press Council:

CHAIRMAN: Apart from the fact that you have not the same powers as we have, you could have constantly kept the economic developments under review the while, bearing in mind that newsprint and general costs had gone up, efficiency had gone down in particular parts of the industry, and restrictive practices were developing? MR. MURRAY: We could have done it if we had had the secretariat and the money; MR. BATE: If you are going to pronounce on the question of restrictive practices, and go into all the details, you have to be in a position to get all the available information and you must be prepared to take sides. A policy of taking sides would be a decisive step towards breaking up the Press Council.

Q.: You prefer to remain an ineffective council? A.: We do not agree we are ineffective.

When Mr. Reddaway suggested that the sensible thing would have been either to amend the constitution or not to pretend to have in its objects things the council did not intend to do, Mr. Campbell replied that had the council at any stage seen a solution to this dilemma it would have been the first to put it forward. When the small financial contributions to the council were criticised, Mr. Murray said there was no comparison between the resources of the editorial bodies and those of the N.P.A. "You may say, 'why not let the N.P.A. pay the whole lot.' Then we would have the criticism that the Press Council is a creature of the N.P.A. It is so easy to talk about adjustments but there are all these other considerations."

CHAIRMAN: If you had carried out these requirements [of Article 2 (vii) of the constitution] there would have been a body of ascertained fact which would have alerted Parliament and the government and public to what was going on and avoided the trouble that occurred at the time the *News-Chronicle* went out of existence? MR. NEWTON: I should have thought everyone knew what was happening to the *News-Chronicle* for years ahead.

Q.: Everyone in the industry, but what of the public? A.: No, but to suggest that the failure of the Press Council to do something about this created a shock, I think that is really going too far.

Q.: This is "far" is it not? If this constant review had taken place as appears to have been envisaged by Article 2 (vii) and (viii) the case for setting up this commission would not have existed. This commission may find no solution but we have been appointed to ascertain the facts. You could have published all the facts? MR. MURRAY: I am sure if we had entered into this sort of inquiry we should have had the criticism of a closed shop levelled at us.

Later Mr. Campbell pointed out that had the council at any point suggested that the *News-Chronicle* was in difficulties that would rapidly have hastened its death, and Mr. Bate added: "It is doubtful if a dry and dreary report on the economics of newspaper production would get much publicity. I doubt if the public would have been very much aware." Or, he might have said, whether they would have very much cared.

CHAIRMAN: I do not want you to think we are really concerning ourselves only with the fact that you have not in the past done the job that has now been imposed upon us, but I would like to have your view on suggestions made for remedies. There is the possibility that you might have some tribunal which would have the power to consent, or otherwise, to take-overs or mergers; an antitrust system limited to the newspaper industry? MR. MURRAY: In the first place, that would not seem to cover the deaths of newspapers; only take-over bids. Some of us hold the opinion that such a body would be very useful. Others do not agree.

Q.: Would any of you care to express an individual view on it? MR. MURRAY: I would say that the concentration of power and finance is part of the trend of the times; and the newspaper industry cannot expect to escape it any more than any other industry. I agree that the newspaper is in a special position but I cannot see the solution to it. It seems to me it is part of the dilemma of our free society. Our free society, for example, allows the expressions of opinion which tend to destroy it. If you stop those expressions of opinion you destroy the freedoms in which you believe. The concentration of opinion into a few newspapers or one newspaper is damaging to the freedom of the press only because it restricts variety of opinion. But it does not kill the fundamental freedom of the press and that freedom consists not only in the ability to start a newspaper but to end one, and if you interfere with that in any way, if you attach any strings to the survival or death of a newspaper, you interfere with the freedom of the press. That is an individual view, not shared by other members of the council.

MR. NEWTON: I think it possible, on paper, to establish a body like the old Capital Issues Committee. . . . Whether it would be right or proper is another matter, because a merger might even help the press by merging weak with strong. All mergers are not bad. They do not destroy. Some can create. . . . I think one is getting oneself into the most appalling complications. Once again it is this question of what is fact and what is right or wrong; you are trying to look into the future . . . and it is going to be difficult. It is quite conceivable it would do more harm than good.

MR. BATE: I think the principle of this should be looked at carefully by the commission. There is no doubt that the public interest is important. It is worth examination to see if it is practicable to put a restraint on mergers which simply amount to a financial improvement for a controlling group. Mr. Newton draws attention to the difficulties in distinguishing between the different kind of mergers, but I think there would be public support for something which prevented this kind of concentration of ownership. There was public opposition to the *Daily Mirror*-Odhams merger. Therefore I think it should be looked at, but I have no precise proposal to put before you.

The inquisition came to an end, and the council representatives emerged feeling somewhat battered by their ordeal. The commission seemed to have given little heed to constant reminders that the Press Council was working on a shoestring, in purse and power. To say, as Lord Shawcross did, that "you have not done the job which has now been imposed on us" was to infer that the council, like the commission, had all the authority of the government and the State behind it, which was, of course, ludicrous.

The council delegation had been told that the body they represented was "ineffective," and they had been lectured on its "poor performance." Lord Shawcross had told them "we are not here to tell you what to do or to try the Press Council at all," which was fair enough, but when he added, "but to show you what you could do," he was almost certainly going beyond the commission's brief. To suggest, as he also did, that if the council had carried out the letter of its constitution the commission need never have been set up was not sound reasoning. The government themselves had boggled at any inquiry into the failure of the *News-Chronicle,* and all the "ascertained fact" in the world (which was readily available) did not stop the *Daily Mirror*-Odhams merger which brought the commission into being.

After the strictures passed on the Press Council one might have expected some new, far-reaching and imaginative proposal to emerge from the Shawcross Commission. But, as everyone who knew anything about the matter had expected, this second mountain brought forth the same mouse as the first one had done, its main recommendation being the continuance of the Press Council, with an insistence, under threatened penalty, that the lay element should at last be included. It can be noted here, however, that in later years the new council had no more to say in such great transactions as the purchase of the *Times* or an attempted take-over of the *News of the World* than the old council had had in the matter of the *News-Chronicle* or Odhams.

The Commission's Report, published in September 1962, noted that since 1949 no fewer than 17 daily and Sunday newspapers had ceased publication in London and the provinces and the ownership of those remaining had become concentrated in fewer hands. London evening newspapers had declined from 3 to 2, provincial morning papers from 28 in 1937 to 18, and provincial evenings from 79 to 74. "The loss of a publication which seeks to provide little more than light entertainment is . . . hardly a grave matter," it said. "What is dangerous is that serious newspapers which are part of the political and social fabric of the community may not be able to survive even when they are supported by substantial numbers of readers."

"It is important to dissociate the facts of concentration from any sinister implications which the word may convey. The growth of circulations or of the number of newspapers controlled by a single undertaking is not necessarily to be attributed to aggressive empire building. It may certainly result from expansionist policies; but it may simply indicate the growing popularity of an undertaking's journals or its enterprise in starting new publications."

The commission did not think the influence of the press was as great as some people suggested, in modern conditions. They would not think it possible for a newspaper or group of newspapers, to swing public opinion overnight. The obvious danger of concentration of ownership lay in the possible stifling of variety of opinion, though this seemed unlikely to be threatened in the quality press. Even in the popular press common ownership did not necessarily entail suppression of independent editorial policies. But "whatever may be the economic implications of amalgamations, it is beyond doubt that there is a special public interest involved in the Press that is not present in industry at large. . . . The potential political and social influences of multiple ownership of newspapers and journals of opinion, although not to be exaggerated, remain matters of serious concern."

Turning its attention to the efficiency, or otherwise, of newspaper production, the report said manpower was being squandered in national newspapers. Some offices could reduce their wages bill by one third. Both management and labour had lacked the incentive to improve efficiency and some were beginning to realise that inefficiency might help to kill at least some of the geese which laid the reputedly golden eggs. When it said that the industry "does not appear to be one in which advances in technique have been strikingly exploited in the past half-century" it was putting the case mildly. As many as seven hundred persons would be tying up parcels of newspapers in one office, though more than one-third of them could be saved by machinery in common use abroad. The unions refused to work these machines and only after four years was their use permitted provided no one was dismissed. As a result, men sat doing little or nothing and going home on full pay after two hours or so. These included not only staff men but regular casuals and, in an emergency, casual casuals because the regulars had gone home.

In another office an increase in the number of copies on the rotary presses was met by a union demand for 75 additional assistants, an increase of 25 percent. Demarcation had prevented the wider use of teletypesetting with transmission because there was a difference between the printing unions and the Press Telegraphists Union as to whether it was typesetting or telegraphy. One newspaper estimated that to cope with a sudden increase in pages from 20 to 24 meant the employment of 70 additional men in an already overstaffed department. One example of the many kinds of house "extras" was that if more pages than normal had to be printed more men had to be called in. If the necessary number of casuals was not available the work was quite easily done by the existing labour force without loss of time, but the wages which would have been paid to the casuals had to be shared out among the crews actually at work, though they had not been at all extended. This was known as "ghost money."

The unions disputed these criticisms. In a statement published in the press after the publication of the Shawcross Report, the Printing and Kindred Trades' Federation (P.K.T.F.) said that its charges of overstaffing were a "gross exaggeration" and could only have been made after an inadequate study of the problems of national newspaper production. The P.K.T.F. also attacked the absence from the report of any suggestions to deal with the serious situation facing the newspaper and periodical industries. This represented, said the statement, "a failure on the part of the Commission to fulfill one of the main purposes for which it was set up."

While dealing with newspaper economics, the report made specific reference to the *News-Chronicle* and *Star*. "The problem is not so much why the *News-Chronicle* could not survive with a circulation of 1,250,000 but how it could get anywhere near to surviving in competition against newspapers with a circulation of over 4,000,000." The proprietors had said that while the *News-Chronicle*'s main trouble was circulation, the *Star*'s difficulty was to get the advertising revenue justified by its circulation. This was a good deal higher than that of its next rival, the *Evening Standard,* but it appealed to readers in the lower income brackets and did not attract the advertising which would have saved it. The formula of the *News-Chronicle* was not adapted to a changing public taste. When newsprint restrictions were eased in 1947 and the struggle for circulation was resumed, it fell behind and the steps taken to bring it into fashion were by that time too late. "We cannot escape the conclusion that the failure of the *News-Chronicle* was not entirely the result of an inevitable law of newspaper economics; different and more consistent managerial and editorial policy might have saved this newspaper."

On general economics the commission thought multiple ownership in the press contributed, on balance, to the maintenance of the number and variety of papers and periodicals. Strong units were essential to a healthy press and strength frequently rested on multiple ownership. "How far this multiple ownership can be carried without harming the public interest is another matter. . . . Although, in our opinion, the public interest is not being seriously injured by the present economic situation of the Press, the future effect of the various economic pressures must cause grave anxiety." However, the way to success lay through the quality of management and editorial direction. Legislation could not produce these qualities, but the question was whether it might mitigate the considerable dangers to which those papers which lacked inspired leadership were exposed.

Many proposals for strengthening weaker newspapers as against the stronger had been examined by the commission. Some were quite unreasonable, while others had a semblance of logic. Many originated from people or organisations who were, in general, opposed to the competitive forces of a capitalist system. Here they are, with the reasons for their rejection.

1. Concessions in the form of cheaper postage, special capital allowances against income tax or relief from death duties: "We can find no justification for special concessions of this kind."

2. Cooperative printing for the smaller papers to reduce overheads: "Impracticable."

3. A National Press Corporation financed partly by an Exchequer grant and partly by a tax on advertising, to provide printing plant at cheap rates: "Not possible to devise an acceptable scheme."

4. Making newspapers sell at a price nearer the cost of production, thus reducing or eliminating dependence on advertising: "No legislation could compel newspapers to charge higher prices."

5. A statutory restriction on the amount of space devoted to advertising. This, it was thought, would compel newspapers who had to reduce this space to charge higher advertising rates so that some of the advertisers' money would be diverted to the weaker papers: "We are unanimous in rejecting this scheme." For several reasons, the most cogent being that advertisers having to pay more to the stronger paper would have even less to spend on the weaker ones.

6. A levy on advertising revenue which would rise with the newspaper's circulation. This would induce proprietors to reduce their circulations. The money would be used to strengthen weak papers and establish new ones: "We reject outright the idea of a statutory scheme which would force the proprietors of the two newspapers primarily affected (the *Mirror* and the *Express*) to have for decades a major objective of progressively reducing their circulations." Such a levy would raise difficult issues of principle. It would also pose difficult political problems.

7. An excise duty on the advertisement revenue of any paper or periodical where this exceeded £2 million a year: "The newspaper publishers, including those publishing newspapers which might have been expected to benefit from the scheme, were virtually unanimous in opposing it, and some did so in strong terms."

Lord Shawcross and Sir Graham Cunningham regarded some of these proposals as divorced from the realities of a free society. "They consider it quite improper in this context to employ statutory devices which, while nominally applicable to all newspapers, are, in fact, deliberately discriminatory against those which are achieving commercial success, in the hope of assisting those which are not." The other three members thought that circumstances might arise in which discriminatory action would be desirable in the public interest. But the commission as a whole concluded that "there is no acceptable legislative or fiscal way of regulating the competitive and economic forces so as to ensure a sufficient diversity of newspapers. The only hope of the weaker newspapers is to secure—as some have done in the past—managers and editors of such enterprise and originality as will enable these publications to overcome the economic forces affecting them."

And, as their last word on multiple ownership: "The potential danger to the public interest of further concentration of ownership and control in the newspaper Press by amalgamations is beyond doubt." It was obvious that the point which the first Royal Commission said could not be contemplated without anxiety had now been reached.

But the Press Council and what it could or could not do was still the nub of the matter. The report said that had the council done what the 1949 Royal Commission recommended, much of the second inquiry might have been unnecessary and public awareness of possible developments might have modified the course which, in the end, these developments took. "Full advantage has certainly not been taken of the existence of a body representing the Press as a whole to enlarge public knowledge of the problems which the Press have to face." It was remarked that representatives of the council had said in evidence that their ability to deal with economic matters was limited by their ability to ask for information, and that their work was limited by lack of money. "We were not told that the Council had ever pressed for a substantial increase in its funds."

(If the commission was not told it was no doubt because that question was not asked. As a result of council pressure on several occasions its income had been doubled during its first ten years. Whether this was or was not a "substantial" increase is a matter of opinion.)

The report did tend to place the blame for what it regarded as shortcomings on to the press as a whole rather than on the council alone. Thus, "the more valid these excuses for the Council's inactivity in the economic field may be, the greater is the criticism against the constituent bodies which have denied it the necessary powers and finance. The council as now constituted has not been, and is not, able to make any significant contribution to the broad problems which we are called upon to consider. If the Press is not willing to invest the Council with the necessary authority and to contribute the necessary finance, the case for a statutory body with definite powers and the right to levy the industry is a clear one."

This, then, was the chief recommendation—that the Press Council should be so reconstituted, with a lay chairman and a substantial lay membership, as to comply with the recommendation of the 1949 commission, and that it should be endowed with the necessary powers and funds. Then came the "Dear Sirs, unless" threat. "The Government should specify a time limit after which legislation would be introduced for the establishment of such a body if, in the meantime, it has not been set up voluntarily." It should have sufficient money not merely to carry out its existing functions, but also to:

1. Note and report on changes in ownership;
2. Publish statistics relating to concentration in the press;
3. See that newspapers bear the name of the company or individual in ultimate control.

(The first two were adopted by the council; the third was not.)

Another important recommendation was for the establishment of a Press Amalgamations Court to examine the purchase of newspaper titles or the controlling interests in newspaper companies owning papers with aggregate weekly sales of dailies or Sundays of more than three million copies. Transactions would be held to be contrary to the public interest unless it could be shown that freedom and variety of opinion were not likely to be reduced.

The obvious objection to such a court would be that it interfered with the freedom of the press. In refutation of such an argument the report quoted a judgment of Mr. Justice Douglas in the U.S. case of *Associated Press* v. *the United States:*

"The argument is made that to apply the Sherman Act to this association of publishers constitutes an abridgement of the freedom of the Press guaranteed by the First Amendment. . . . It would be strange, indeed, however, if the grave concern for the freedom of the Press which prompted the adoption of the First Amendment should be read as a command that the government was without power to protect that freedom. The First Amendment, far from providing an argument against the Sherman Act, here provides powerful reasons to the contrary. That Amendment rests on the assumption that the widest possible dissemination of information from diverse and antagonistic sources is essential to the welfare of the public, that a free Press is a condition of a free society. Surely a command that the government itself shall not impede the free flow of ideas does not afford non-governmental combinations a refuge if they impose restraints upon that constitutionally guaranteed freedom. Freedom to publish is guaranteed by the Constitution but freedom to combine to keep others from publishing, is not. Freedom of the Press from governmental interference under the First Amendment does not sanction repression of that freedom by private interests. The First Amendment provides not the slightest support for the contention that a combination to restrain trade in news and views has any constitutional immunity."

The commission's proposal for an Amalgamations Court came to nothing, however. Three years later the Labour government rejected it because, in the words of Mr. Douglas Jay, the president of the Board of Trade, "decisions on freedom of speech, free expression of opinion and the public interest simply are not justiciable issues." Since the issues raised by newspaper mergers were so different from normal take-overs, a special panel of experts to consider press transactions was attached to the Monopolies Commission, under the Monopolies and Mergers Act of 1965. The panel included two members of the Press Council, Mr. Henry Bate, its vice-chairman, and Mr. Donald Tyerman.

Since this section of the act can be traced to the circumstances attending the appointment of the Royal Commission, it may be considered here, though it is out of chronological context. The act provides that the transfer of a newspaper to another proprietor whose papers, with the proposed acquisition, had a circulation of five hundred thousand or more copies, must have the permission of the Board of Trade, acting on a favourable report from the Monopolies Commission. The board could, however, grant permission without a report from the commission if the newspaper to be taken over would otherwise close down. Any person knowingly concerned in the transfer of a newspaper without consent, or in breach of the conditions of transfer, would be liable to imprisonment for up to two years, or to an unspecified fine, or both.

These penal provisions shook the newspaper world. The Press Council announced that the freedom of the British press was in issue. This was founded largely on the absence of special press laws which alloted the exercise of government controls. "The penal effect envisaged in clause 8 of the Monopolies and Mergers Bill would effectively make the measure Britain's first Press law. The Council sees a need for close scrutiny of any action that might make the Press more vulnerable to attack." It also pointed out that since the law allowed any man to start a newspaper it automatically gave him the right to sell it.

A statement issued by the Thomson Organisation, criticising the Monopolies legislation, was also an outspoken attack on the Shawcross Commission. It challenged the two basic assumptions made by the commission: 1. That it is contrary to the public interest for newspapers to go out of business; 2. That it is contrary to the public interest for the group ownership of newspapers to be extended. The statement said that if a newspaper was no longer filling a need it was difficult to see what rational grounds could be adduced for its continued existence. The public were the only qualified judges of need.

Running through the Shawcross Report was the inarticulate premise that newspapers were primarily organs of opinion and persuasion and existed to provide a platform for whoever owned them, so that any reduction in their number meant a stifling of free expression. This was not so, said the statement. Newspapers were primarily organs of communication and information, and their effect on readers operated mainly in that area and not in the other. Nowhere in the report was any substantial evidence that public opinion was materially influenced by newspaper persuasion. There was assertion to that effect but no social scientists were called in to speak on the considerable body of research material on the subject, accumulated mainly in the United States, the bulk of which showed that the effect of newspaper persuasion on public opinion was inconsiderable.

"It cannot reasonably be argued that London was better served when it had nine evening newspapers than it is now with only two. . . . There is not one particle of evidence to suggest that the public interest was adversely affected by the closures of the *Empire News* or the *Sunday Graphic*." Then came a rather cruel thrust. The statement said that "while no causal relationship can be inferred, it is not without interest that the renaissance of the Liberal Party was broadly coincidental with the death of the *News-Chronicle*."

The impending death of that paper, it continued, was obvious long before it ceased publication. Under the proposed act, it would be impossible for some better-off group to buy such a property except with a delay and lack of secrecy which would make the whole thing impracticable. But if it had gone so far that its position was irrecoverable, it could be bought without reference to the Monopolies Commission.

Therefore two propositions were implicit in the bill: 1. That it is in the public interest for a dying newspaper to be acquired for what could be scavenged from its corpse; 2. That it is not in the public interest for it to be acquired by a group capable of restoring it before it had deteriorated too far.

On group ownership the statement said the circumstances of national and regional newspapers were entirely different, yet these differences had been largely glossed over in the Shawcross Report and no reference was made to them in the bill. That report had asserted that "the potential danger to the public interest of further concentration and control in the newspaper Press by amalgamation is beyond doubt," yet nowhere was "the public interest" adequately defined. The phrase was incorporated, equally without definition, in the proposed bill. What it seemed to boil down to was a belief that editorial and journalistic integrity and independence were more likely to be guaranteed by singly-owned newspapers, or small groups, than by larger groups. But proprietorial pressure was no more likely to be applied by a single proprietor of ten newspapers than by ten proprietors of single newspapers. On the contrary, the more remote the proprietor the less likely the pressure.

Under the bill the owner of a provincial daily paper who wished to dispose of it would have three possible courses: 1. To find a newspaper purchaser whose scale of activities was so small that the transaction would not be covered by the bill; 2. To find someone prepared to demonstrate that it was in "the public interest" and willing to brave the damaging publicity of the procedure; 3. To find a purchaser unconnected with newspaper publishing. The bill, as drafted, could only encourage alternative 3, and it was hard to believe that that would be in the public interest.

Thus the statement from the Thomson Organisation. By one of those ironies which bespangle recent newspaper history, Thomson's application for the purchase of the *Times* was the first newspaper takeover to be examined under the Monopolies and Mergers Act of 1965. The purchase was approved in 1967.

We may here break off to look briefly at what happened, in the first few years, to Lord Thomson's venture. In a television interview of March 22, 1970, he said he had told the Monopolies Commission that he was prepared to put £1 million a year into the *Times* in order to make it a paying proposition. Now he said: "A million a year is nothing compared to what has happened. We've lost, or invested – I consider it an investment, but the money's gone – over £5 million in the three years. And we're not out of the wood by any means.

"We gave an undertaking that we would make the *Times* viable, that it will continue in existence, and it will. But I might say this: that the unions have got to make some contribution. I can't keep pouring in this kind of money and have some of it drained away in make-work practices and stupid manning requirements." He agreed that a big circulation might result if the *Times* was made more in line with the popular papers. But, he said: "I don't want to do that. I want the *Times* to be a journal of record. I want it to be a better newspaper than it's ever been, not a worse one."

When he was asked why the New York *Times* could pay its way while the London *Times* could not, Lord Thomson said: "Because there are only two morning newspapers in New York, the *News* and the *Times*. If the *Times* was only one of two newspapers here, one of only three or four, we'd make a lot of money. But it isn't; it's one of seven or eight or nine morning newspapers – dailies here, and there are too many of them. . . . More papers on Fleet-street today are losing money than are making money. Well – that's a hell of a way to do business." A few months later it was announced that Thomson Scottish Associates Ltd. had undertaken to operate the *Times* "which continues to incur substantial losses."

Incidentally, the Thomson view (contradicting the opinion of the two Royal Commissions) that the public interest does not necessarily suffer when newspapers shut down was supported by a report on the national newspapers issued by the National Board for Prices and Incomes (the P.I.B.) in February 1970.

The P.I.B. was set up in 1965 by the Wilson government under the chairmanship of Mr. Aubrey Jones as part of Labour's prices and incomes policies. Its duty is to investigate proposed increases in prices and wages, having regard to the overriding need for higher national productivity. In practice all price rises on an industrial scale are investigated while wage increases have come to be largely determined by unofficial strikes.

It was a proposed increase in the price of newspapers which produced the P.I.B. report on the industry. A previous report, in 1967, had concluded that the difficulties of the press stemmed from the nature of competition in the industry, failure to meet effectively competition from commercial television and failure to control manning costs and other forms of expenditure.

Now, the 1970 report said, there were at least four national newspapers not covering their direct costs and some doubt must hang over their future while that continued. Discussing the possibility of some further reduction in the number of papers, the report asked whether any special action should be taken by the government to prevent this happening. "There are a number of arguments that can be made against such action," it said. "There is nothing sacrosanct about the present number of newspapers, and the possibility of contraction should be seen in the context of the whole range of communication media now available — radio, television, provincial newspapers, magazines, and so on. The view could well be taken, moreover, that the quality and range of view of the Press is of more consequence than mere numbers."

The report went on to say that "there is no doubt that the national newspaper industry is making an effort to achieve more realistic manning levels. . . . In the production departments investigated we found that manning levels had been reduced by an average of 5 percent, ranging from an increase of 5 percent in one newspaper to a reduction of 15 percent in another." Productivity had increased by 9 percent but the average increase in production wage costs was 12 percent, reflecting increased earnings per capita of 18 percent. There was still considerable room for improvement and in many cases manning agreements merely replaced one unrealistic manning by another less so. "Restrictive labour practices do undoubtedly constitute an important constraint on the introduction of new and improved techniques, though in our view they are not the only important constraint." Present methods of production, the report went on, were well behind available technology and further developments were on the way, involving large capital investment. But even in the short term many possible changes would lead to economies in labour costs. "The benefits would be nullified, however, if existing manpower practices were simply taken over in the new technological conditions."

Paradoxically, it was the printers' strike in the national newspaper offices during the general election of June 1970, which promised the first break in the long history of anarchy and confusion in the economics of the press.

The stoppage was called by the Society of Graphical and Allied Trades (SOGAT) the largest print union formed of an amalgamation of smaller unions whose demand for a 25 percent interim wage increase was rejected by the N.P.A. Instead, the newspaper publishers offered a cash bonus of 5 percent which, in its turn, was rejected as "derisory." It was estimated that the cost of meeting SOGAT's claim would have been £22 million a year, whereas the entire national newspaper industry's profits for 1969 had been only £7 million.

The wage-and-holiday settlement finally reached was estimated to cost £5 million a year. But it also established the vitally important principle that the whole complex of wages and manpower would be overhauled so that future bargains would be made, not with separate unions but with all unions in the industry; not with separate offices but across the board of the industry as a whole. It seemed that, at last, "leapfrogging" might come to an end and some sanity be injected into a senseless structure as the result of the inquiry set in motion.

Let us return now to events following the Shawcross Commission's Report. Its insistence on a lay element in the Press Council was still unwelcome to the newspaper industry, and to a strong body of opinion within the council which was opposed to any alteration. The chairman, however, argued that public opinion would no longer tolerate a continuance of the old-style council and that changes had to come. This view prevailed. Had it not done so, a difficult situation would have arisen, not least for the government who would have had the thankless task of imposing some form of statutory control on the free press.

In the foreword to the council's ninth annual report in 1962 the chairman remarked that the commission's recommendations had come as no surprise and that the sole purpose of lay membership was to satisfy the public. Without some form of control the new body could exert no more power or authority than did the existing one, but any control would be a blow to press freedom. That was the crux of a question of vital importance to the liberties of the British people. The 1949 commission's dictum that "the body we have in mind would depend for its effectiveness on its moral authority rather than on any statutory sanctions" was recalled. "It takes many years of precept and practice, trial and error, to build up such an authority," said the foreword, "but it has been the claim of successive chairmen of the Council, and I repeat it, that we are succeeding in this difficult task.

"It remains for the journalistic profession and the newspaper industry to decide the future shape of the Press Council in the light of the Shawcross Report. Whatever form it may take, the existing Council, if it has done nothing else, has served its generation well in at least one way. It has accustomed the British Press to a form of restraint which has caused it to search its own conscience, and has thus paved the way to the possible acceptance of some limits to its economic freedom."

Now followed a period of many meetings and intensive discussion among the constituent bodies of the council, the committees and the council itself on its future shape and form, and possible changes in its constitution. In the end, the council's objects were reduced from eight to seven, though the two most important were retained unaltered. These were, and are: 1. To preserve the established freedom of the British press; 2. To maintain the character of the British press in accordance with the highest professional and commercial standards. The new articles omitted mention of training, education, and technical research, and placed greater emphasis on reviewing and reporting publicly on newspaper developments.

All this took time. The Shawcross Report had been published in September 1962, and when by March 1963, nothing had been heard, people began to ask what was happening. One M.P. said in a television programme that the council had done nothing. It was this same M.P. who, in a speech to editors in 1967, said: "Far too often journalists are content to skim the surface of events, to take statements at their face value instead of digging down and finding out what is really happening."

Had he dug down in 1963 the council might not have found it necessary to issue the following statement, dated March 28, 1963, on what they had been doing during an apparently passive six months:

"These Shawcross recommendations, and others, have been discussed at more than a dozen meetings of the Press Council, its General Purposes Committee, and conferences of delegates from its constituent bodies. The first meeting was held on September 20, the day after publication of the Commission's Report. As was to be expected in so diverse an organisation the recommendations have met with some opposition and many amendments have been proposed. Every member organisation has been asked for ideas and full consideration has rightly been given to all points of view.

"The Council is composed of active journalists or managers nominated by seven constituent organisations. They are scattered throughout England, Scotland, and Wales and their sponsoring bodies meet on different dates and at varying intervals.

"It is therefore inevitable that weeks should have elapsed before the views of the constituent bodies could be collated. In these circumstances it is not unreasonable that deliberations on a matter of such far-reaching importance should have been spread over six months. Such a delay may be regrettable, but this is how democracy works."

A few weeks later the chairman was able to issue a public statement saying that the council had, by a majority, agreed to a lay chairman and a proportion of lay members.

11 Journalists in Jail

WHILE these matters were pending an event had involved the newspapers in a notoriety which impelled the National Council of Civil Liberties to say that "relations between the Press and the public have probably never been worse." This was the Vassall Tribunal, leading to the imprisonment of two journalists for refusing to reveal the sources of their published information.

William John Christopher Vassall, an Admiralty clerk, had been sentenced to a long term of imprisonment as a spy for the Russian secret service during more than seven years. According to the report of the Tribunal he was a homosexual and a man of "limited mental capacity." After his trial and conviction certain allegations rumbled on in some newspapers. In particular it was alleged that the presence of another spy within the Admiralty had been known to the First Lord (Lord Carrington) and his service chiefs after other naval spies had been convicted in the Portland case eighteen months previously. There were also hints and innuendoes that Vassall had received special consideration from some of his superiors which seemed to reflect on the honour and integrity of ministers, naval officers, and civil servants. The First Lord and the Hon. T. G. D. Galbraith, who had been a civil lord of the Admiralty, were especially concerned. These reports reached such a pitch of scandal that in November 1962, the government appointed a tribunal under the Tribunals of Inquiry Act, 1921, to inquire into the whole affair. All the allegations were shown to be unfounded, and all the persons who had been subjected to rumour and insinuation were absolutely cleared.

The press, however, did not emerge so cleanly. The tribunal found that what appeared to be positive statements of fact in certain newspapers were "either pure comment expressed in the form of as-

sertion of fact or else inferences put together from other readily acceptable sources, such as matters already published in other newspapers or elsewhere, or general public knowledge." Reporters from
several papers were closely questioned about their published stories,
and from whom they had obtained information. In most cases there
was no secret about that, but in the case of two reporters, Mr. Brendan
Mulholland of the *Daily Mail* and Mr. Reginald Foster, contributing
to the *Daily Sketch,* the tribunal was unable to prove their reports, and
both men refused to give the sources of their information. The tribunal had no power to punish them but it could, and did, remit them
to the High Court. Here they were again required to reveal the names
of their informants, but again both refused. Mr. Mulholland was then
sentenced to three concurrent terms of six months' imprisonment, and
Mr. Foster was given three months in jail, for contempt of court.

Press and public were in an uproar. What infuriated the newspapers almost as much as the jailing of the journalists was this remark,
during the case, by Lord Chief Justice Parker: "How can you say that
there is any dishonour (in disclosing the source of information) if you
do what is your duty in the ordinary way as a citizen to put the interests of the State above everything." The obvious retort was that the
liberty of the subject came before the interests of the State.

The *Times* commented: "However sound in law, the judgment
that two journalists must be imprisoned because they refused to disclose their sources of information is against the public interest. No
doubt there will be many people, some in positions of authority who
ought to know better, who will be rejoicing today because 'The Press
has been put in its place.' Others will say it is outrageous that the
journalists should claim an immunity that is withheld from the doctor
and the priest. Yet others will pay lip service to the inviolability of
sources and add that it was not worth fighting for in this case. This is
not the matter of jealous privilege or special pleading. The people are
being placed more and more at the mercy of the Executive."

The chairman of the Press Council, giving his personal views in
the *Daily Mail,* wrote: "This is a black day in the history of a free
Press and a free people. When the laws of England can imprison two
reporters for refusing to dishonour themselves by refusing to disclose
their source of published information, they have taken a big, back-
ward step into the dark age of British constitutional development. It is

clear that the Tribunals of Inquiry Act under which this scandal became possible is a mortal blow at the liberty of the Press, and therefore at the liberty of the subject."

Such arguments failed to impress more than a minority of the public. They were received in many quarters with the sceptical comment that the newspapers were concerned not so much with the liberty of the subject as with their own commercial interests. The two imprisoned journalists were thought by some people to have had no sources to reveal – in other words, that they had invented part of their reports. This unworthy accusation served to show the low esteem into which the press appeared to have fallen.

The *Times* returned to the subject in a now-famous leading article headed "It *Can* Happen Here." This piece was written by the editor, Sir William Haley, and has certainly taken its place among the historic editorials of British journalism. A comparison of this article with that of Delane, written in 1852, shows the way the press had gone in 111 years, and brings us back to de Tocqueville's proposition that "in order to enjoy the inestimable benefits which the liberty of the Press ensures, it is necessary to submit to the inevitable evils which it engenders."

The Haley editorial said: "The predominant note in the letters the *Times* has received about the two imprisoned journalists has been that of hostility to the Press. The bitterness has gone beyond what could be justified by a reasonable reading of the published proceedings of the Vassall Tribunal. It has overflowed and at times has sought to sweep away the principle at stake in these cases. They have broken the dam to a long-pent-up, ever-rising flood of resentment against the practices of some newspapers. Intrusion, triviality, distortion, muck-raking, the inversion of values – the list of offences is long. They are real offences. The newspapers were warned years ago that if they went on in the way they were going they would end by alienating those very sections of society upon whose goodwill the freedom and the working conventions of the Press depend. This has now happened. . . . The lesson of the events of the past month is that, in the final analysis, the only people who can preserve the freedom of the Press are the journalists themselves. It will not be done by law or Government; it cannot be done by Parliament. It is mistaken escapism to believe that the responsibility can be concentrated in the Press Council."

Nevertheless, the cry went up for the council to do something, a demand heard with scepticism by some newspapers. The *Daily Herald* said the appointment of a lay chairman of the council must be the first step, but others would be needed. The *Guardian* said the council was a feeble body whose word counted for little and its dealing with press conduct would appear more dispassionate if it were not drawn wholly from the industry. The *Daily Telegraph:* "If it be thought that a stronger Press Council will compel reporters to break their pledged word not to reveal their sources of information, then the Council is being conceived as one more weapon for destroying the freedom of the Press."

The council, after a discussion on the Vassall affair, issued this statement in May 1963:

1. The Press Council has considered the report of the tribunal appointed to inquire into the Vassall case;

2. The press has the right and, indeed, the duty to investigate and comment on matters concerning national security, but the council condemns, in some London newspapers, false information and damaging innuendoes based on nothing more than conjecture, assumption, and speculation. It regards these reports as a serious lowering of the standards of a responsible press;

3. The council, however, expresses its deep anxiety about the severe penalties of imprisonment imposed on two reporters for declining to depart from the journalistic code of honour to respect confidences. It is vital that newspapers, which depend so much on confidential information, should continue to be in a position to investigate and ventilate matters of public importance. A precedent has now been established which may hinder the press in performing this duty;

4. The two reporters were punished for contempt of court committed under the Tribunals of Inquiry (Evidence) Act of 1921. The council believes there should be early reexamination of the rules which govern contempt, especially as they are applied under this Act.

Perhaps the last observations in this business should be those of Lord Devlin who told the Winnipeg Press Club in 1964 that if the Press Council failed, the only alternative would be control of the press by law. There were enough people in high places, he said, who would like to see press freedom restricted. The role of the press was opposite to that of the Establishment in which both government and opposition tended to coalesce. The press must constantly criticise the government, although it must retain the respect of those criticised because

otherwise it could not rally supporters against the erosion of its freedom. Such erosion, rather than the outright muzzling of the press, was
the greatest danger. The explosion against the press over the Vassall
case, he ended, was deliberately provoked by the government, and it
had cleared the air.

These words were important for Lord Devlin was to be the first lay
chairman of the Press Council, an appointment for which he was,
even then, preparing.

The revised constitution came into being on July 1, 1963, and the
new council began operations on January 1, 1964. But before this
chapter opens we must cast a valedictory glance on the old council
and what it had, or had not, accomplished. A summing-up was attempted in the chairman's foreword of the tenth annual report:

"The conclusion of the Press Council's first decade has coincided
exactly with its end as a voluntary organisation solely within the newspaper profession and industry. It is not often that Time provides so
neat a conjunction. . . . If I were asked to say briefly what I considered our greatest achievement I should adopt the quip of the Abbé
Sieyès when asked what he had done during the French Revolution.
I should say: 'We survived.'" Speaking of the rejection of lay membership after its formation: "It was not unreasonable that journalism,
with its long immunity from interference of any kind, should have
taken a cautious first step towards an unaccustomed regulation. It
therefore settled on this compromise—and thus made a typically British approach to the problem.

"What I must now call the 'old Council' formed a link between the
time when the Press was subjected to no outside restraints (apart from
those provided by the law) and today, when the public, whom it
serves, will help to keep an eye on it. By its mere survival the Council has accustomed newspaper editors to the existence of a body constantly on the watch to see that they maintain the standards expected
of a decent and responsible Press. In this matter alone the Council
has fulfilled a valuable function and is able to pass on to the new
Council a name and an organisation which have won acceptance by
the newspapers and the people."

Having seen the transformation through, the last journalist chairman resigned. A tribute in the annual report noted that he had contributed "a wealth of able and painstaking work which will always
secure him a premier place in the Council's history."

12 The New Council

THE most obvious difference between the old council and the new was, of course, the infusion of the lay element, particularly in the person of the chairman. The Press Council was fortunate to obtain the services of Lord Devlin, who had been eminent in the law for many years, and a distinguished public servant in other fields. Besides having been a High Court judge, a lord justice of appeal, and a lord of appeal in ordinary, he had also headed several Royal Commissions, the best known of which had been those inquiring into dock labour, and into the political situation of Nyasaland. Lord Devlin, after a brilliant career at the bar, had attained high judicial office at the unusually early age of forty-three and was able to retire from the bench at a time when many other judges began to occupy positions which he was now leaving. His appointment came through the good offices of Mr. Cecil King, who had approached Lord Shawcross in the matter. Lord Devlin brought to the council a disinterested mind which was of great value to it, and a quality of forensic adjudication which gave it a status and prestige which it had previously lacked.

His nomination assuredly made history. It was the first admission by the press that outsiders had the right to say (apart from legal prohibitions) what was, or was not, proper for the newspapers to print. On the other hand, it was also an indication of the importance assigned by authority to the newspaper press in the modern scheme. When Lord Devlin accepted the Press Council post there were some in judicial circles who deprecated the step he was taking. After all, it was the courts who had once sent journalists to prison for daring to criticise the Establishment. Now an eminent judge was ready, willing, and able to defend the freedom of the press against the encroachments of government. The British democracy had come a long way since the eighteenth century.

It may be convenient to remark, at this point, that Lord Devlin served the council with distinction for five years, retiring in September 1969. The annual report for that year noted that his "warm personality and skilled leadership of a team composed of various sections of the Press and representatives of the public, won the high esteem of all members of the Council and played a very big part in ensuring that the reconstruction fulfilled all expectations. In his public utterances and in the preparation of statements of Council policy, Lord Devlin showed the deepest understanding of the problems involved in maintaining the freedom of the Press and under his chairmanship the Council grew in stature and authority. Members of the Council have placed on record their appreciation of his outstanding service to the Council and to the British Press as a whole."

In his final foreword Lord Devlin dealt with the attitude of British editors towards the Press Council. He recalled that in June 1969, the *UK Press Gazette* had published the result of a survey among editors made by Dr. Paul B. Snider of Bradley University, Illinois. More than two-thirds of those who responded welcomed the Press Council, about a quarter were neutral, and a small minority "resented" it. There were 58 percent who thought the council effective, while 86 percent considered that the spread of a Press Council movement throughout the world would be desirable.

"My predecessor in his foreword six years ago," wrote Lord Devlin, "claimed no more for the Press Council in 1963 than that, in the *mot* of the Abbé Sieyès, it had survived. He put it too modestly. Drawing on his period of office as well as on my own, I think I can now claim on behalf of the Council that it has succeeded. Success brings with it its own problems. In the early days of the Press Council the prime danger was thought to be that nobody would pay any attention to it. Today the greater danger is thought to be that its decisions may force conformity on a profession which thrives on diversity. The founders of the Council laid upon it a perhaps more difficult task than they realised when they charged it with the double burden of preserving freedom and maintaining standards."

Lord Devlin went on to ask the question which so many others (including de Tocqueville) have found unanswerable. "At what point does the imposition of standards begin to interfere with true freedom?" And, as a corollary: "Where lies the happy mean between a state of affairs in which the adjudications of the Press Council are disregarded and one in which they are accepted with such submission that the Press might as well be ruled by a statutory body?" He said he was tempted to try his hand at framing a theoretical answer to the problem but it was not a problem that could be solved theoretically. As yet none of the Council's problems had been so solved. "The theoretical defect that the Press Council was without 'teeth' was cured by the at first uncoordinated decisions of editors invariably to publish adverse adjudications against their newspapers. The delicate balance of forces that is needed to make standards effective without being suppressive will come from experience and not from the application of a formula settled in advance."

Having said this he added that it was most opportune that, at this stage in its growth, the council should have obtained as its new chairman a judge who during his rise to the top had acquired, almost as his distinguishing mark, a reputation for finding the sensible and practical solution of the many problems with which he had dealt.

Lord Devlin's successor in the chair was Lord Pearce, who, after a distinguished career on the judicial bench, had retired as a lord of appeal in ordinary. He was called to the Bar in 1925, became a High Court judge in 1948, and a lord justice of appeal in 1957. He, too, had served on public bodies, including the Committee on Ship-building Costs, and the Royal Commission of Marriage and Divorce, having been chairman of both.

In a final word Lord Devlin said he left the council "proud to have played a part in a great work, refreshed by a sojourn in a new and strange world, rewarded by the friendship of men I have learnt to admire and confident that Lord Pearce will do for the Council all, and more than all, that a good chairman can do."

The other lay members of the council were not chosen on any system because it was felt that if particular interests were selected for representation as, for example, the churches, education, the trade unions, and so on, those not brought in might feel aggrieved. Names were therefore put forward in committee—to cover as wide a field as possible—and were put to the vote in council. The first lay membership, however, did seem to give undue weight to the scholastic profession. They were: Professor Alexander Haddow, an international name in medical research; Lord James, a schoolmaster and vice-chancellor of York University; Mrs. Elaine Kellett, barrister, farmer, and first choice of the Women's Institute Federation for Britain's No. 1 country housewife; the Rev. Ronald G. L. Lunt, Chief Master of King Edward's School, Birmingham; Mrs. Marie Patterson, the youngest member of the General Council of the Trades Union Congress to that date.

Having given five valuable years of service to the council, Lord Devlin retired in October 1969, and was succeeded by Lord Pearce, whose legal career had followed an almost exactly similar course to his own. The new chairman besides being a High Court judge, a lord justice of appeal, and a lord of appeal in ordinary, had also headed several important committees and commissions of inquiry. He took up his appointment with the Press Council at the age of sixty-eight.

Another big difference between the old council and the new lay in finance. All the work in the old council (except that of the secretariat) had been voluntary, and fares were the only expenses allowed. Now the chairman was to be paid £4,000 a year (of which £1,000 ranked as expenses), and lay members were to be given subsistence allowances in addition to fares. The income was raised immediately to £14,000, and in the following year to just over £20,000. The N.P.A. now paid £10,500, the Newspaper Society £4,500, the N.U.J. £1,500, the Institute £450, the Guild £300, the Scottish Daily Newspaper Society £525, and the Scottish N.P.A. £337. An additional £2,000 was contributed by the Periodical Proprietors' Association which was represented for the first time. The permanent staff of the old council was one secretary and one assistant; today it is one secretary, two assistant secretaries and two office assistants.

The annual reports now list the names and publishers of all newspapers and periodicals in the kingdom, with global circulations, while the council keeps up-to-date, but confidential, records on ownership, control, finance, changes, and other details of press undertakings. There is also a section in which the structure of some of the big British newspaper publishing houses is analysed.

The volume of information about the British press now available in these reports presents an informative record and examination of ownership interests which have not been given anywhere before. When the Monopolies Commission examined the application for the *Times* take-over, they went to the council's secretary for statistical detail and acknowledged his assistance in their report.

The council has been able to fulfill these duties because of its bigger income, which also enables it to examine more witnesses in person than was previously possible. In these respects it is much more active than before. But although its scope has been enlarged and its judgments are now backed by legal expertise, its power and purpose remain exactly the same as they were.

It wields no sanctions beyond those of rebuke and persuasion. It has no authority to intervene when press mergers or take-overs are in the offing—nor can it claim that its records would be of any great value in making obvious a trend towards monopoly. Its request for the information from publishers it needs to discharge the duty laid upon it by the Shawcross Commission states specifically that the circulations of weekly newspapers (those of most dailies and some weeklies are published by the Audit Bureau of Circulations) will not be disclosed to anybody and would not even be circulated to council members. Requests that other information supplied should also remain confidential are given close attention and no publication of such matters is made without the consent of the informant. In view of such restrictions, it is hard to see how the public could ever be warned that another *News-Chronicle* tragedy, large or small, was impending. Indeed, it is paradoxical that the new council, with its quadrupled income, is not required, like its impoverished predecessor, "to study developments in the Press which may tend towards greater concentration or monopoly"—a duty perforce neglected, before it got into hot water before the Shawcross Commission.

Nor are its adjudications any more severe. On the contrary many judgments of the all-newspaper council against newspapers were in much harsher terms than those of the latter-day council. Among them were such phrases as "callous and indecent regard for the feelings of the family"; "a flagrant violation of good manners"; "a grave violation of journalistic standards deserving of the strongest censure"; "condemned in the severest possible terms"; "grossly lewd and offensive"; "a disgrace to British journalism." These were the verdicts of a council which had been called a "whitewashing machine," and was said to be "judge and jury in its own case." Compared with them, the dicta of the new council are mild indeed. They rarely consist of more than a balanced view of the pros and cons of the case, ending with one of two phrases—"the complaint is upheld," or "the complaint is rejected." The language of these judgments is no doubt more judicial, but it is certainly less robust.

The old council also appears to have tempered justice with less mercy to its constituents than does the new one. The first analysis of cases considered appeared in the annual report for 1961–62, when 58 complaints were adjudicated. Of these, 35 were upheld and 23 rejected. In the next year 36 were upheld and 39 rejected. After the first year of lay membership 39 were upheld and 47 rejected, and in the next year 49 were upheld and 54 rejected. By 1968–69 the figure was 28 upheld and 36 rejected. On these records, the old council may claim to have done its work with as little fear or favour as its successor. Nevertheless, criticism has been largely stilled, for as Lord Devlin remarked in his first foreword (to the eleventh annual report), the participation of lay members in sifting complaints "ought to satisfy the public that the Press is not acting simply as a judge in its own cause. In this respect the council has an asset which, so far, no other similar body has cared to acquire." This ensured, he said, that the reaction of an ordinary member of the public to any complaint would be heard and understood.

One thing which used to anger the critics was that the all-newspaper council reached its decisions on a majority basis, the extent of which was not announced. From the fuss that was sometimes made, anyone would think such a procedure something new and rather shameful. But when Lord Devlin took over he confirmed that adjudications "must seek acceptance on the usual democratic basis as a decision reached, after careful deliberation, by a majority of elected men and women."

He also remarked that the inclusion of lay members had caused no breach in continuity. "That this is due to the fact that the Council in the past never dealt with complaints in a partisan way. Under the guidance of a succession of high-principled and wise chairmen there has already been established a firm tradition of impartiality. The task of the Press Council in dealing with complaints is not always easy. There is no settled code for it to administer. Press ethics are still in the formative stage. Press criticism may give the impression . . . that the Council is an alien body whose activities the Press can survey from a position of detachment. This is not so. The Council is the creature of the Press. It serves the Press in the same sort of way though in a very different field, as Reuters or the Press Association. Its membership is designed to make it responsive to Press opinion."

That was well said, and perhaps could only be said by a layman of authority, as, indeed, could many other pronouncements on the rights and duties of the press which reflected a trained legal mind and became a valuable feature of the annual reports. The first of them appeared in this particular report and arose from the case of the Great Train Robbery of August 1963, when a railway train was held up in Buckinghamshire by a gang of robbers who got away with bank notes worth £2.5 million.

During the committal proceedings in this case, counsel for some of the defendants submitted that the press should be asked to exercise great discretion in reporting the evidence which might otherwise prejudice a fair trial. The chairman of the bench then asked the press to be considerate and to report "only what is necessary." The Press Council considered this the sort of request it was impossible for the press to comply with. The only definitive characteristic this evidence possessed to distinguish it from any other evidence in the case was that one counsel contended that it was admissible, while another thought not. "A reporter in such a situation cannot be expected to judge what should be reported and what should not," said the council.

After some of the disputed evidence had been given, one counsel for the defence stated in open court that if any part of it were published by press, radio, or television the matter would be reported to the attorney general to see if he thought fit to bring proceedings for contempt of court. In a statement issued in May 1964, council said: "There is no authority whatever for the suggestion that newspapers which publish what has taken place in open court, there being no ruling from the Bench to the contrary, can be punished for contempt of court. The further suggestion that the Press will be acting contemptuously unless it takes steps, which the court itself has not taken, to ensure for the defendants what their counsel thinks necessary for a fair trial and to remedy what he deems to be the injustice done by the ruling of the court is, in the opinion of the Council, absurd. The Council hopes that editors and reporters will not be deterred by threats of this sort from the performance of their duty to the public. The Council has expressed itself strongly because this is not the only occasion upon which suggestions of contempt of court have been made by members of the Bar."

Having defended the newspapers in this matter, the report went on to rebuke certain of them for their handling of the Profumo case, the social-political scandal which rocked the country. This affair was investigated by Lord Denning, a distinguished jurist and master of the rolls who, among other things, probed the scandalous rumours concerning well-known people which were being whispered at cocktail parties and hinted at in the newspapers. He had been asked by the prime minister "to examine in the light of the circumstances leading to the resignation of the former Secretary of State for War, Mr. J. D. Profumo, the operation of the security services and the adequacy of their co-operation with the police in matters of security, to investigate any information or material which may come to his attention in this connection and to consider any evidence there may be for believing that national security had been, or may be, endangered, and to report thereon." In his report, published in September 1963, Lord Denning said that these rumours had been thought by some people to be a symptom of a decline in the integrity of British public life, but he did not believe that to be true. But public men were more vulnerable than they were and it behoved them, even more than ever to, give no cause for scandal.

He went on: "Scandalous information about well-known people has become a marketable commodity. True or false, actual or invented, it can be sold. The greater the scandal the higher the price it commands. . . . The story improves with the telling. It is offered to those newspapers—there are only a few of them—who deal in this commodity. . . . They publish what they can but there remains a substantial part which is not fit for publication. This unpublished part goes round by word of mouth. It does not stop at Fleet-street. It goes to Westminster. It crosses the Channel, even the Atlantic, and back again, swelling all the time. Yet without the original purchase it might never have got started on its way. When such deplorable consequences are seen to ensue, the one thing that is clear is that something should be done to stop the trafficking in scandal for reward. The machinery is ready to hand. There is a new Press Council already in being."

The council had already received shoals of complaints about the conduct of the press in reports, articles, and illustrations of the activities of Miss Christine Keeler, Mr. Stephen Ward, the osteopath who was convicted on two charges of living on immoral earnings, but who killed himself before sentence was passed, and their associates. These complaints were not only concerned with the detailed reporting of court proceedings involving evidence of immorality and vice but also, in the words of Lord Shawcross "the publicising of pimps, prostitutes or perverts in highly-paid interviews or feature articles." In particular, some people objected to the publication of Miss Keeler's confessions in the *News of the World,* feeling that the large financial rewards for such contributions falsely glamourised such behaviour and tempted young people to try to do likewise.

In a statement issued from its meeting in September 1963, the council said it was important to differentiate between the reporting of news and its elaboration in memoirs and other articles. The press had a responsibility to record what was going on and extensive reporting of court proceedings in the Ward case was not only justified but necessary, however much the facts may have shocked or dismayed many people. Newspapers could not ignore matters of that kind because of the risk that reports might be read by the young. They had to deal with adult questions in an adult manner.

The editor of the *News of the World* argued that the Keeler memoirs were news. The only difference between his paper and others, he said, was that it was the first to publish material with an authentic basis and for that they had to pay. But the council did not accept that contention and went on: "The Council recognises that in the competitive world of the Press the publication of personal stories, even though objectionable to some people, may be legitimate and of public interest, but in the Council's opinion there are few things today which are doing more to discredit the Press as a whole than the memoirs of immoral or criminal people." In an adjudication the council repeated these views and specifically deplored the action of the *News of the World* in paying twenty-three thousand pounds for the confessions of Miss Keeler and publishing in the articles details of her sordid life story. "By thus exploiting vice and sex for commercial reward the *News of the World* has done a disservice both to public welfare and the Press," it said.

This judgment was issued before Lord Devlin had taken office. When he did so, he recorded that the duties of chairman had been discharged in the interregnum by the able and experienced vice-chairman, Mr. Bate. "The Council," he wrote, "has reason to be grateful to him for the skill and care with which he conducted its affairs during that period; and I, also, for the way in which he initiated me into my duties."

After having accustomed himself to his environment, the new chairman contributed a number of observations on the press and the council which proved a valuable guidance to both and could be of service elsewhere. Thus, in the thirteenth annual report issued in 1966 he named six factors which he regarded as essential to the creation and proper working of a Press Council. They were:

1. There should be a general acceptance by the press itself that it is a desirable thing to have;

2. The government of the country must be responsive to public opinion and must accept that the press has a constitutional part to play in the formation and expression of opinion;

3. The press must accept its corresponding obligation—i.e., there must be standards of conduct to which the press conforms;

4. A newspaper accepts the obligation to publish adjudications against itself;

5. The public is represented on the Press Council;

6. The council must stand for the freedom and rights of the press as well as censuring misconduct.

In the next report, published in the autumn of 1967, the chairman discussed secret sources of information and the journalist's refusal to disclose them. He said the problem was theoretically insoluble because there lay at its roots a conflict between the power of the State and the conscience of the individual and such a conflict could not, in the last resort, be decided otherwise than by the use of force, physical or moral. If the State were willing to put freedom of conscience above its own security there would be no conflict, and so no problem. But no State had ever been willing to offer the unlimited protection of the law to individual consciences; on the contrary, *salus populi suprema lex esto*. Likewise (and this seemed, intentionally or not, to be an answer to Lord Chief Justice Parker's observation in the Vassall case), "no individual in a free society can be expected to place his conscience unreservedly at the disposal of the State. . . . Thus each in his or her own sphere, the individual and the nation, claims full sovereignty and between sovereigns an insoluble conflict means war.

"The practical solution in this sort of situation is, as in the case of nations with conflicting interests, to reduce, if possible to vanishing point, the occasions on which a clash can occur. . . . A reasonable attitude on both sides can probably stop issues of principle from rising to dangerous heights. Compromise is aided by the thought that the two sides are more evenly matched than the State's monopoly of bayonets would suggest. It can hardly be doubted, for example, that an attempt by the State to smash the secrecy of the confessional would fail. Journalists are not in as strong position as priests. Inevitably in many cases when they seek to protect their sources, they are also seeking to protect their own livelihood.

"The real strength of their position lies in the fact that, whether or not they are serving their own interests, they are serving the public interest. Decisions taken in the name of the State are, in fact, taken by individuals who also have consciences and these consciences tell them that they are not, and ought not to be, above criticism. They know that well-informed criticism in a free society plays a vital part in the process of government and that the streams of well-informed criticism would soon dry up if they were filled by tributaries openly flowing into them, and took nothing from underground springs. . . .

"Whatever the law of libel may say, no journalist is ethically at fault simply because what he has written turns out to be untrue. His duty is to check and to cross-check, the degree of care he takes varying with the importance of the subject-matter, but he cannot be asked to guarantee the truth of what he writes. His professional duty is to act responsibly. If a complaint is made to the Press Council alleging the falsity of a statement in a newspaper, accompanied, it may be, by a charge of irresponsible reporting, and if the editor denies the falsity and relies on sources which he says are unimpeachable but which he cannot disclose, how should the Council deal with the case?

". . . The public cannot accept, and ought not to be asked to accept, that an editor or journalist, any more than any other type of citizen, can be a good judge in his own cause. When a journalist decides whether he will or will not act on information received . . . he is not, as it were, adjudicating on the point; he is making a professional decision. If, thereafter, there is a case for adjudication, he cannot review his own decision impartially. This is how the public looks at it, and if the Press Council does no more than pass on to the public the judgment of the editor in his own favour, it will command no respect.

"From the point of view of the Press also, it is highly desirable that the Council should act wherever it can. If a charge of irresponsible reporting be made to which a newspaper is convinced it has a good defence, it is not in the interests of the newspaper nor of the Press as a whole that the slur should remain unremoved."

Lord Devlin went on to point the difficulties of getting at the truth. For example, the idea of disclosing the sources of information confidentially to a small committee of the council was open to the objection that the identity of the informant would be made known to rival newspapermen. Then there was the difficulty that the name could not be disclosed without the permission of the informant. Some might refuse. Others might accept, though wishing to refuse, and newspapers might be reluctant to present them with an embarrassing choice. "From the public point of view it is, at least, as reasonable for a complainant to refuse to publish confidential matters in furtherance of his complaint as it is for a journalist to refuse to disclose confidential sources in furtherance of his defence. This produces deadlock."

Having traversed other pros and cons the article concluded that machinery could not speedily be designed to enable the council to deal satisfactorily with all cases of this type. But lack of the perfect machinery would not excuse the council from dealing with as many cases as it could. Nor would it excuse an editor from considering afresh in the circumstances of each case how far he could go without infringing the journalist's code of honour so as to enable the Press Council to give an adjudication satisfactory to the public.

So much for that. The question of what journalists should or should not do, whether they should or should not tell, would become academic if there were no newspapers in which they could spread themselves. And, at this time, the possible demise of some great and famous national newspapers became more than a theoretical talking-point. The *Guardian*, which had started publishing in London as well as in its hometown, Manchester, was in low water. This newspaper, with the *Times*, had been named as among the best twenty in the world. Now both seemed near the point of extinction. Economies of £500,-000 had to be made to save the *Guardian* and these were effected in agreement with the unions. The *Times* survived because it was taken over by Lord Thomson, who was prepared to lose £3 million in the process of rebuilding it.

The joint board for the national newspaper industry which had already made its own survey after the disclosures of the Shawcross Commission, decided to order an exhaustive investigation into the structure and organisation of the industry, and employed the Economist Intelligence Unit to conduct it. The outcome was a report of 150,000 words, and a bill for £47,000. The Unit found that in 1966 only three out of eight national daily newspapers were operating at a profit. This, however, was not a new situation, for it is doubtful whether for fifty years past more than four nationals had, at any one time, been profitable.

Before the report was published, the *Guardian* published a report of what it was said to contain. The chairman of the joint board was Lord Devlin who was also, of course, chairman of the Press Council which had more than once declared that the words "private and confidential" on a document should not prevent a newspaper revealing the contents if it was in the public interest to do so. Now by another of those quirks of the Spirit Ironic, it fell to Lord Devlin to rebuke the *Guardian* for doing exactly what his council might, in other circumstances, have permitted. He said the EIU report was a strictly confidential document and was so marked. "The board deplores the premature publication in the *Guardian* of parts of the report which gave a misleading impression of the conclusions reached by the EIU, and records its view that the action of the *Guardian* has done a disservice to labour relations in the newspaper industry." History does not record that the matter was referred to the Press Council.

What the EIU had to say confirmed many of the findings of the Shawcross Commission. It said, ominously, that unless the existing cost structure remained unchanged, at least four national newspapers would have to close down by 1970. (The *Sunday Citizen,* formerly *Reynolds Sunday News,* owned by the Co-operative Society, did cease publication in 1967.) Five daily and two Sunday newspapers were making "impossible" losses amounting to several million pounds annually. In 1965 four daily papers had made a total profit of £9,462,-000 while four had made a loss of £3,541,000. Profits had risen very much slower than wage costs during the eight years to 1964. Profits had gone up by 29 percent whereas editorial costs had risen 98 percent and production wages by 130 percent.

These figures told their own story. The report rubbed in the lesson when it said that the wages structure, as far as one existed, was made up of a multitude of extras many of which had no bearing on the needs of the job. The employees appeared to have little knowledge of wages and conditions in other industries, and saw nothing unusual in unskilled men earning, say, £1,750 a year for doing very little work. Newspaper workers did not realise that their industry was almost unique in the degree to which control of labour was in the hands of the unions.

Thus labour was scarified—but management did not escape either. Some proprietors, the report said, had little interest in modern management methods and techniques, yet retained almost absolute authority over their organisations. Some of them were not too interested in making profits as was a professional manager in industry for whom that was the yardstick of efficiency and success. The press lord was prepared to consider keeping an ailing newspaper subsidised by its sister papers, or perhaps by other financial interests.

That last comment could be construed as more a matter for praise than reproach for newspaper proprietors. A newspaper in the red would only be kept alive for one of three excellent reasons—a sense of public duty, a reluctance to see a famous name disappear, or a desire to keep newspaper workers in employment; and all three reasons have operated in the Street of Ink.

Indeed, the EIU report itself continued: "No one would suggest that profits should be the only criterion, but an inefficient industry is really an unhealthy industry . . . it is difficult to see how an efficient and prosperous industry can be achieved unless all proprietors become as interested in running an efficient business as they are in producing a good newspaper."

In a letter to his staff, the Hon. Gavin Astor, chairman of the *Times,* before its take-over, said that that development "recognised that the age when newspaper proprietors could successfully run their newspapers as a sideline is fading into an age where the survival and prosperity of newspapers depended upon brilliant commercial and professional management." Which was putting into a nutshell what all the bother, all the inquiries by Royal Commissions and Intelligence Units, had been about. But still the essential problem remained: The newspaper, as an industry, is in a special category, but what can be done about it? And still there was no answer.

The EIU report said there was not much career structure for management, that too few journalists were brought in at the top or encouraged to take any role in management, that there was little training, and weakness in handling the unions. At middle management there was often a failure of communication from the top downwards so that there was no awareness of company policy. The responsibility for handling labour had long been abdicated to the trade unions and the Father of the Chapel was much more powerful than middle or junior management. Inevitably that had led to overmanning, restrictive practices, and waste. But restrictive practices were not as bad as generally believed. They did exist but did not materially affect the final success or failure of any newspaper, although they naturally affected the level of profit or loss.

The report, described by Lord Thomson as "a devastating indictment of Fleet-street," included one thought which journalists could take to heart: "Possibly brilliant editorial can carry poor management, whereas brilliant management cannot carry poor editorial."

By this time the press had been battered and buffetted by so many inquiries that it had good reason for feeling punch drunk. There had been the two Royal Commissions, the EIU, the Vassall inquiry, the two Prices and Incomes Board inquiries, besides the Cameron inquiry into the printing industry, which also impinged on the newspapers.

In a debate in the Commons the prime minister, Mr. Wilson, said that restrictive practices in the newspaper industry had "reached the dimensions of a national scandal," and blamed management for fear and timidity. The House of Lords went over the familiar ground again, but expressed the general view (with the expected dissentients) that it would be fatal for the press to accept any kind of financial help. Lord Rothermere said the press must remain financially independent, and even if one or two papers should lapse, that would be far better than taking government help. Lord Thomson said the British press was not efficient by good American or Canadian standards, and he admitted that about his own outfit. There was some very amateur management in Fleet-street. "What appals me is that some do not seem to realise their shortcomings and don't know what they should do about it."

In that, however, it seems that he was wrong because there began a tightening-up of efficiency, a recasting of company structures and an introduction of new methods into some of the most important newspaper houses.

In the fifteenth report of the Press Council, issued in the autumn of 1968, the chairman returned to the subject of "private and confidential," perhaps having in mind the episode of the *Guardian* and the EIU report. He said the council would not accept that when a document contained material of public interest the author could, by rubber-stamping it, impose an obligation of confidence on everyone into whose hands it might fall. If an editor came by it fairly and was not himself bound by the confidence, he must use his discretion about publishing it, satisfying himself first that it really was a public and not a private matter, and then asking himself whether its publication would do more harm than good.

He mentioned the case of the *Express and Star,* Wolverhampton, which was threatened with a libel action if it published a confidential report commissioned by the Dudley, Worcestershire, town council. The editor withheld publication to give the council a chance to apply to the court, but in the meantime the *Birmingham Post* got hold of the report and published it. The council took no action.

"This is a heartening example of editorial courage," wrote Lord Devlin, "which is the only quality that can, in the end, prevail against legal obscurity. . . . The great vice of obscurity is that it frightens the poor and the timid out of what may well be their legal rights. What the courageous editor has to appreciate is that only rarely will he be provided by his own lawyer with a safe conduct through the intricacies of libel. . . . The right demand to make upon him is for his estimate of the risks involved and on that and on the other factors in the case, the editor must take his own decision."

In most cases the lawyer could give him some idea of what the damages would be. Cases of libel were among the few that were still sent for trial by jury. The result was that the amount of damages awarded was always unpredictable and could be crippling; conceivably it could be so astronomical that an expensive appellate process was required to bring it down to earth.

A notorious example of a case such as Lord Devlin mentioned was the libel suits brought by a London company against the *Daily Mail* and the *Daily Telegraph,* both of whom had reported that the City of London fraud squad had been inquiring into the company's affairs. There had, in fact, been a police inquiry, but not of that nature. The chairman of the company issued a denial which the *Telegraph* published, but which the *Mail* did not. The jury awarded the company and its chairman between them, £117,000 damages against the *Mail,* and £100,000 against the *Telegraph*—an enormous tax-free total for the plaintiffs, and a record for British libel damages.

There was then no appeal against libel damages and the newspapers' only recourse was to apply for new trials on the question of damages. After a ten days' hearing these were ordered. One of the lords justices remarked that the damages awarded were "wholly unreasonable and out of all proportion to the injury suffered." The company appealed to the House of Lords against the order for new trials, but the appeal was dismissed and the damages were again described as "ridiculously out of proportion to the injury suffered." Later the actions were settled out of court and the total damages paid to the company and its chairman were agreed at £22,000. That sum alone could have bankrupted less opulent newspapers, and silenced two voices of a free press.

Even as it was, this case had a deplorable effect. The report on "Law and the Press" (issued by a joint committee of lawyers called Justice, and headed by Lord Shawcross and the International Press Institute) said: "Legal advisers of newspapers said that after these cases newspapers had been anxious to settle libel actions whatever the cost, and sometimes with little regard for advice that negotiations might effect a more economical settlement; they further stated that a result of such awards had been to revive dormant actions. For a time after these cases, it appeared that each newspaper was most reluctant to be the next to take a case to trial irrespective of its merit for fear it might be the victim of another astronomical award."

To continue with the Press Council. Its 1968 report recorded with great regret the resignation of Colonel Clissitt, at the age of seventy, from the secretaryship. Lord Devlin said he had done much to consolidate the council's position as a national institution and to win it international recognition. Colonel Clissitt was succeeded by Mr. Noel S. Paul who had been assistant secretary since 1964 after an all-round journalistic career on the Press Association, Home Counties newspapers, and the Liverpool *Daily Post,* where he was features editor. He had also served for seven years on the National Executive of the N.U.J.

The 1968 report carried an account of a complaint of intrusion made against the *Daily Sketch* in 1964 which had been held up by the council because legal proceedings had been instituted. The importance of the case, which concerned the publication of private matrimonial matters after an interview by a reporter, lay not in its details but because it was quoted by the council as an example of an improvement in the level of journalism. "The standards of 1964," said the adjudication, "would no longer apply, and it seems very unlikely that this kind of interview would now take place."

It was, indeed, a significant change, resulting in large measure from the public's aversion to certain journalistic practices, as shown by the Vassall affair, but due, also, to the influence of the Press Council. The fifteenth report noted that, for the second year in succession, the number of complaints had shown a fall. The total of 412 in 1966–67 was about 5 percent below that for the preceding year, while the figure for 1967–68 had decreased by a further 8 percent.

It would appear that the public were finding less to complain about in the newspapers, and the council now seemed to be placing more emphasis on its first object—"to preserve the established freedom of the British Press"—than on its third—"to consider complaints about the conduct of the Press." Although it cannot be said that the newspapers were more sinned against than sinning there were, as there nearly always had been, constant attempts in the courts and elsewhere to curb the powers and privileges of the press. That the price of liberty is eternal vigilance is much more than a cliché to the Press Council. The many instances in which it has fought for, or at the least pronounced on, the freedom of the press will be found in the following chapter, listing some of the typical cases it has dealt with, and some of the work it has performed.

13 Royalty—and Others

As has already been noted, one of the Press Council's first actions was to rebuke a newspaper for its handling of Princess Margaret's private affairs. The activities of the royal family, and the way they were recorded in the newspapers, continued to exercise it for some time. When it began, relations between the palace and the press were far from satisfactory, but after a few years they were put on a better footing, an outcome for which the council may claim much of the credit.

Soon after the Princess Margaret affair, a complaint was received from a member of the public about a series of articles in the *Sunday Pictorial* during 1954 by a former valet of Prince Philip who wrote about his life in royal employment. The editor said the material was authentic and was not offensive. The council took his side and told the complainant that it had long been the custom for members of the staffs of royal households to write books about life therein, and no objection had usually been taken provided they did not betray intimate confidences or cause distress.

This view was challenged by Commander (afterwards Sir Richard) Colville, the press secretary to the Queen, who disclosed that one of the conditions of service of people entering the royal household was a ban on giving information to the press about the royal family. Only a small number had broken this trust. The commander added: "You will, I am sure, readily agree that the Queen is entitled to expect that her family will attain the privacy at home which all other families are entitled to enjoy."

The council welcomed this statement as clarifying the position in January 1955, and issued it for publication, expressing the hope that newspapers and periodicals would act upon it. Later, Commander

Colville called attention to a series of articles in *Woman* by a former
deputy controller of Supply entitled, "I Shopped for the Royal Family."
There was no suggestion that these articles, which appeared in 1956
were offensive or indiscreet, but the council were reminded of the
request that the press should respect the Queen's privacy. The writer
of these articles, it transpired, had given no specific undertaking not to
communicate with the press.

This case triggered off an article in the council's third annual report, of 1951, discussing the whole relationship between palace and
press. It recalled all that had gone before and commented that English
literature had been enriched by the writings of royal servants who,
through personal glimpses of the great, had made an invaluable contribution to the history of the country. Nevertheless, it continued,
"there is a marked difference between the reminiscences of discerning
and cultured minds set down at a later date than the events they por-
tray, and the current, ill-informed, and tasteless tittle-tattle of people
who may not even be able to write readable English. It is as a protection against this sort of offensive trivia that servants in the Household have, of recent years, been forbidden under contract to communicate to the Press information about the Royal Family.

"When, however, the Press Secretary at the Palace says, 'the Queen
is entitled to expect that her family will attain the privacy at home
which all other families are entitled to enjoy,' it must be asked whether
the Royal Family can be compared with any other family or put on
the same plane as ordinary people. The private lives of public men and
women, especially Royal persons, have always been the subject of a
natural curiosity. That this is so is one of the consequences of fame or
eminence or sincere national affection. Everything, therefore, that
touches the Crown is of public interest and concern.

"It is the duty of newspapers to record the movements of Her
Majesty and the members of her family, and it is the pleasure of the
Queen's subjects to read of them if only as a token of the affection
existing between Crown and people. But, plainly, there are limits
beyond which Royal tolerance or endurance should not be asked to
go. Where should these limits be set? On the one hand is the desire
of newspapers to obtain the news. Interest in the Royal Family is so
intense that if newspapers do not obtain satisfaction from official
channels they are almost forced to consult unofficial sources. It was to

prevent this less desirable alternative that there evolved over the years a Press Secretariat at Buckingham Palace. If the relations between this Department and the Press were all that could be desired there would perhaps be fewer complaints about the newspapers than there are now.

"But, unfortunately, this is not always the case. The comment is sometimes heard from news editors that the Secretariat neither understands nor gives the news they want, or the necessary guidance on what is, or is not, likely to become news. The Council records this with regret, but it would be lacking in candour if it pretended that dealings between the Press and the Press Department in the Royal Household were always happy or harmonious. As against this it must be said that some newspapers descended to the lowest levels of bad taste and worse manners in their references, over many weeks, to Princess Margaret and Group-Captain Townsend."

The article went on to mention the *Daily Mirror*'s headlines: COME ON MARGARET! PLEASE MAKE UP YOUR MIND. FOR PETE'S SAKE PUT HIM OUT OF HIS MISERY. Such coarse impertinence, it said, was an insult to the Princess and an offence against the decencies of British public life, and added: "The Council has thought it right to recount these matters at length in order that some of the difficulties as well as some of the sins of the Press may be better understood. The newspapers always must, and always will, give every possible scrap of news about the Royal Family, but the selection and presentation of each item comes down, in the end, to a matter of taste, and upon that the public must be the judge."

The council offered three suggestions:

1. That an improvement in the quality and supply of news and guidance from the press secretariat to the press should be sought;

2. That newspapers should refrain from tempting royal servants to break their contracts by offering large sums for their "stories";

3. That royal news should at all times be handled with discretion.

The council also issued the following statement for general circulation: "It must be stressed that public interest in the lives of the Royal Family is intense, and rightly so, and that newspaper comment on, for example, Princess Margaret's future is justified, but this involves newspapers in a great responsibility in the way they deal with both fact and comment, and in maintaining a standard of good taste. The Council feels that certain newspapers have offended against good taste and have done considerable ill services to the reputation of the Press."

The council asked editors to state why they thought the news service from the palace to be inadequate, and to give instances. They were collated and discussed several times by the General Purposes Committee with Commander Colville who attended committee meetings for that purpose. An example of the view held by newspapers was quoted in the next annual report. It was from the *News-Chronicle,* which said: "The lack of confidence which now exists between Fleet-street and the Palace does genuine harm not only at home but abroad. It is a positive encouragement to rumour-mongers."

Commander Colville came to a meeting of the full council in 1958 at which the matter was thrashed out against a background of complaints and suggestions from newspapers and news agencies. One of the chief criticisms was that the press department at the palace was understaffed. With the Queen's approval an additional press secretary was appointed, after which there was greater flexibility and the news flowed more smoothly.

There were still, however, times when the royal family found the pressure of newspaper intrusion well-nigh intolerable. When Prince Charles, as a young boy, attended a gymnasium in Chelsea, the parents of other boys were so badgered by reporters that the Prince had to discontinue. There was an occasion when Princess Margaret refused an invitation to go skiing in Austria because she realised that she would get no peace from newspapermen. The Queen herself sometimes thought seriously of giving up attending the polo games at Windsor because she was the constant target of photographers when she was trying to relax away from the castle or the palace. But when the council began circulating requests that the press, after being given facilities at the start, should allow the royal children to pursue their education and recreation without the embarrassment of constant publicity, the situation improved.

That the sense of strain between palace and press had diminished by 1968 was shown when some members of the public complained to the council about pictures showing the Queen in bed after the birth of Prince Edward, published on October 2 in the *Daily Express.*

In printing these pictures the newspaper thought it necessary to give the reasons why it had done so. It said: "Already they have been published in France. The American magazine *Life* has bought them. They are appearing in Australia, Canada, and other Commonwealth countries, as well as throughout Europe. While it was never the Queen's intention that these informal photographs should have been circulated, their world-wide publication outside of Britain has created an anomaly which can only be resolved by letting the British people see them."

On the day the pictures were published it was reported that a Buckingham Palace spokesman had said: "The Queen would have preferred that these photographs which are of so personal a nature had not been published." A few hours later the Press Council issued the following statement: "The Press Council announces that the circumstances attending the publication in the *Daily Express* on 2 October 1968 of two photographs of Her Majesty the Queen in bed after the birth of Prince Edward are to be considered by the Council."

On the next day the *Daily Express* published more pictures and, in a leading article, criticised the issue of the statement by the council, saying that the Editor had been given no opportunity to answer it.

Subsequently, Mr. Derek Marks, the editor, told the council that when the pictures were offered to him he telephoned the palace to that effect. He also sent copies of the pictures to the palace. He said that while approval for their publication was not given, no specific request was made to him not to publish. "I was told that it was a matter entirely within my discretion," he wrote. "That discretion was exercised in the light of the fact that the pictures were, in any case, going to be published throughout the world, and in the absence of any direct prohibition from the Palace there was no reason for not publishing them in Britain. The pictures themselves were of a most seemly nature and could be calculated only to show the Queen and the Royal family in a most favourable light.

"Since the pictures have been published no one connected with the Palace has made any complaint to your Council or to me. Indeed, the first reaction that I received to the statement issued by your Council on the day of publication (to which I shall be referring later) was a telephone call from the Palace to say that they had no hand in it and did not wish to make any complaint. That, so far as I am concerned, should be an end to the matter. The more so since in the past the Palace has not hesitated to complain to your Council when it was deemed necessary.

"I feel that there is an important question of principle raised here. Having received the information that I did from the Palace I do not feel obliged to defend myself in answer to complaints made by people in no way connected with Her Majesty, and complaints, moreover, which it seems to me on any view of the matter were for the most part, if not entirely, invited by the premature and, in my considered opinion, ill-judged statement issued by your Council on the day of publication. You must be aware that this statement was issued without any reference to me. No inquiry was made to ascertain whether or not I had made any approach to the Palace and, if so, with what result. So far as I can recall no similar statement has ever been issued by the Press Council. If my recollection is at fault I suggest that the precedent is a bad one and should never in future be followed."

Here, once again, were two familiar grievances of editors about Press Council procedure: 1. That statements are issued concerning their newspapers without giving them an opportunity of rebuttal; 2. That complaints come from sources which have no concern, apart from being newspaper readers, of the matter at issue.

Mr. William Heseltine, an Australian who succeeded Sir Richard Colville as press secretary to the Queen in 1968, issued a statement saying that as the Queen had made no complaint to the council she did not wish that the matter should be pursued on her account. "Her Majesty trusts, however, that it will not be allowed to form a precedent for the future publication of private photographs, either of her own family or those of any of her people."

The council, in its adjudication, replied to the editor's two points of principle. It said:

"The Council has from its inception taken the view that, since it is concerned with the standards which ought to be maintained by the Press, it will entertain a complaint from any member of the public alleging a lapse from such standards, whether or not the complainant is personally concerned. Furthermore, the Council considers that, once it is plain that the conduct of a newspaper has rightly or wrongly aroused widespread questioning, the Council's duty to consider it does not depend solely on whether or not a formal complaint is made. The Council is expressly charged under its constitution with the task of maintaining the character of the British Press in accordance with the highest professional and commercial standards. Any deviation from these standards by a British newspaper inevitably reflects on the credit of the British Press as a whole. The Council cannot therefore uphold the editor's objection that he is not required to answer any complaint that is not made by or on behalf of Her Majesty.

"The Council also approved the statement issued on its behalf on October 2 and does not regard it as premature or ill-judged. The publication of the pictures coincided with a meeting of the Council's Complaints Committee. Having regard to the announcement from the Palace published at the same time and quoted above and to criticism in other papers than the *Daily Express,* it appeared to the Committee that the Council could not, without shirking its responsibility, ignore the question of whether the *Daily Express* had acted properly or improperly. The Committee resolved that the matter should be considered at its next meeting; and in response to a number of inquiries about what action, if any, the Council was taking, authorised the announcement that the circumstances attending publication would be considered by the Council. As a matter of courtesy the *Daily Express* was notified shortly before the announcement was made. The editor of the *Daily Express* seems to have read into the announcement some sort of condemnation of his action, and on that reading is naturally aggrieved that he was offered no opportunity of stating his case. The Council does not believe that the statement is capable of any such construction. It said that the Council would consider the circumstances, and it meant that and no more.

"The Council has considered the circumstances and is greatly indebted to Her Majesty's Press Secretary for setting them out so fully. The Council finds that the editor acted promptly in notifying the Palace of his possession of the photographs. If the Queen had directly requested that they should not be published, it would plainly have been wrong of the *Daily Express* to have done so. But it is clear that in the case of these particular photographs the publication was left to the discretion of the editor. The Council considers that the editor did not exercise his discretion improperly. The complaints are rejected."

One fear which haunts British newspaper editors is of falling into contempt of court, a judicial power so ill-defined and subject to such personal interpretations from the bench that it is often hard to say where it begins and ends. Newspapers are also extremely shy of criticising judicial verdicts, even though some judges have stated that the press is absolutely free to question their decisions so long as prejudice is not imputed to them. In general, "contempt," as applied to newspapers, insists that nothing must be said or done by way of newsgathering, of report or comment, to impede the processes of the law or to prejudice a fair trial. This is as it should be, although it does lead to journalistic subterfuges so transparent as to become ridiculous. For example, if one man shoots another and is apprehended, the newspapers can only say that "a man is assisting the police in their inquiries" even though everyone knows who has done it. Only when he is charged can he be named and from that moment he disappears from the news until court proceedings begin.

All very right and proper, no doubt; but constant attempts are made to enlarge the net of contempt. Since the Press Council was established, the law of contempt as defined in an Edinburgh judgment presses far more harshly on Scottish than on English newspapers. In England papers have been punished for offences against "contempt" which they did not know existed. There has been a movement, also, to push contempt beyond the courts of justice and to make it apply to tribunals of inquiry. All these provocations have been resisted by the Press Council.

Its 1958 report noted with concern serious encroachments on press freedom resulting from new rulings on contempt of court. All senior editorial workers, it said, had known for many years of the dangers of this law. It had been little written about and there were few decided cases to give guidance. Three contemporary cases were mentioned:

1. The *People* was on October 11, 1956, convicted of contempt because it published an article relating to legal proceedings about which it had no knowledge, and was admitted to have no knowledge. It had to pay, in all, fines of two thousand pounds: This judgment meant that a newspaper could be found guilty of contempt of court if it printed a report about a man in financial difficulties in one part of the country without being aware (which it could not reasonably be) that he was on remand for fraud one hundred miles away.

2. Newsagents who circulated an American journal commenting on a notorious murder case then proceeding in England on May 10, 1957, were found guilty of contempt and told that the defence of innocent dissemination was not available to them: Such a verdict obviously put

serious obstacles in the way of the flow of international news and comment, because the distributors would find it impracticable to ensure that what they sold of foreign origin respected the requirements of our law. They might therefore decide not to sell foreign publications.

3. The *Daily Mail* was on February 13, 1957, fined for contempt and ordered to pay costs for reporting matters heard before a judge in chambers (customarily in private): This was thought to be the most dangerous judgment of the three because no question of prejudicing a fair trial could arise from publishing the result of proceedings in chambers.

These cases caused grave disquietude. The *Times* argued that, quietly and unobtrusively, within two years, while parts of the press were under a cloud, judges had acquired new powers to punish for contempt, without jury or right of appeal, newspapers which had incurred the displeasure of the courts. There were protests from legal journals and leading jurists who demanded changes in the law. The Bar Council urged the right of appeal in contempt cases, and Justice, that influential body of lawyers and journalists, set up a subcommittee to consider the question. The Press Council said the freedom of the courts to administer the law without interference, and the right of the citizen to fair process without being prejudiced by irresponsible newspaper comments were as necessary to the liberty of the subject as was the freedom of the press. Nevertheless, the press was seriously disturbed by any change in the application of the law which would tend to muzzle newspapers unfairly.

Two years later the council reported a much more serious inroad, this time in Scotland. A man had been detained by the English police in connection with a murder in Scotland, and before he was charged the *Scottish Daily Mail* published an article about him and the crime, including interviews with people who might be witnesses at a trial, and a photograph of the man and his wife taken on their wedding day. This was admittedly a risky thing for the paper to do, and its plea that there was some distinction between reports concerning a man who had been arrested but not charged, and one who had been charged was, perhaps not surprisingly, rejected.

But, fining the editor five hundred pounds and his company five thousand pounds, Lord Clyde, the lord justice general, delivered a judgment which, for all practical purposes, stopped newspapers from making any extensive reporting of criminal cases. "It is no part of our system," he said, "that there should be a sort of preliminary trial of the case conducted in public by a newspaper, feeding to its readers pieces of evidence that the newspaper has unearthed, and which may be ultimately brought out in their proper setting at a trial in court. . . . All these investigations, and all these interrogations of possible witnesses should be done by the criminal authorities and not by the Press, and the results should only be published to the world when the ultimate trial takes place . . . if the criminal authorities have not specifically asked for a photograph to be published in the Press, the Press must not procure or obtain a photograph of any person involved in the investigation and publish it either during the investigations by the criminal authorities or during the trial itself."

The effect of this judgment was to prevent newspapers writing anything beyond the bare facts at any stage of a criminal action, or to publish pictures of any incident which might possibly end in legal proceedings. It could be dangerous even to print pictures of cars involved in road accidents.

The Press Council took this matter up with the Scottish Home Office, saying that the judgment of Lord Clyde might prevent press publication of information which the public had a right to know. It asked for clarification of the law and said there should be, in Scotland, a right of appeal against findings of contempt of court as there was to be introduced in England and Wales in the Administration of Justice Bill. The Scottish Daily Newspaper Society also presented a Memorial to the secretary of state for Scotland asking that Scottish law on contempt should be brought into line with English law which, in several important respects, was less severe. The minister, however, considered that the stricter rules conformed to the needs of Scottish criminal procedure and said the public interest did not call for any amendment in the law of contempt.

The most disquieting episode came with the Aberfan disaster of 1966. A coal tip at Aberfan, in South Wales, collapsed and overwhelmed a school, some cottages and a farm, killing 144 people of whom 116 were children. The government set up a tribunal under the Tribunals of Inquiry Act to investigate the calamity. In announcing it Sir Elwyn Jones, the attorney general, gave warning that it was undesirable for the press, radio, or television to make any comment on matters which the inquiry would have to probe. These, he said, might have legal consquences which were perhaps not appreciated. The tribunal would have to consider whether such comments would demand investigation by the High Court as to whether there had been contempt of the tribunal. His remarks aroused strong criticism in press and Parliament to which Lord Gardiner, the lord chancellor, replied that it was high time somebody reminded the newspapers and television what the law was. He thought it possible that they imagined the law of contempt did not apply to a tribunal. "But it does," he added, "and they were rightly reminded that it does."

This facile statement was severely handled by the Press Council in a special twenty-page pamphlet, *The Aberfan Inquiry and Contempt of Court* (1967), examining all the considerations involved. These are of such great importance to journalists that extensive quotation is now offered.

The pamphlet said the council accepted that when a body was set up to ascertain facts and report on a matter of public importance it was undesirable that it should be hampered by embarrassing comment or that wide-ranging discussion should lead the public to jump prematurely to conclusions.

"But to refrain from embarrassing comment or discussion does not mean complete silence. Comment can be useful and helpful and then it is not undesirable. Anyway, undesirable comment is not illegal. It is doubtful if even a complete discussion of the merits of a case awaiting trial by a judge would amount to contempt of court, at any rate in England. It is only when there is a real risk that publication of matter is likely to interfere with the course of justice or prejudice the impartial trial of an action that contempt of court occurs."

The lord chief justice was quoted as saying that embarrassment which has no effect on impartiality is not necessarily contempt of court. "This distinction—between any comment and prejudiced comment— becomes of the first importance if this branch of the law of contempt is to be applied to tribunals under the 1921 Act. If the rule is that all comment is prejudicial, it is applicable with as much ease to tribunals of inquiry as to courts of law. But if the rule is qualified, it will be found, for reasons further developed in this memorandum, to be very difficult to apply to a tribunal of inquiry."

The House of Commons barred reference to matters it had sent to a tribunal until the report was published, but resolutions of the Commons formed no part of the law of the land. "It would be a serious interference with the freedom of speech if it were ever established that subjects which Parliament chooses not to discuss should not be discussed at all." Admitting that it was alive to the dangers that could arise from persistent questioning of potential witnesses, the pamphlet said: "But interference, intentional or unintentional, with witnesses differs completely from comment, well-advised or ill-advised, on the issues with which the tribunal has to deal. Remedies designed to cure the former need not touch the latter. Yet it will be found that, repeatedly, Government spokesmen in both Houses defended the position which the Government had taken up on the right to comment, by reference to the need for protecting potential witnesses.

"To sum up, the existing law, as decided by the courts, is that publication of information or comment on issues pending in a court of law is contempt of court only when there is a real risk that it will be likely to interfere with the impartiality of the court. The courts have never yet been invited to embark on the task of applying this principle of law to a public inquiry.

"The 1921 Act expressly applies the law of contempt to inquiries under it. Contempt can broadly be divided into contempt in the face of the court and contempt by outside interference in various ways with the course of justice. Contempt of the first sort covers misconduct at the proceedings, such as the refusal of a witness to answer questions. A tribunal under the 1921 Act is given power to order witnesses to attend and answer questions, and so there must obviously be some sanction for disobedience. It is contempt of the second sort that gives rise to difficulties."

There were obvious differences between the administration of justice by trial and the eliciting of facts by inquiry. "The result of a trial is a verdict or judgment and if justice miscarries a grievous wrong may be done for which it is difficult to find a remedy. Hence the need for protection over-riding the ordinary right to comment on public matters. The result of an inquiry is a report to Parliament. If the judgment of the tribunal is influenced or distracted, the worst that can happen is that Parliament is misinformed. That is very undesirable, but the possibility that Parliament may be misinformed as a result of Press or outside comment is not a ground for suppressing it.

"A trial often means trial by jury. An inquiry under the 1921 Act is held by persons of high judicial or professional qualifications.

"A trial is upon evidence which is confined by rules; an inquiry raises no precise issues and any sort of material can be considered.

"A trial is conducted before permanent members of a judiciary. An inquiry is conducted *ad hoc* by the Government of the day."

Since the susceptibility of the lay mind to outside influence may be considerable, "where there is trial by jury . . . virtually any comment on the issues before the jury may amount to contempt." Since most cases which excited public comment were trials by jury this probably accounted for the popular belief that all comment on matters *sub judice* was prohibited. But judges (as opposed to juries) should be able to put out of their minds the embarrassing, irrelevant, and inadmissible, so that their impartiality was unlikely to be affected by it. "There is, in fact, no record of any case of importance in which comment has been held to prejudice a fair trial by a judge alone.

"If the members of a 1921 tribunal are to be likened either to judges or to jurymen, it is obviously the former that they resemble; so it seems at the outset very unlikely that any comment on the issues before the tribunal would be held to be prejudicial. But one must go further than that. There is a distinction between judges and juries on the one hand and the members of a tribunal on the other, which makes it almost impossible to visualise a case in which comment on the matters pending before a tribunal could amount to contempt of court. The distinction is that judges and juries cannot decide for themselves what facts they will consider, whereas the members of a tribunal can. . . . The area of their investigation is usually contained in terms of reference so wide as to make it a description and not a definition. . . . If a newspaper article suggests to a member a point that he thinks worth following up, so much the better. . . .

"No member of a tribunal is going to certify that he was, or was likely to be, influenced by silly comment or information he considered irrelevant. But he would hardly be doing his duty if he put out of his mind valuable comment or information simply because he read it in a newspaper. Thus the application of this branch of the law of contempt to tribunals of inquiry would produce the absurd result that silly and irresponsible comment on trivial and irrelevant information would not be contempt because it would not be effective, while serious and helpful comment and information that the tribunal thought following up would be contempt because attention was paid to it."

There were other significant differences between a trial and a tribunal. One was that trial judges were not chosen by governments, whereas the judge presiding at a tribunal and its members were so chosen, and this gave an immense advantage to the government. "There is no known case in which a government has consciously abused this advantage . . . but there have been cases in the past where the choice has been thought to reflect too closely, no doubt unconsciously, the government's choice of what is sound. There ought, therefore, to be complete freedom to criticise any appointment."

Another difference was that cases determined before a court of law were determined by the law. Cases before a 1921 tribunal were determined by the government of the day. "There must be as complete freedom to criticise the motives of the government in taking this decision as there is when it takes any other decision of policy. The resentment caused by the insinuation [made in a television interview] that the Aberfan inquiry would be only a whitewashing one is understandable. Nevertheless, it is wrong to use the law to drive this sort of comment underground.

"In some, at least, of the cases in which there has been Press interference in the administration of justice, some part of the blame must be borne by the uncertain state of the law. It is quite wrong to suppose that the demands of justice would be automatically overridden by newspapers in search of sensation unless they were deterred by the threat of heavy penalties. There is not, so far as the Press Council is aware, a single case in which a request (although no sanction is attached to it) made by the judiciary not to publish definite material has been deliberately disregarded. . . . If, to the existing uncertainty, there is to be added the profound obscurity which at present surrounds the application of the law to tribunals under the 1921 Act, the editor's dilemma will become intolerable."

Finally, the pamphlet suggested that a Royal Commission or a committee should be appointed to inquire whether it was necessary or desirable that comment or information on matters which are the subject of an inquiry under the 1921 Act should be restricted.

As a direct result of the pamphlet, the home secretary, Mr. Callaghan, appointed Lord Justice Salmon in April 1968 to be chairman of a committee "to review the law of contempt as it affects comments on, or statements made about, matters referred to a tribunal of inquiry under the Tribunals of Inquiry (Evidence) Act, 1921."

The Salmon Committee reported in June 1969. It recommended that comment should not be prohibited at any time on the subject matter of an inquiry, and that nothing said or done before a tribunal had been actually appointed should constitute contempt. In other words comment would be unrestricted after the government had announced its intention of setting up a tribunal but before the members had been named.

After the appointment it would be contempt if anything was said or done about any evidence relevant to the inquiry which was intended or obviously likely to alter, distort, destroy, or withhold such evidence from the tribunal. The committee also recommended that the chairman of a tribunal might request that no interview with certain named persons should be published, though he should not impose a legal obligation to comply.

Another recommendation was that the law of contempt should be retained for any unjustifiable attack on the integrity of a tribunal member, and for anything said or done before a tribunal which, had it been a court of law, would have been punishable as contempt. It was felt that a tribunal was no more likely to be influenced by comment than a judge sitting alone or in an appellate court. When there was a crisis of public confidence in a matter of nationwide concern it was much more in the public interest that there should be complete freedom of discussion by press, radio, and television. To curtail or prohibit such discussion was likely to increase public unease and was contrary to our concept of a free society. Freedom of comment might also lead to fresh factors being brought to light or the airing of new theories which might help the tribunal to arrive at the truth.

These recommendations were open to such wide and endless interpretations that they have done little to reassure editors. So concerned was the press over this whole question that, in 1969, a two-year research project into it, partly financed by the International Publishing Corporation, the N.P.A., and the Midland News Association, was begun at Birmingham University.

Successful endeavours were made by the Press Council concerning a less momentous matter in the courts of law. It drew attention to the neglect of some clerks to the justices to provide reporters with the proper identification of defendants, who often appeared in the dock without any reference to their names and addresses. If these were wrongly given in a newspaper and an action for defamation was brought, it was not enough to plead that they appeared on the charge sheet in court, for that document was not legally privileged. If, however, a defendant was asked at the beginning of a case to state his name and address, the information so given would be privileged and the newspaper could not be held liable if it were false. As a result of personal representations by Lord Devlin the Home Office circularised all clerks to the justices inviting them to adopt the practice of having names and addresses clearly mentioned in open court, or else supplying reporters beforehand with copies of lists already prepared for court purposes.

The Bodkins Adams case of 1956, in which a doctor was accused of murdering one of his patients, and was acquitted, led to a re-examination of reporting such cases in the press, and to an ultimate change in the law.

Evidence in serious criminal offences is first heard in a magistrates' court, or court of first instance, to decide whether there is enough substance in the charge to send the accused for trial by jury. Usually, only the case for the prosecution is outlined, the defence being reserved for the trial. It has often been held, and as often denied, that these proceedings may prejudice the accused at his trial. The argument came to a head when certain adverse evidence was given against Dr. Bodkin Adams before the magistrates, but was not repeated in the Assize court, and it was thought that that could conceivably have led to his being found guilty because the jury might have been influenced by what they had previously read of the case. In his summing-up at the trial the judge thought it would have been wiser if the magistrates had sat in private, as they were entitled to do if they so wished.

After this, the situation threatened to become chaotic because various benches took different views of their duty. In one murder case the public were excluded, while in another, an application to hear a murder charge in private was refused. The Institute of Journalists, hoping to have the confusion cleared up, asked the government to appoint a committee of inquiry. As a result the home secretary, Mr.

R. A. (afterwards Lord) Butler, set up a committee in 1957 under Lord Tucker "to consider whether proceedings before examining magistrates should continue to take place in open court and if so whether it is necessary or desirable that any restriction should be placed on the publication of reports of such proceedings."

The Press Council at once submitted a memorandum to the committee opposing any change in the procedure, and making these points:

1. The argument that preliminary hearings should be in private is based on inadequate knowledge of the workings of justice. The opening of a case before magistrates puts a salutary check on gossip;

2. At this hearing the accused learns at least the outline of the case against him. So does the public and witnesses sometimes come forward with valuable evidence, for or against;

3. Those who wished to curb press reports seemed ready to admit the public into court. This meant an inadequate and often misleading method of reporting by word of mouth;

4. The Press Council dismissed the suggestion that jurymen could be prejudiced by reading reports of the preliminary hearings. The ability of juries to come to decisions only on evidence they had themselves heard, had been proved;

5. The work of magistrates should be done within the full knowledge of the public;

6. The council thought it unnecessary to give magistrates any more power than they already possessed to hear in private evidence about indictable offences.

The council was invited to submit written evidence to support its statement that witnesses sometimes came forward with valuable evidence, and this it did. There are cases on record. One concerns a motorist who was alleged to have ignored traffic lights and, as a result, to have caused a fatal accident. Another man, who read about the proceedings in a local paper, happened to know that those lights were out of order on the material day and his evidence prevented what could have been a grave miscarriage of justice. The murderer in the notorious brides-in-the-bath case many years ago was brought to justice because someone read in a paper the report of a coroner's inquest on a woman found dead in a bath, which reminded him of an exactly similar occurrence reported in the press some time before, and many miles away. And even while the Tucker Committee was being discussed a man who had been "identified" was committed for trial for robbery with violence, but another man, who had read the committal proceedings came forward and confessed to the crime.

The Tucker Committee reported in 1958. While agreeing that it could not be established that trials were prejudiced by reports of committal proceedings, it said there was a widespread belief that they were, and recommended that newspaper reports should record only the name of the accused, the charge, and the court's decision until the trial or unless the accused had been discharged by the magistrates. The hearings should, however, continue to be open to the public.

In spite of the authority of the Tucker Report, the Press Council insisted that there should be no restriction on reports of criminal proceedings. It acknowledged that the fair trial of an accused person must always be the paramount consideration but pointed out that the report itself had remarked that "it is a serious matter to fetter the freedom of the Press to report what is done in public by a public body." It considered that the decision to recommend a breach of this fundamental principle was based on a misunderstanding of the nature of publicity in a modern society and of the functions of the press in relation to it.

The Tucker Committee recognised as weighty objections to committal proceedings being held in camera: (a) A general distaste for the idea of justice being administered in a court of law behind closed doors; (b) If examining justices were to dismiss a charge when sitting in camera it might be suspected that some favouritism had been shown to the accused; (c) There might be suspicion that the conduct of the proceedings did not come up to the normal high standard of magistrates' courts.

The Press Council said it was unreal to suppose that such objections could be overcome simply by admitting the public to the court. In the ordinary, unsensational case, the public might not even be present. In the exceptional case the court might be crowded with sensation seekers who would not be qualified to detect signs of favouritism or judicial misbehaviour. The only way suspicion could be dispelled was the presence of trained reporters with the means of criticism at their disposal. To admit the public while denying facilities to the organs of publicity was to mistake the forms of publicity for the substance.

After further arguments the council submitted that the compromise solution proposed by the Tucker Committee was bad in principle and in practice would not meet at all realistically the weighty objections which the report itself set forth. The council's attitude was largely supported by the Law Society. The government took no action on the report, and it was not until 1965, seven years later, when a Labour government was in power, that the proposals were to be adopted, with the proviso that if the accused applied for a removal of the restriction the court would allow a full report.

These provisions were included in the Criminal Justice Bill which did not pass into an act without considerable protests from the press. Early in 1967 a deputation of newspaper proprietors, editors, and other journalists waited on the home secretary, Mr. Roy Jenkins, and told him that the restrictions were contrary to the public interest and would create new difficulties in newspaper production. Later, the Press Council put out a statement condemning the bill's provision to allow the public to attend committal proceedings but to deny newspapers the right to publish more than a formal record. This acceptance of the principle that justice should be administered in public, it said, with a restriction that confined knowledge of what was done to the few members of the community who could afford time to attend the court made a mockery of the principle it professed to support.

"The absurdity of the provision is heightened by the fact that whereas newspaper proprietors, editors, and publishers responsible for a written report of a committal hearing unauthorised by the bill would be liable to a heavy fine (of up to five hundred pounds), any member of the public could go away from the court and talk freely about what is said and done without danger of prosecution. Apparently he could relate his version of the proceedings to a public meeting with the same immunity. The dangers of rumour and distortion of fact that could arise from this state of affairs ought not to need emphasis. The Press Council continues to protest against mock publicity whether it relates to legal proceedings or anything else."

The council's objections were of no avail. The proposals passed into law, and thus one more gag was applied to the voice of a free press.

One matter which had troubled the press and also the Press Council almost from its outset was the tendency of some local authorities to exclude newspaper reporters from meetings which they were entitled to attend. Their rights were secured under the Local Authorities (Admission of the Press to Meetings) Act of 1908. This measure did allow local authorities temporarily to exclude the press when, in the opinion of a majority of council members, the nature of the business made it advisable to do so in the public interest. Reporters had no statutory right to be present at committee meetings. Some councils, therefore, adopted the practice of resolving themselves into a committee of their whole membership with the sole purpose of keeping their discussions secret. The Press Council and other journalistic bodies had more than once protested against this practice and had asked for a tightening of the law. But in 1959 Mr. Henry (afterwards Lord) Brooke, the minister concerned with local government, had said the argument could be better resolved by good will than by legislation.

But things took a more dramatic turn when the printing industry dispute of 1959 stopped publication of provincial newspapers. Emergency editions were prepared in some cities but several Labour-controlled councils declared these to be "black," and instructed members and council officials to refuse to give any information to their reporters. The Nottingham City Council excluded the press from its meetings, but allowed the BBC to be present, the town clerk having advised that the BBC was "the public," but the press was not. The Press Council, in an emergency resolution, condemned the action of these councils as a "gross violation of the right of the subject to be kept informed of the proceedings of his elected representatives," and sent it to the minister.

The ministry at once wrote to the Nottingham Council reminding them of the legal rights of the press and saying the council's action was contrary to the spirit of the act and to the principles which local authorities should observe in their relations with the press. The minister was wholly out of sympathy with any council which deprived the local electors of the opportunity to inform themselves from press reports about council business, and with any local authorities who took sides in an industrial dispute. He was "gravely concerned" that the actions of some authorities during the printing dispute suggested that they attached little importance to keeping the electorate informed. The sting of this severe rebuke came in the tail which threatened new statutory obligations and a new procedure to force recalcitrant councils to come to heel.

A sequel to this affair was the Public Bodies (Admission to Meetings) Act of 1960, a private member's measure which had the support of the government. Under it the press gained the right of admission to any committee of a public body specified in the schedule of the act whose members consisted of the whole membership of the body. Local authorities and other bodies were authorised to receive advice in private, as the difficulty of receiving it from officials and others in the presence of the press was recognised. The press could be excluded, but only after a resolution, whenever publicity was deemed to be prejudicial to the public interest.

Thus obscurantist councils were deprived of the device to keep the press out by going, as a body, into committee. But they quickly discovered that if only one member were absent it would be legal to resolve the remainder into committee, which they did. So, in some places, the public are still being deprived of their right to full information by local jacks-in-office who dislike the press.

What has come to be known as "cheque-book journalism," or the purchase of news or articles from prominent or nefarious people, takes several forms. One is "body-snatching," or the spiriting away of a person in the public eye by a newspaper which has bought the exclusive rights to his story. Another is buying, usually at high prices, of unsavoury or criminal memoirs. A third is payment to witnesses at notorious trials. These various facets of the same practice—or malpractice—came within the purview of the Press Council, which denounced them all.

Its first use of the phrase "cheque-book journalism" in an annual report, that of 1963, arose from an undignified scramble among a number of Glasgow journalists anxious to secure the story of a man who had been discharged on a "not proven" verdict from a charge of murder. As he left the court he was met by a "surging, jostling crowd of reporters" and some "tough thugs." It was stated that, in the mêlée, reporters were struck to the ground, an iron gate was torn from its hinges, a policeman was injured, and a knife was flashed. An inquiry by the Glasgow branch of the N.U.J. elicited that three reporters had been felled; that the man whose story was wanted—the "quarry" he might be called—was, in the confusion, bundled by the representatives of one newspaper into the car belonging to another; that one of his friends was "hitting out at everyone in sight with a pair of crutches"; that three separate newspapers believed they had signed up the quarry;

and that one of them succeeded in taking him to a hideout. The N.U.J. blamed editors and news-desk pressure for this unseemly episode and asked the Press Council to condemn cheque-book journalism and body-snatching techniques.

The incident occurred in November 1961 and was reported in 1962 to the council which then examined statements by seventeen witnesses, including the chief constable of Glasgow, who denied that some of the more lurid incidents had taken place. Four editors supported the traditional right to purchase a story deemed to be of interest, but three opposed it. The council found that it was not clear to what extent the journalists had been responsible for the fracas and thought accounts of it had been exaggerated. It did, however, regard this deplorable affair as a lowering of journalistic standards and condemned the methods used.

The subject came up again when, in May 1963, the Vassall Report was debated in Parliament. On that occasion, Mr. Harold Wilson, then the leader of the Opposition, said the press should stop the odious practice of buying for large sums the memoirs of convicted criminals. It had long been the practice in Britain that no one could make a profit out of proven crime. "This ought to be stopped, along with the undignified scramble in court if a man is found guilty, as journalists jostle one another in their efforts to buy his memoirs." A few months later the government were asked in the House of Lords if such practices by some newspapers could be referred to the Press Council. Lord Hailsham, the then leader of that House, replied that the council was reconstituting itself but might well consider this an appropriate subject on which to express an opinion.

As previously mentioned, it did so towards the end of 1963 in its pronouncement on the press and the Profumo affair. But a definitive statement was still needed, and this was issued in 1965, after long and careful examination of the whole question.

Noting that the phrase "cheque-book journalism" was of recent introduction, the council said it could cover many things from entertaining a contact to buying discreditable memoirs for thousands of pounds. It was fundamentally the power of the purse, a power which, misused, could give the wealthy newspaper an unfair advantage over less well-to-do rivals. There was nothing inherently wrong in the purchase of knowledge from a willing seller, nor had a notable person a greater right to benefit himself financially by the sale of autobiographical matter than had the rogue. An objectionable element in the practice was the power of the purse to deny competitors access to news or facts that the public ought to know. If the public good required that news should be generally known, it was completely unethical for any newspaper by the exercise of such power to block dissemination.

A second undesirable element was the tendency to induce unseemly conduct in the quest of special-purchase stories – and here the Glasgow case was mentioned. The practice of body-snatching was most objectionable. But the aspects of cheque-book journalism which made the biggest impact on the public were the glamourisation of vice and the rewarding of criminals. "The Press Council has not hesitated to condemn this practice and it is heartening to note that since its outspoken comments on the Christine Keeler memoirs in 1963 there has been a marked improvement in the standards of newspaper approach to the publication of unsavoury matters which are not dealt with in the way of public duty. . . . When the Press exceeds its duty to inform in these events, it panders to the baser element in man's nature and descends to the level of trafficking in scandal. The claim that a large section of the population demands this sort of journalism is no excuse for providing it. One does not give a sick man poison because he demands it."

Some reservations were expressed within the council about publication of disclosures by convicted spies because the spy, in the minds of many, was a criminal only to the side he injured. On the whole, however, the council felt it was contrary to public welfare to reward criminals whether they were vicious or treasonable.

The council said it could not provide an all-embracing definition of cheque-book journalism. That would, let us add, be an invidious task, for it would have to take account of adventures and enterprises of the highest order which are financed by newspapers. We may reflect that the one which springs most readily to mind is H. M. Stanley's 1871 assignment by Gordon Bennett's *New York Herald* in association with the London *Daily Telegraph* to find Dr. Livingstone in darkest Africa. But even that was considered hardly respectable in Victorian times and Stanley's account of his journey was (says the *Encyclopaedia Britannica,* 13th ed.) "at first received in London with some incredulity, owing in part to his connection with American journalism of a type then unfamiliar and distasteful."

What would unquestionably come into the less reputable categories of cheque-book journalism would be payments to a witness. In the Moors murder trial of 1966, which concerned the sadistic killing of young people by a man and a woman, the chief witness for the prosecution disclosed that he had received weekly payments from a newspaper to provide a series of articles about the crime. He refused to give the name of the paper, but the *News of the World* announced that it was the one concerned and had informed the attorney general to that effect. The witness was to be paid one thousand pounds for his story, plus syndication rights. The Press Council asked the paper to furnish a statement but waited until the trial was over before considering the ethical implications.

The attorney general, who was the leading prosecutor in the case, said later there was no evidence that the testimony of any witness had been affected by these payments, nor was there any question of a larger sum being offered in the event of a conviction. He had decided not to proceed against the newspaper for contempt because he was satisfied that an interference with the course of justice had not occurred. But the government proposed to examine the question of paying witnesses in this way with a view to making such changes in the law as might be necessary. He hoped, nevertheless, that before the government took any such action Fleet-street would put its house in order in this respect.

The threat of legislation led to such anxiety that Lord Devlin saw the prime minister and the attorney general in person and promised the urgent consideration of the Press Council. It was thought that nothing less than a declaration of principle backed by the press as a whole would meet the case. Such a declaration was drafted by a committee of the council and was sent to national and provincial newspapers, seeking their views.

The replies from editors were of great interest. They generally agreed that there should be no ban on the questioning of people likely to be, or certain to be, witnesses in legal proceedings. Among the arguments put forward were: newspapers often had to prepare background information to be published when a case was over, and questions to witnesses in such a situation would not influence their evidence; any ban would prevent the sort of character study of the psychopaths figuring in the Moors trial; newspapers had more than once exposed criminal or illegal practices by paid information from people who would be key witnesses when proceedings were begun; press interviews with witnesses might bring to light facts which would assist the course of justice. And so on. Many editors were also opposed to an outright prohibition of the publication of unsavoury stories and feature articles. A newspaper's job, said one editor, was to reflect the society in which we lived, warts and all. Another said the Press Council should not try to restrict in advance the judgment of newspapers as to what they might or might not buy or publish. These were matters for the judgment and integrity of editors.

From these and many other points put forward by responsible journalists, the council bent to the difficult task of hammering out its Declaration of Principle. This was published in the annual report for 1967 and is certainly one of the most important documents issued since its formation, because it attempted to embody the invited views of the press at large. This is what it said:

1. No payment or offer of payment should be made by a newspaper to any person known, or reasonably expected, to be a witness in criminal proceedings already begun, in exchange for any story or information in connection with the proceedings, until they have been concluded;

2. No witness in committal proceedings should be questioned on behalf of any newspaper about the subject matter of his evidence until the trial has been concluded;

3. No payment should be made for feature articles to persons engaged in crime or other notorious misbehaviour where the public interest does not warrant it; as the Council has previously declared, it deplores publication of personal articles of an unsavoury nature by persons who have been concerned in criminal acts or vicious conduct.

In making this declaration the Press Council acknowledges the wide support given by editors to the broad principles set out. The Council does not intend that the principles enunciated shall preclude reasonable contemporaneous inquiries in relation to the commission of crime when these are carried out with due regard to the administration of justice. There may be occasions when the activities of newspapers are affected by overriding questions of public interest, such as the exposure of wrongdoing. No code can cover every case. Satisfactory observance of the principles must depend upon the discretion and sense of responsibility of editors and newspaper proprietors.

In 1969 the Declaration of Principle was cited by Mr. M. Christiansen, the editor of the *Sunday Mirror,* after a member of the public had complained about a series of articles in his newspaper. These articles were by Mrs. Frances Reynolds who described her experiences while on the run with her husband, Bruce Reynolds, one of those convicted in the case of the Great Train Robbery. The complainant thought it wrong for the newspaper to pay Mrs. Reynolds for articles concerning his crime, for such a practice tended to promote rather than to discourage crime.

Mr. Christiansen told the council that, in deciding to publish, he had in mind that part of its Declaration of Principle which said: "Satisfactory observances of the principles must depend upon the discretion and sense of responsibility of editors and newspaper proprietors." He submitted that the articles in the *Sunday Mirror* were not unsavoury or sensational and did not glamorise crime. There was a legitimate public interest in how Reynolds evaded capture and what he did with his share of the loot. The thought left with the reader at the conclusion of the series was that crime, even on the scale of a train robbery, did not pay.

The council's verdict was: "In previous adjudications given under the Declaration of Principle the Press Council has held that the Declaration leaves it to an Editor's discretion to make a payment to a criminal or his wife for an article or information about the crime or its aftermath provided that two conditions are satisfied.

"The first is that the crime is of a wholly exceptional character which arouses a serious-minded demand for information among the public at large—information of a sort which, if not provided through the Press, would properly be provided through some other medium. The second condition is that the article should be written in a way that does not glamorise the crime or the criminal.

"Since the Declaration of Principle was issued in November, 1966, the Council has not received a complaint of its infringement in any case in which the first condition has not clearly been satisfied. The Council notes this with satisfaction, since a primary object of the Declaration was to prevent the publication of articles publicising sordid and unsavoury crime. But the Council also draws attention to this point, so that it should not be thought that its adjudications, which have so far concerned only crimes that have aroused world-wide interest, are in any way applicable to ordinary crime.

"The second condition is one that is not easy to apply and is bound to produce decisions that are one side or the other of a narrow line. In the present case the Press Council considers that the articles in the *Sunday Mirror* are a factual account of the years spent by Mr. and Mrs. Reynolds between the commission of the crime and his arrest and as such are of legitimate interest to the public; and that they do not glamorise the crime or the criminal.

"The complaint is not upheld."

The forecasting of election results by opinion polls is regarded with disfavour by many politicians who believe that the advance figures induce some voters to desert the losing party and climb on the band wagon of the prospective winners. With this in mind the Speaker's Parliamentary Conference on Electoral Law recommended that public opinion polls or betting odds on the likely results of Parliamentary elections should not be allowed to be published or broadcast within seventy-two hours of the poll. The Press Council was at once up in arms, and issued the following statement in its 1966–67 report:

"It is obviously a very grave matter to interfere in any way with the conduct of a public opinion poll. These polls have become one of the recognised ways by which, in a democracy, the people can express their views. . . . If these activities are thought to be harmful why are they not prohibited altogether, or at least their publication in any form . . . ? The clear and immediate danger is that what is not published for all to know will be the subject of rumour and speculation which, in the closing days of an election, could be far more injurious than full disclosure. . . .

"It is, or should be, an absolute requirement of the freedom of the Press that the Press should be allowed to report and comment on whatever is done in public. A Press that cannot comment on what everyone is talking about is muzzled simply because it is the Press. Moreover the Press must be free to choose from out of all that is happening in the public sphere those events which it thinks the public ought to know about. Any restriction on this freedom of choice, however slight, is dangerous because it may lead to a situation in which the Press can publish only what the State thinks it ought to publish—and then it ceases to be entirely free.

"Of all the ways open to the State for interference with the freedom of the Press this is the most insidious. On the plea that there is no wish to impose secrecy, but only to prevent the harmful effects of excessive publicity, the State can drive underground information which, if it is to be made public at all, ought to circulate freely and openly. The Press Council sincerely hopes that Parliament will refuse to countenance any further encroachment on this fundamental principle."

Up to the time of writing that was the last that was heard of this latest of innumerable attempts by legislators to shackle the press.

Relations between the press and the police occupied the council on several occasions. The first time was in 1958 when the Association of Chief Police Officers submitted a memorandum on the subject. This recognised the importance of a happy relationship but said that many senior officers thought that difficulties between press and police had increased in recent years. This was mainly due to the larger number of reporters and photographers who arrived on the scene of major incidents. They included not only local newspapermen known to the police in their areas, but representatives of many national newspapers and also a number of people who called themselves free-lance journalists. These were not so careful of their relations with the local police as were the known reporters.

In particular, the memorandum mentioned an aircraft crash in Lancashire when 35 passengers were killed. The machine came down on a hilltop to which the only known access was a narrow moorland road blocked by snow. There were 60 police officers, firemen, and ambulance men, with some 30 volunteers on the scene and, in addition, about 40 photographers and reporters. Their presence, hampering the work of rescue, was "a very great nuisance." While acknowledging that the press must fulfill its normal functions the police argued that there should be some form of control.

Here, of course, was the old problem of "blanket coverage," which had been before the council several times but to which no solution had been found. This time, a deputation of chief police officers discussed the question with the council's General Purposes Committee, but once again no remedy was found. It did emerge, however, that the newspapermen were not the only nor, perhaps, the chief offenders. A number of radio and television vans also rushed to the scene of the accident, and these must have caused a much greater obstruction than the cars of the newspapermen.

In 1958 the council made representations to the chief commissioner of Metropolitan Police about a police witness who had described himself as a journalist and had carried a press identity card in a case concerning a club in London's West End. That this had happened was admitted by the police. The council pointed out that such an incident was likely to discredit the identification card system which had worked well for many years. The commissioner replied that while he could not think that any real harm had been done, he appreciated the council's anxiety and had ordered that this subterfuge should be discontinued.

In 1961 a Royal Commission on the Police invited the Press Council to give evidence, but the council declined on the ground that it had no direct contact with the police and could therefore be of little assistance. But the council's chairman attended for consultation and agreed to have investigated four typical instances in which the police said the press had published biased or misleading articles showing them in a bad light. In one case the chief constable concerned refused to cooperate in the investigation, and, in a second one, the chief constable withdrew his complaint. The third case concerned the reporting of the Law Society's evidence before the commission. This paid generous tribute to the integrity and ability of the police, but also mentioned isolated examples of police behaviour which fell short of customary high standards. Such practices as "planting stolen goods," "fabrication of evidence," and the omission of relevant evidence, were mentioned. The newspapers, it was complained, had stressed these adverse aspects to the detriment of the good points, and had thus distorted the news. Four newspapers were mentioned. The council, after investigation, decided that three of the accounts were neither unfair nor unbalanced, but they found fault with the headlines in three cases.

The fourth case remitted to the council from the Royal Commission was to do with the treatment, handling, and disposal of a police dog. The dossier on this mountain made out of a molehill ran to about twelve thousand words—an example of the time and care the council spent on its work. The evidence was so conflicting that it was impossible to reach any conclusion one way or the other.

So much for police grievances about the press!

The relations between Parliament and the press, never cordial, showed no improvement as the years went by. The Press Council's annual report for 1969 said that the gap had considerably widened during the year. "It is no bad thing in itself for there to be such a gap," the report continued. "When one exists there can be no suggestion of collusion and the public can feel happier that the needs of democracy are being served. After all, what most people know and understand of Parliament and what goodwill they may have towards the Government of the day depends largely upon the interpretation they gain from the Press, radio, and television. Unfortunately the drift this year has been away from healthy respect and there has been a mutual increase in suspicion, combined with failure by both parties always to appreciate the other's problems. It is one thing to realise and accept the fact that there are problems, even if it is impolitic to deal with them. It is an entirely different matter to refuse to see the problems."

During the twelve months under review, there had been no major legislation to the advantage of the press. A Freedom of Publication (Protection) Bill which aimed at helping newspapers in respect of contempt of court, official secrets, and libel, was on the verge of becoming law when it was "talked out" by a back bencher who continued his speech until the time limit for consideration of the bill had expired.

However, there had been legislation not directed at the press but wide enough to include the press, nearly always in a restrictive way and the feeling existed that when such bills were drafted no thought was given to any incidental effects they might have on the media of communication. Recognising this, the Press Council during the year set up a small parliamentary subcommittee to study pending legislation and to suggest action where necessary.

In August 1970 the council was criticised for doing what it had always tried to avoid, namely to rebuke a newspaper for an expression of political opinion.

The Earl of Arran, who does not mince words in his weekly column in London's *Evening News,* mentioned Israel's bombing of an Egyptian factory when seventy were killed, and added: "Go to it, Israel, and push those Egyptian bastards into the Quattara Depression."

The paper published a letter of complaint from the embassy of the United Arab Republic and added a footnote by Lord Arran, who wrote: "It ill becomes some UAR functionary to ask for apologies.

My advice to the Counsellor is to keep his trap very shut and lie very low for the time being."

When a reader of the *Evening News* complained to the Press Council about these examples of "gutter journalism," the council issued the following statement:

"The expression of controversial views is an important function of a free Press, and matters of taste are, in general, matters of opinion, but in this case the Press Council deplores the use of abusive and inflammatory phraseology which can contribute nothing to the calm consideration of a serious international situation." The complaint was upheld.

There were some who recalled the words of Mr. Justice Salmon during the libel action brought by Liberace against the *Daily Mirror* in 1959, when he said: "We are all free to state fearlessly to anyone our real opinion, honestly held, upon any matter of public interest. We are free to state such opinions in any way we like, diffidently, decorously, politely and discreetly, or pungently, provocatively, rudely, and even brutally."

Lord Arran's comments unquestionably fell into the last category, but however much their crudity may be deprecated few would doubt that they expressed a "real opinion, honestly held."

In upholding the complaint against him the council appeared to be indicating how far a writer could go in political comment, and to be giving its own opinion on a particular international situation.

That would be a perilous path to pursue.

14 The Will of the People

THE Press Council was born of a welter of confused issues and contending interests. Its origins were in part political, in part material, in part moral. The political aspect appeared to die with its birth, for it has no connection with government, Parliament, or party. The moral has come to outweigh the material by at least ten to one, for though moral tendencies can be influenced by persuasion, material authority depends upon power, and the Press Council has no real power. It is a typical British compromise, a hybrid characteristic of a democratic society. While existing to defend the freedom of the press and to raise the tone of newspaper offerings, it also enables the industry to lay a virtuous hand on a virtuous heart and declare that "something is being done."

But while all this is true, the council cannot be dismissed – as many have tried to dismiss it – as something of no account, a harmless eccentricity, a hollow turnip. Setting aside all the speeches, debates, arguments, criticisms, and quarrels, it came into being in response to the instinctive feeling of the British people that the power of the press had increased, was increasing, and ought to be diminished. It was a true instinct. Since the growth of modern newspapers and the inescapable diminution in their numbers and variety, there had been a time when great press lords seemed to be reaching positions of unbridled power in the life of the nation, and had even sought to dictate to prime ministers. However ardent may be the feeling for the liberty of the subject; however profound the belief in the freedom of the press, it must be agreed that government by newspaper would be the antithesis of parliamentary democracy. The government must govern by the will of the people through their elected representatives and the press, which also speaks for the people, must be constantly on the

214

alert to see that they do it. The function of the press is not to govern but to keep watch and ward, to disclose, guide, criticise, and suggest, with a due sense of decency and responsibility. To keep the press on these lines is the purpose of the Press Council.

But, inevitably, its main duty has been to act as a court of honour. Such statistical records as are available show that between 1963 and 1968 the council received about 3,000 complaints against the newspapers. Many of these were frivolous or without substance, and others were not followed through by the complainants. About one-quarter were pursued to a verdict and some 750 adjudications had therefore been issued during this period. Complaints averaged about 65 a year in the first seven years and rose to 150 in the next three years. After the appointment of the new council there was a swift increase to about 400 a year, laying a great burden on the Complaints Committee. As the annual report for 1968 remarked: "The labours of members of this committee are best described as 'massive.' " The last two years under review showed a tendency for the total to fall, an indication, no doubt, of lessened causes for complaint about the newspapers. The downward trend continued. In 1968–69 the council adjudicated in fewer cases than in any year since 1962, an indication that frivolous complaints were being reduced and that the status of the Press Council was being increasingly recognised.

The bulk of grievances transmitted to the council concerned inaccuracy, alleged breaches of confidence, bad taste, vulgarity, distortion, intrusion, and unfairness. Some of the complaints heard by the council, and listed by the secretary were: objectionable statements about the royal family; misleading advertisements; unnecessary identification of innocent persons with people accused of grave offences; offensive photographs; unfair criticism of theatrical shows; smear campaigns; errors in reports; unbalanced reports; distortion of facts by slanted writing; reporters attempting to stir up trouble; callous indifference to private tragedy; misleading edition titles; refusal to accept advertisements; publication of "confidential" documents; failure to allow an author to reply to an unfavourable book review; undue emphasis on one of several suspected foods in a poison epidemic; interpretation of the expression "phone-call girl"; disallowances of readers' letters; nondeclaration of an interest in commercial television; withholding reasoned official reply to an attack on an institution;

interviewing personnel and taking pictures at a fire station without permission; gross intrusions into private grief; publication of an un-confirmed report received by telephone; misleading contents bills—and so on, through the calendar of real or fancied newspaper mis-demeanour.

In this field the council does provide a redress for people who feel that they have been injured by a newspaper in a way that falls short of libel. There is no reason why inaccuracies concerning people or things should go unchallenged or uncorrected and why there should not be some check on the ever-present temptation of a newspaper to pretend to omniscience.

It may well be that a Press Council was felt to be especially ap-propriate to Britain which has the unique possession of national news-papers and where an error or misstatement will cover the entire country. But its formation gave impetus to the conceptions of self-discipline and self-regulation among newspapers elsewhere. It is true that Sweden had begun long before with a Council of Conduct founded in 1916 but this, like Norway's, formed in 1927, was of a more limited scope than the later British body. Switzerland instituted a Mixed Press Policy Commission in 1938, but though it claimed to have "per-formed duties which similar institutions in the free world have adopted in recent times," its intention was almost purely political. It was "to protect the Swiss Press from uncontrollable foreign influences" and to see that press foreign policy was in line with the principles proclaimed by the Swiss government and Parliament. Latterly it has dealt with ethical questions as well.

The first important foreign council after 1953 was the Deutscher Presserat of Western Germany in 1957, and those who founded it looked to the British body for guidance. In 1959 Mr. Murray, the then vice-chairman of the Press Council, visited Bonn at the invitation of the Presserat and addressed an audience which included the federal president, Dr. Lübke, several ministers, and many M.P.'s and journal-ists. The German Council operates in much the same way as the British, though there are certain press laws to which journalists have to conform.

A Press Council for India came into being in 1966. The words of its constitution are almost identical with those of its British predecessor, but there the resemblance ends. The Indian Council is tied to the government, which finances and regulates it, and upon which it is represented. The same adviser from the Press Council attended a seminar in Delhi in 1966 and pointed to these divergencies, but local conditions appear to have made a government-sponsored council for India inevitable.

Among other countries to have formed Press Councils of various kinds in recent years are Israel, Pakistan, Denmark, Holland, the Philippines, South Korea, South Africa, and Turkey. In the last-named country, the court of honour, founded in 1960, was soon in disarray. Disputes arose between newspapers, and between press and government, leading to the cancellation, for some, of the official advertising upon which they depended to keep going. This, said a Turkish commentator, "naturally made a dent in the solidarity and confidence which self-discipline ought to command."

As is to be expected, Press Councils best succeed in countries which have a long tradition of parliamentary democracy. Journalists and politicians seeking information about British newspapers or desiring to form councils of their own, come to London to find it. Since the Press Council began, the representatives of more than forty nations have been sent to it by the Foreign Office, the Commonwealth Office, and the Central Office of Information, apart from those who come independently. Many of these visitors are astonished to find that neither the executive nor the legislative branch of government has any connection with the council and cannot demand any action from it.

Much of its work goes on behind the scenes. It keeps a careful watch on all matters affecting the press, especially on bills introduced into Parliament and judgments in the courts affecting newspapers and their freedom of expression in any way. The council has become a kind of public relations office for the press. People write to it with all sorts of problems connected with newspapers, and the staff always do their best to help.

Will the council be permitted to jog along as it is going now, or will authority interfere at some future date? Merely to ask the question is to be reminded that, after centuries of struggle, the British press won its freedom and that no government today would attempt to tell the Press Council what it should or should not do. But can anyone be sure that such conditions will continue? The original all-Press Council was, to many journalists, an ominous step in the wrong direction. Next, the loose rein on which the first body was running was tightened by the inclusion of lay members, a development to which nearly every press organisation was opposed, and which was brought about only by the threat of statutory action.

At this point some thought must be given to the nature of liberty. The late unlamented Mussolini once said: "There is such a thing as too much liberty," a statement denounced by every liberal in Europe. But, in a different context, the excesses of the permissive society have shown that there was some truth in his remark. One is reminded of the elderly Russian woman who, after the revolution of 1917, was seen walking in the thick of the Moscow traffic, which was dislocated as a result. When someone remonstrated with her she said she could walk where she liked, "because we have liberty now." It had not occurred to her that if she was free to walk in the road, the traffic would be equally free to encroach on the sidewalk. The incident illustrates how easy it is to imagine that "liberty" is all, whereas, of course, the high ideal of civilisation is "liberty under the law."

To exercise unrestricted freedom of professional action and expression is the constant temptation of those who communicate with the public, but who know that there are many times when it must be resisted. They also know that what ought, or ought not, to be printed occupies a vague, borderline territory (apart from the definitions of the law) made up of conscience, convention, good taste, a sense of responsibility and humanity, and other imponderables which may change with the passing of time. It is mainly on that borderline that the Press Council operates, feeling its way, interpreting motives, investigating denunciations, offering guidance, compiling its own "law" in ways which could not possibly be handled by an act of the legislature.

The council is, at once, an accuser of the press and a defender of the press against the centripetal tendencies of the twentieth century. In the modern State, even though a democracy, the executive encroaches more and more upon the liberties of the individual and the self-determination of private enterprise. The newspaper industry is not immune from these tendencies. It is often claimed that there are no press laws in Britain and that free speech is unimpeded. It is true that, apart from the special provision of the Monopolies and Mergers Act, no statute puts up any specific bars against the press. Yet (as already mentioned) successive enactments in the past thirty or forty years have forbidden the reporting of evidence in divorce cases, the taking of photographs within the precincts of the courts, and the reporting of evidence in cases before the magistrates. As has been shown, the laws of libel and the rules of contempt are applied to newspapers much more than to anything or anyone else. The Official Secrets Acts also bear hardly upon them. Free speech has been curtailed by the Race Relations Act to an extent that has yet to be tested at law. It is conceivable that this act could imperil an English barroom humourist who told a funny story about an Irishman, a Scotsman, a Welshman, and a Jew, to say nothing about an African or an Indian.

As always, legislators itch to control or regulate the newspapers, and from time to time attempt to do so by the introduction of private members' bills into Parliament. These usually get short shrift, but they may not always do so. Nor can the Press Council be certain that it will be allowed to retain complete independence for ever.

Much depends upon its own conduct and also that of the newspapers. The council's verdicts, reached in private session and by majority vote, are not always accepted without question. Some people believe that both "complainants" and "defendants" should be represented legally, if only by counsel on watching briefs. Others think that once barristers obtained a foothold the council would be turned into what would be virtually a court of law, but without the backing of the law. If that situation arose, the council would inevitably be hedged about with statutory regulations.

Its treatment by the newspapers is also of great importance. Some of them still tend to shrug it off as of small account. But if they were to treat it with open disdain to the extent of ignoring its strictures or refusing to publish its condemnations of themselves, some legislator would soon get busy on new restrictions.

All such considerations must be kept constantly in mind by those performing what is inevitably a thankless task. Be that as it may, the council in its present form has abundantly proved its value. It has become rooted in the British system and will undoubtedly endure.

Appendixes
Bibliography
Index

Appendix A
Founder Members of 1st Press Council, 1953

Chairman: Col. the Hon. J. J. Astor (The *Times*)
Vice-Chairman: Sir Linton Andrews (The *Yorkshire Post*)

Editorial representatives

National Newspaper Editors:
H. Ainsworth (The *People*)
A. L. Cranfield (The *Star*)
Guy Schofield (The *Daily Mail*)

Provincial Editors Elected by Newspaper Society:
Francis Graves (Windsor, Slough & Eton *Express*)
J. L. Palmer (The *Cornishman*), O.B.E.

Provincial Editors Elected by Editors' Guild:
Sir Linton Andrews
R. E. Wilson (*Stockport Advertiser*)

Scottish Newspaper Editor:
A. C. Trotter (*Scottish Daily Express*)

National Union of Journalists:
Henry Bate (London)
A. J. Gibson (Lancaster), J.P.
H. D. Nichols (Manchester)
John Taylor (Motherwell)

Institute of Journalists:
G. R. French (Maidstone)
George Murray (London)
John Sherret (Glasgow)

Managerial Representatives

Newspaper Proprietors' Association:
Col. Astor W. Emsley Carr (*News of the World*)

Stuart McClean (Associated Newspapers)
Frank Waters (*News Chronicle*)

Newspaper Society:
Kenneth Brown (*Hornsey Journal*)
E. M. Clayson (*Birmingham Post*)
W. T. Curtis-Willson (Brighton & Hove *Herald*), M.B.E., J.P.
R. P. T. Gibson (Westminster Press Provincial Newspapers)

Scottish Daily Newspaper Society:
William Veitch (Aberdeen *Journal*), C.B.E., J.P.

Scottish Newspaper Proprietors' Association:
F. M. Johnston (*Falkirk Herald*)

Officials of Organisations:
Bernard Alton (N.P.A.)
H. J. Bradley (N.U.J.)
H. R. Davies (Newspaper Society)
A. Watson McCarroll (Scottish D. N. S.)
Stewart Nicholson (Institute of Journalists)
J. Forbes Fowler (Scottish N.P.A.)

Secretary:
Alan Pitt Robbins, C.B.E.

Assistant Secretary:
Phyllis Deakin

ARTICLES OF CONSTITUTION OF 1ST PRESS COUNCIL

1. Constitution—The General Council of the Press, hereinafter called the Council, is constituted, on and from the first day of July 1953, by the Organisations named in the Schedule hereto, hereinafter referred to as the constituent organisations, as a voluntary organisation of twenty-five members.

2. Objects—The objects of the Council shall be:
   (i) To preserve the established freedom of the British Press.
   (ii) To maintain the character of the British Press in accordance with the highest professional and commercial standards.
   (iii) To keep under review any developments likely to restrict the supply of information of public interest and importance.
   (iv) To promote and encourage methods of recruitment, education, and training of journalists.
   (v) To promote a proper functional relation among all sections of the profession.

(vi) To promote technical and other research.

(vii) To study developments in the Press which may tend towards greater concentration or monopoly.

(viii) To publish periodical reports recording its own work and re-viewing from time to time the various developments in the Press and the factors affecting them.

3. Procedure—The Council is empowered by the constituent organisations to regulate and control all its procedure and action for the furtherance and attainment of the objects defined in Clause 2 hereof as the Council may decide, provided that in dealing with representations which it may receive about the conduct of the Press or of any persons towards the Press, the Council shall be required to consider only those from complainants actually affected, and shall deal with such in whatever manner may seem to it practical and appropriate.

Note—It was agreed at the first meeting of the Council in July 1953, that, while the Council is "required" to consider only complaints from complainants actually affected, it may, at its discretion, consider complaints reaching it from any source.

4. Membership—

(i) The Council shall consist of fifteen editorial representatives and ten managerial representatives, elected or nominated as provided in this Clause.

(ii) Membership of the Council shall be restricted to persons who have the qualification of being full-time directors or employees on the editorial or managerial staffs of newspapers, periodicals, or news agencies supplying a regular service of news to daily newspapers, which qualification shall also include full-time pro-fessional free lance journalists regularly engaged in supplying news or articles to such newspapers, periodicals, or news agen-cies. Any member ceasing to be so qualified shall notify the secretary or acting secretary of the Council within one month and shall terminate his membership of the Council within three months of such cessation of qualification.

(iii) The fifteen editorial representatives shall comprise:

National newspaper editors elected in accordance with the provisions of section (vi) hereof 3

* Provincial newspaper editors elected in accordance with the provisions of section (vi) hereof 2

* Provincial newspaper editors nominated by the Guild of Brit-ish Newspaper Editors 2

Scottish newspaper editor elected in accordance with the provisions of section (vi) hereof 1

* The term "Provincial newspaper editors" shall be deemed to include editors of London suburban newspapers.

Nominees of the National Union of Journalists 4
Nominees of the Institute of Journalists 3

(iv) The ten managerial representatives shall comprise:
Nominees of the Newspaper Proprietors Association . . . 4
Nominees of the Newspaper Society 4
Nominee of the Scottish Daily Newspaper Society 1
Nominee of the Scottish Newspaper Proprietors' Association 1

(v) The method of selecting nominated members of the Council shall be left to the discretion of the organisations by which their nominations are made but in deciding upon their nominees the organisations concerned shall have regard to the desirability of ensuring as wide a representation of the categories of morning, evening, Sunday, and other weekly newspapers as possible.

(vi) The national newspaper editors shall be elected by the editors of newspapers in membership of the Newspaper Proprietors Association; two provincial newspaper editors shall be elected by the editors of newspapers in membership of the Newspaper Society; and the Scottish newspaper editor elected by editors of the Scottish Daily Newspaper Society and the Scottish Newspaper Proprietors' Association. The procedure by which these elections shall be carried out shall be determined by the respective organisations.

(vii) On or before June 1, 1953, names of nominees and elected members shall be sent by the constituent organisations to the secretary or acting secretary of the Council for the time being accompanied by the written consent of the persons nominated to serve. In the event of the same nomination being put forward by more than one organisation, the nomination first made shall have priority and the organisation or organisations submitting the subsequent nomination of the same person shall be asked to put forward another nomination.

5. Chairman—At its first meeting the Council shall appoint from its members a Chairman and Vice-Chairman, each of whom shall hold office until the first meeting of the Council in 1954 and be eligible for reelection. At the first meeting in 1954 and each subsequent year the Council shall elect a Chairman and Vice-Chairman who shall hold office for the ensuing twelve months. Persons so appointed shall be eligible for reelection.

6. Retirement of members—Members of the Council shall be members for at least three years. At the end of the first three years of the Council's existence, eight members, chosen by lot, shall retire. At the end of the fourth year, another eight members, chosen by lot, shall retire. At the end of the fifth year, the remaining nine members out of the original twenty-five shall retire. The same procedure of retirement shall continue after the sixth year. Members retiring shall, subject to qualification, be eligible for renomination

or reelection. Vacancies arising from retirements shall be filled in like manner to that by which the persons retiring were originally elected or nominated.

7. Casual vacancies—Persons filling casual vacancies shall be nominated or elected in like manner to that by which the persons whose vacancies they fill were nominated or elected, and in so far as the process of retirement is concerned shall stand in the same relation thereto as those whose places they fill.

8. Quorum—A quorum shall consist of fourteen members of the Council.

9. Legal advice—The Council may seek legal advice as to any course of action which may be proposed in regard to any matter under consideration.

10. Meetings—Meetings shall be held quarterly. The Chairman shall have power to call a special meeting if the volume or importance of business necessitates this. A special meeting shall be called by the secretary on the requisition of not fewer than eight members; such requisition shall be addressed to the secretary at the office of the Council for the time being. Not less than seven days' notice shall be given in writing of any meeting of the Council unless all the members thereof are agreed that a meeting should be convened at shorter notice.

11. Officials of constituent organisations—Each constituent organisation shall be entitled to nominate an official to attend all meetings of the Council in a consultative capacity. Such nominees may speak but not vote at Council meetings. The first nomination shall be made on or before June 1, 1953, and the organisations concerned may change the name of their nominee at any time by giving notice of such change to the secretary or acting secretary of the Council for the time being.

12. Notices—Notices of meetings shall be sent to members of the Council and officials nominated by the constituent bodies at the addresses provided by them for the purpose. The accidental omission to notify any of the said persons or the nonreceipt by any of them of the notice shall not invalidate the proceedings of the meeting to which the notice relates.

13. Secretarial duties—The secretarial work of the Council shall be carried out by a staff appointed for the purpose on terms and conditions laid down by the Council from time to time.

14. Subscription—The expenditure of the Council shall be met by annual subscriptions paid by the constituent organisations in the proportions shown in the Schedule hereto. Until otherwise decided by the Council the annual subscription shall be collected on the basis of an estimated expenditure of £3,000 per annum, and no increase in this amount shall be made without the written consent of the constituent organisations. Subscriptions shall be payable on the first day of July in each year beginning July 1, 1953.

15. Travelling expenses of members—Members of the Council attending meetings shall be entitled to receive their first-class return railway fare payable from the funds of the Council.

16. Committees—The Council shall have power to refer any matter under consideration to a committee of its members. No committee appointed shall have executive authority unless expressly authorised to that effect by the Council.

17. Dissolution—The Council, being a voluntary organisation to preserve the established freedom of the British Press, may at any time terminate its existence if it appear to the members that the voluntary nature and independence of the Council are threatened. A resolution to dissolve the Council must be passed by a two-thirds majority of its members present and voting at a meeting specially called for the purpose, which two-thirds majority shall be not less than a simple majority of the members. Not less than twenty-one days' notice shall be given of any meeting at which it is intended to propose the dissolution of the Council. Such notice shall give particulars of the purpose for which the meeting is called and in addition to being sent to all persons entitled to receive notices of meetings of the Council shall also be sent to the secretaries of the constituent organisations.

18. Alterations of constitution—Alterations to these Articles of Constitution shall require the approval of a two-thirds majority of the members present and voting at a meeting, which two-thirds majority shall not be less than a simple majority of the members. No alteration shall be effective unless at least one month's notice of the proposed alteration shall have been given to all persons entitled to attend meetings of the Council and to the secretaries of the constituent organisations, and no alteration of clauses 1, 2, 3, 4, or 14 hereof shall be submitted under the provisions of this article unless such alteration has first received the approval in writing of the constituent organisations.

SCHEDULE

	Subscription
1. The Newspaper Proprietors Association	20/60ths.
2. The Newspaper Society	16/60ths.
3. The Scottish Daily Newspaper Society	3/60ths.
4. The Scottish Newspaper Proprietors' Association	3/60ths.
5. The National Union of Journalists	8/60ths.
6. The Institute of Journalists	6/60ths.
7. The Guild of British Newspaper Editors	4/60ths.

Appendix B
Original Members of 2nd Press Council, 1964

Independent Chairman: *†Rt. Hon. the Lord Devlin, P.C.
Vice-Chairman: *†Henry Bate

The Newspaper Proprietors Association Ltd.:

M. Chapman-Walker, C.B.E., M.V.O. (*News of the World*)
† Trevor Evans, C.B.E. (Beaverbrook Newspapers Ltd.)
C. D. Hamilton, D.S.O. (*Sunday Times*)
* Edward Pickering (Daily Mirror Newspapers Ltd.)
* G. R. Pope (The Times Publishing Co. Ltd.)

The Newspaper Society:
Sir Eric Clayson (*Birmingham Post*)
David Greenslade (*Mansfield Chronicle Advertiser*)
† Charlse A. Ramsden (*Halifax Courier*)

The Scottish Daily Newspaper Society:
A. Fraser Anderson (*Daily Record*)

Scottish Newspaper Proprietors' Association:
† F. M. Johnston (*Falkirk Herald*)

The Periodical Proprietors Association Ltd.:
† Sir James Waterlow, Bt. C.B.E., T.D. (P.P.A.)
† Donald Tyerman, B.A. (The *Economist*)

The Guild of British Newspaper Editors:
† Mrs. Gordon Clemetson (*Kent* and *Sussex Courier*)
* Charles Jervis (Press Association)

National Union of Journalists:
*† Henry Bate (*Daily Telegraph*)
A. E. Hargrave (Freelance, Glasgow)
* Allan Lofts (Thomson Newspapers)
* Kenneth Holmes (*Eastern Evening News*)

The Institute of Journalists:
G. R. French (Freelance, Maidstone)
* Alfred M. Lee (*Huddersfield Examiner*)

Lay Members:
 * Prof. Alexander Haddow, F.R.S. (London)
 Rt. Hon. the Lord James of Rusholme (York)
 * Mrs. Elaine Kellett, M.A. (Bucks.)
 † Rev. Ronald G. Lunt, M.C., M.A. (Birmingham)
 † Mrs. Marie Patterson, B.A. (London)

Officials of Constituent Organisations entitled to attend meetings in a consultative capacity under the provisions of Article 3

W. Barrie Abbott, Scottish Newspaper Proprietors' Association
Bernard Alton, M.V.O., The Newspaper Proprietors Association Ltd.
H. J. Bradley, National Union of Journalists
R. F. Farmer, The Institute of Journalists
A. Watson McCarroll, J. P., Scottish Daily Newspaper Society
H. MacDougall, The Periodical Proprietors Association Ltd.
N. Richards, M.A., Guild of British Newspaper Editors
William G. Ridd, M.V.O., The Newspaper Society
Secretary: Col. Willie C. Clissitt, T.D.

ARTICLES OF CONSTITUTION OF 2ND PRESS COUNCIL

Articles of Constitution of The Press Council approved by The Newspaper Proprietors Association Ltd., The Newspaper Society, Periodical Publishers Association Ltd., The Scottish Daily Newspaper Society, Scottish Newspaper Proprietors' Association, The Institute of Journalists, the National Union of Journalists, and The Guild of British Newspaper Editors hereinafter referred to as the constituent bodies.

1. Foundation—The Press Council, hereinafter called the Council, is voluntarily constituted on and from the first day of July 1953, in the designation "The General Council of the Press." The Council revokes that style and title on and from the first day of July 1963, but accepts responsibility for all acts performed by The General Council of the Press as though they had been done by The Press Council.

2. Objects—The objects of the Council are:
   (i) To preserve the established freedom of the British Press.
   (ii) To maintain the character of the British Press in accordance with the highest professional and commercial standards.

* Member of Complaints Committee.
† Member of General Purposes Committee.

(iii) To consider complaints about the conduct of the Press or the conduct of persons and organisations towards the Press; to deal with these complaints in whatever manner might seem practical and appropriate and record resultant action.

(iv) To keep under review developments likely to restrict the supply of information of public interest and importance.

(v) To report publicly on developments that may tend towards greater concentration or monopoly in the Press (including changes in ownership, control and growth of Press undertakings) and to publish statistical information relating thereto.

(vi) To make representations on appropriate occasions to the Government, organs of the United Nations and to Press organisations abroad.

(vii) To publish periodical reports recording the Council's work and to review, from time to time, developments in the Press and the factors affecting them.

3. Membership—The Council shall consist of:

(i) A Chairman who shall be a person otherwise unconnected with the Press.

(ii) Twenty members nominated by the following bodies in the proportions indicated:

The Newspaper Proprietors Association Ltd.	5
At least two of whom shall be editorial—as distinct from managerial—nominees	
The Newspaper Society	3
At least one of whom shall be an editorial nominee.	
Periodical Publishers Association Ltd., including one editorial nominee	2
The Scottish Daily Newspaper Society	1
Scottish Newspaper Proprietors' Association	1
The Guild of British Newspaper Editors	2
The National Union of Journalists	4
The Institute of Journalists	2

(iii) Representatives of the Public who shall not exceed 20 percent of the Council's total membership entitled to vote   5

4. Methods of Appointment—

(i) The Chairman shall be invited to accept office on such terms as shall be agreed mutually by him and the Council.

(ii) Members nominated within the provisions of Clause 3 (ii) shall be persons who, at the time of appointment, are full-time directors of newspapers, periodicals, news agencies supplying a daily service of news to newspapers in Great Britain and/or overseas OR full-time editorial or managerial employees on the staffs of such organisations. Editorial qualification shall extend to include also full-time professional freelance journalists regularly engaged in supplying news and/or articles to recognised newspapers, periodicals or news agencies. A member ceasing to be so qualified shall notify the secretary or acting secretary of the Council in writing within one calendar month and his membership shall terminate within three calendar months.

(iii) Representatives of the Public co-opted to the Council shall be chosen by the Chairman and other members of the Council in consultation. These representatives shall rank equal with members nominated by the constituent bodies in the rights, privileges and duties inherent in membership of the Council other than qualification for election to the vice-chairmanship.

5. Retirement—On nomination to the Council a person shall be entitled to membership for three consecutive years. At the end of this period the nominee, if he is qualified, shall be eligible for reelection. On first appointment of the group of members specified in Clause 3 (ii) seven shall serve for only one year before retirement and a further seven for an initial period of two years. These members shall be decided by lot. They will be eligible for reelection and thereafter the normal period of their membership of the Council and that of their successors shall be three years. On first appointment of the group of members specified in Clause 3 (iii) one shall retire at the end of the first year of service and a further two at the end of two years' membership in similar manner and conditions.

6. Casual vacancies—A person filling a casual vacancy shall be appointed to membership in like manner to that by which the person whose vacancy he fills was appointed. On initial appointment he shall retain membership only for the unexpired portion of the period which remained to the person whose place in the Council he takes.

7. Procedure—The Council is empowered by the constituent bodies to regulate and control all its procedure and action for the furtherance and attainment of the objects defined in Clause 2 hereof as the Council may decide. The Chairman and members shall each be entitled to cast one vote in any matter decided by them on a show of hands or by ballot, but if a division should result in an equal number of votes being cast for and against a motion the Chairman shall be entitled to exercise a casting vote.

8. Quorum—A quorum at a Council meeting shall be 13 members.

9. Vice-Chairman—At its first meeting following the thirtieth day of June in each and every year the Council shall appoint from its members nominated under the provisions of Clause 3 (ii) a Vice-Chairman, who shall hold office until the first meeting of the Council in the following financial year and subject to possession of qualification, shall then be eligible for reelection. Nominations in writing, duly proposed and seconded, with the written consent of the nominee, must be submitted to the secretary not later than fourteen days before the meeting of the Council at which the election

is to take place. In the absence of written nomination, oral nomination may be made at the appropriate meeting of the Council. If no nomination is made, the existing holder of the office shall be declared to have been re-elected. In the absence of the Chairman the Vice-Chairman shall preside at Council meetings and he shall fulfill all the functions of the Chairman should that office be not occupied.

10. Meetings—Meetings shall be held at least five times a year. The Chairman is empowered to call a special meeting, if, in his opinion, the business to be transacted warrants this action. A special meeting shall be convened by the secretary on the requisition of not fewer than eight members. Such requisition shall be addressed to the secretary at the office of the Council for the time being. Not less than seven days' notice shall be given in writing of any meeting of the Council unless members agree to accept shorter notice.

11. Committees—The Council shall have power to appoint committees of its members for the discharge of such duties as shall be specified. A committee shall not have executive authority unless this is expressly delegated to it by the Council. At the last Council meeting preceding the thirtieth day of June each year the Chairman and Vice-Chairman shall submit to the Council for its approval a list of members willing to serve on committees. Members of committees shall hold office from the date on which the list in which they are named is approved or the first day of July, whichever is the later, until the date on which their successors similarly take office. Upon the occurrence of one or more casual vacancies in the membership of a committee the Chairman and the Vice-Chairman may, at their discretion, submit to the Council for its approval the names of members willing to fill the vacancies and such members shall hold office on like terms as those whom they replace. Each committee shall appoint a Chairman from amongst its members. The Council Chairman and Vice-Chairman shall be ex officio members of all committees.

12. Notices—Notice of meetings shall be sent to members of the Council at the addresses indicated by them to the secretary. Accidental omission to notify any of the said persons or nonreceipt by any of them of such notice shall not invalidate the proceedings of the meeting to which the notice relates.

13. Finance—The monetary expenditure of the Council shall be met by annual subscriptions payable by the constituent bodies as set out in the Schedule hereto. No variation in these amounts shall be made without the prior written consent of the constituent bodies. Subscriptions shall be payable on the first day of July in each year.

All cheques issued in the name of the Council shall be signed by any two of the following persons: the Chairman, the Vice-Chairman, the secretary, the assistant secretary and any other specially designated members of the Council.

14. Travelling expenses—A member attending a meeting of the Council or of any of its committees shall be entitled to receive his first-class return railway fare from the funds of the Council.

15. Subsistence allowances—Members of the Council appointed under Clause 3 (iii) shall be entitled to receive from Council funds subsistence expenses incurred in attending council and/or committee meetings in accordance with rates to be fixed by the Council from time to time.

16. Dissolution—The Council may at any time terminate its existence if it appears to the members that the Council's voluntary nature and independence are threatened. A resolution to dissolve the Council, to be binding, must be passed by a two-thirds majority of its members present and voting at a meeting specially called for the purpose, which two-thirds majority shall be not less than a simple majority of the membership of the Council. Not less than twenty-one days' notice shall be given of any such meeting and this shall give particulars of the purpose for which the meeting is called. The Council shall notify secretaries of the constituent bodies of such meeting at the time it summons members.

17. Alteration of constitution—Alteration of these Articles of Constitution shall require the approval of a two-thirds majority of the members present and voting at a meeting, which two-thirds majority shall be not less than a simple majority of the membership of the Council. No alteration shall be effective unless at least 28 days' notice of a proposed alteration shall have been given to Council members and secretaries of the constituent bodies.

18. Staff—The secretarial and administrative work of the Council shall be carried out by an appointed secretary and a staff engaged for the purpose on terms and conditions decided by the Council from time to time.

19. Revocation of previous Articles of Constitution—These Articles of Constitution shall have effect on and from the first day of July 1963. They supersede the original Articles of Constitution, dated the first day of July 1953, as amended in January 1959, and again in the financial year 1961–62 which are hereby revoked by resolution of the General Council of the Press this eighteenth day of June 1963.

SCHEDULE

The Newspaper Proprietors Association Ltd.		£10,500
The Newspaper Society		4,500
The Periodical Proprietors Association Ltd.		2,000
The Scottish Daily Newspaper Society		525
Scottish Newspaper Proprietors' Association		337
The National Union of Journalists		1,500
The Institute of Journalists		450
The Guild of British Newspaper Editors		300
	Total	£20,112

Appendix C
Organisations Forming the Press Council

THE NEWSPAPER SOCIETY

The Newspaper Society, founded in 1836, is the oldest, largest, and most representative organisation of newspaper proprietors in the United Kingdom. For many years it was the only body representing the publishers of newspapers and magazines. In 1889 the London newspapers joined the society, but in 1906 these formed their own organisation, though they did not retire from the society until 1916. Today the society represents mainly the provincial and London suburban press. In 1837 it had 23 members. Today, its 365 members publish 26 morning papers, 78 evenings, and 1,200 weekly or biweeklies.

The main purpose of the society is to act as a central organisation for the British press, with the exception of the London national and evening newspapers. It exercises a close and constant vigilance over the interests of newspapers in Parliament, Whitehall, the law courts, and in their relations with the police, hospitals, and so on. Down the years it has performed valuable service in forwarding and preserving the freedom of the press. It was mainly responsible for forming the Press Association, the chief domestic news agency in Britain, which is owned by the provincial press, and is now in partnership with Reuters. The society is a member of the International Federation of Newspaper Publishers.

THE INSTITUTE OF JOURNALISTS

The institute is the senior professional body for journalists. It began as the National Association of Journalists in 1884, was converted into the institute in 1889, and incorporated by royal charter in 1890. It is the only organisation giving equal rights of membership to all qualified journalists from editor-proprietors to junior reporters; it therefore claims to speak uniquely for the profession as a whole.

For many years there was bitter rivalry between this small professional body and the much larger, more industrially minded National Union. In 1967, however, after the failure of several previous efforts, the two bodies came together in an arrangement whereby full members of the one also became members of the other, the institute being responsible for the professional interests and the union for the trade union interests of the whole joint membership.

The institute maintains a generous scale of unemployment benefit; it has a benevolent fund for all journalists, members or not, and an orphan fund with a capital of more than fifty thousand pounds, which has helped in the education of the children of former members. Funds exist to assist widows, help sick and aged journalists, and provide life pensions. The institute has also established attractive hostel estates for old journalists.

It is a certified trade union, which means that it is not affiliated to the Trades Union Congress, but has the right to negotiate with employers.

THE NATIONAL UNION OF JOURNALISTS

The N.U.J. is the largest organisation of journalists in Europe and the Commonwealth. It was founded in Manchester in 1906, as a breakaway from the institute. Its membership grew from 738 at the end of its first year, to 22,100 in 1968. It also looks after the trade union interests of nearly 2,000 members of the institute.

Though founded primarily to improve the salaries and working conditions of journalists, the N.U.J. has striven to raise professional standards, promote training, and defend the freedom of the press. It promoted the first Admission of the Press Act (1908) and was the first British organisation to draw up a code of conduct. It has taken an active part in the International Federation of Journalists for which, since 1930, it has provided four presidents.

In addition to holding national agreements with publishers and radio and television organisations throughout the British Isles, the N.U.J. does a great deal of benevolent work. Its Widow and Orphan fund distributes some twenty-two thousand pounds annually to journalists' dependents.

The N.U.J. is a registered trade union, affiliated to the Printing and Kindred Trades' Federation, the National Federation of Professional Workers, and the Trades Union Congress. It has no attachment to any political party.

NEWSPAPERS PUBLISHERS' ASSOCIATION

The N.P.A., formed in 1906, comprises the twenty-one daily, Sunday, and London evening newspapers. Its function is to represent and safeguard the interests of national newspapers and to provide for collective action.

The original reason for setting up the N.P.A. was to enable individual newspaper proprietors to negotiate collectively with the printing trade unions.

This involves continuous negotiation with the unions, and the association is responsible for the settlement of all labour disputes in its section of the industry. Advisory services are also provided for individual newspapers, a facility becoming increasingly important with the development of plant bargaining. Among other important services, administrative and advisory, the N.P.A. is responsible for distribution arrangements by road, rail, and air for member newspapers, and for the allocation of reporting and photographic facilities at important events.

The association is controlled by a council consisting of one representative of each member newspaper.

THE PERIODICAL PUBLISHERS' ASSOCIATION

The P.P.A., the most recent recruit to the Press Council, was founded in 1913 to safeguard the common interests of members and to promote an increase in circulation, readership, and advertising of British periodicals. Member companies vary in size from one-publication firms to the largest periodical group in the world. The annual turnover of the membership is £120 million, and the publications listed include general interest, news, opinion, trade, technical, business, and specialised magazines.

THE GUILD OF BRITISH NEWSPAPER EDITORS

The guild was founded in 1946 to provide editors with a medium for collective consultation, without infringing their editorial independence. Its basic objects are to sustain the dignity of editorship; to raise and safeguard the professional status of editors; to protect the rights and freedom of the press; to provide information and discussion on editors' problems; to improve the education and training of junior journalists.

Full membership is open to all editors in chief, managing editors, and editors of morning, evening, weekly, and Sunday newspapers in membership of the Newspaper Society, the Scottish Daily Newspaper Society, or the Scottish Newspaper Proprietors' Association. The guild is affiliated to the Newspaper Society.

THE SCOTTISH NEWSPAPER PROPRIETORS' ASSOCIATION

The Scottish N.P.A., unlike its English equivalent, represents the weekly newspapers in Scotland. It was founded in the early 1900s, with the object of safeguarding newspaper interests by all practicable means, and to promote cooperation within the industry. It has been an affiliated association of what is now the Society of Master Printers of Scotland for just over forty years, thus creating a closer relationship between the weekly newspapers and the general printing industry in Scotland than exists in England and Wales.

THE SCOTTISH DAILY NEWSPAPER SOCIETY

No official information about this body was forthcoming.

Bibliography

Costin, W. C., and J. Steven Watson. *The Law and Working of the Constitution.* 2 vols. London: A. and C. Black Ltd., 1964.

Herd, Harold. *The March of Journalism.* London: George Allen and Unwin, 1952.

History of the London "Times." 4 vols. London: Office of the *Times,* 1935–48.

Longford, Elizabeth. *Victoria R. I.* London: Weidenfeld and Nicolson Ltd., 1964.

Martell, Edward, and Ewan Butler. *The Murder of the "News-Chronicle."* London: Christopher Johnson, 1960.

Performance of the Press: Planning Pamphlet No. 397. London: Political and Economic Planning Institute (P.E.P.), 1956.

Pound, Reginald, and Geoffrey Harmsworth. *Northcliffe.* London: Cassell and Co. Ltd., 1959.

Press Councils and Press Codes. Zurich: International Press Institute, 1966.

Report of the Royal Commission on the Press, 1947–1949. London: H. M. Stationery Office.

Report of the Royal Commission on the Press, 1961–1962. London: H. M. Stationery Office.

Report on the British Press. London: Political and Economic Planning Institute (P.E.P.), 1938.

Report on the Vassall Case. London: H. M. Stationery Office, n.d.

The Press and the People. The 16 annual reports of the Press Council, 1954–69.

Thomas, Harford. *Newspaper Crisis.* Zurich: International Press Institute, 1967.

Index